Learn Faster, Perform Better

Praise for *Learn Faster, Perform Better*

"Dr. Molly Gebrian gifts us with a truly compelling new book. A highly trained performing musician and pedagogue, Dr. Gebrian has also made a life-long study of neuroscience, especially as it relates to 'music and the brain.' In this book, she marries the two disciplines in a way that is understandable to the lay reader, with complete descriptions of the 'why' and the 'how' of applying each new principle. Dr. Gebrian's 'Introduction' is captivating, and the easy cadence of her writing invites us forward with every important technique presented. This is a book for every library—I know I will be using these concepts in my own teaching . . . and my own learning!"
—**James F. Dunham**, Professor of Viola
and Chamber Music, Shepherd School of Music, Rice University

"Finally, a clear and informative book by a musician with neuroscience expertise explaining how to learn music faster and better! Everyone interested in music performance should read this book to get old monkeys off their back (practicing as much as possible, the myths of talent and early achievement, etc.) and to learn what really does work in music practice and why."
—**Jacqueline Leclair**, Associate Professor of Oboe,
Schulich School of Music, McGill University

"This book is pure gold. Scrupulously researched and substantiated by both scientific studies and data culled from her lived experience as a performer and pedagogue, Dr. Gebrian provides musicians with an empowering and practical guide to making profound and lasting progress in their work."
—**Carol Rodland**, Professor of Viola
and Chamber Music, The Juilliard School

"Kudos to Molly Gebrian for gathering such a compendium of valuable information in one place! If you're a growing young artist—you need this book to develop optimal work habits to get the most out of your dedication. If you're a top-flight teacher, you may know many of the techniques described in this book, but you need this book to understand how and why they work.

I look forward to making this book mandatory for my students. It's the perfect combination of information and inspiration! Did I say you need this book?"

—**Peter Slowik**, Professor of Viola, Oberlin Conservatory

"After 40 years of experience as a performer and teacher, you imagine there's nothing new and useful to be said on the subject of practice. Molly Gebrian proved me wrong, and brilliantly so, in *Learn Faster, Perform Better*. Gebrian details fascinating insights from the neuroscience of learning, and then turns those research insights into actionable techniques for the practice room or rehearsal hall. Her book is required reading for my students because it profoundly helps them not just in learning music but in learning anything they set their minds to. Moreover, Gebrian's insights have transformed my own work habits of the last 40 years and helped make me a more confident and reliable performer. Her book is a must-read for anyone who wants to wring every ounce of learning from their practice sessions."

—**Jeffrey Sykes**, pianist, University of California–Berkeley, Artistic Director, Bach Dancing and Dynamite Society (Madison, Wisconsin) and Cactus Pear Music Festival (San Antonio, Texas)

Learn Faster, Perform Better

A Musician's Guide to the Neuroscience of Practicing

MOLLY GEBRIAN

Oxford University Press is a department of the University of Oxford. It furthers
the University's objective of excellence in research, scholarship, and education
by publishing worldwide. Oxford is a registered trade mark of Oxford University
Press in the UK and certain other countries.

Published in the United States of America by Oxford University Press
198 Madison Avenue, New York, NY 10016, United States of America.

© Oxford University Press 2024

All rights reserved. No part of this publication may be reproduced, stored in
a retrieval system, or transmitted, in any form or by any means, without the
prior permission in writing of Oxford University Press, or as expressly permitted
by law, by license, or under terms agreed with the appropriate reproduction
rights organization. Inquiries concerning reproduction outside the scope of the
above should be sent to the Rights Department, Oxford University Press, at the
address above.

You must not circulate this work in any other form
and you must impose this same condition on any acquirer.

Library of Congress Cataloging-in-Publication Data
Names: Gebrian, Molly, author.
Title: Learn faster, perform better : a musician's guide to the
neuroscience of practicing / Molly Gebrian.
Description: [1.] | New York, NY : Oxford University Press, 2024. |
Includes bibliographical references and index.
Identifiers: LCCN 2024013827 | ISBN 9780197680070 (paperback) |
ISBN 9780197680063 (hardback) | ISBN 9780197680087 (epub) |
ISBN 9780197680100 (ebook)
Subjects: LCSH: Practicing (Music)—Psychological aspects. |
Music memorizing.
Classification: LCC ML3838 .G315 2024 | DDC 781.44—dc23/eng/20240327
LC record available at https://lccn.loc.gov/2024013827

DOI: 10.1093/oso/9780197680063.001.0001

To my parents, without whom none of this would be possible.
And to all of my teachers and students, from whom I've learned so much.

Contents

Foreword by Dr. Noa Kageyama	xi
Acknowledgments	xv
Introduction: My Musical Journey	1

SECTION I: BRAIN BASICS

1. Good Practicing and How It Changes the Brain	9
2. Practice Like a Pro	23
3. Use Errors to Your Advantage	35

SECTION II: USING YOUR TIME WELL

4. The Fastest Way to Learn Music: Take More Breaks	47
5. Can You Learn Music in Your Sleep?	59
6. What's the Perfect Schedule of Breaks?	71
7. Be More Consistent in Performance	79
8. Why Exact Repetitions May Not Be the Best Goal	95

SECTION III: THE POWER OF THE MIND

9. The Power of Mental Practice	107
10. Mental Practice and the Brain	121
11. How to Focus to Play Your Best	133
12. The Most Effective Ways to Memorize Music	145
13. Boost Confidence in Memorized Performance	159

SECTION IV: CHALLENGES SPECIFIC TO MUSIC

14. Improving Rhythm and Tempo   173

15. Improving Pitch and Intonation   181

16. How to Play Faster   189

Conclusion: Bringing It All Together   201

Appendix A: Complete List of Practice Strategies   213
Appendix B: Sample Spaced Practice Calendars   221
Appendix C: Variable Practice Strategies   223
Appendix D: Bonus Rhythms   229
Glossary   231
Notes   237
Index   251

Foreword

I was 13 years old, and had recently begun studying with a prominent musician at a prestigious conservatory who rarely accepted students that young.

So I was mortified, when at the end of a lesson, my mom prompted me to ask my teacher if he would explain to me how to practice.

My teacher was speechless for a moment and clearly confused. From the outside looking in, I probably appeared to be doing just fine. I was winning prizes in competitions, playing alongside older and more experienced college students in summer festival orchestras, and had even performed as soloist with several local orchestras.

How could I not know how to practice?

The truth though, is that my mom was right to have me ask. Because I had no clue what I was doing in the practice room, and every day was a struggle to fill the hours that I knew I ought to be devoting to my violin.

The problem was that to that point in my life, "practicing" simply meant repeating the same passage over and over until it sounded better. And while I did improve over time, progress was slow, every minute felt like an eternity, and no matter how many hours I put in, performances were always inconsistent and unpredictable.

Nearly a decade later, as I was completing my graduate studies at The Juilliard School, something finally clicked. And for once, I found myself practicing in a thoughtful, intentional, strategic, and "deliberate" way.

The change was transformative. I began to hear tangible and lasting improvements from one day to the next. I felt more in control on stage than ever before, and feelings of anxiety were replaced by excitement.

The experience was incredibly empowering, and inspired me to pursue a path I never anticipated—a PhD in psychology. I was driven to learn more about the mental foundations of peak performance, and throughout my doctoral studies at Indiana University, one of the questions that consumed me was: did it really have to take nearly two decades for me to figure out how to practice?

If only there had been a handbook on how to practice! A user's manual, drawing from the latest research in motor learning, psychology, and

xii FOREWORD

neuroscience, with clear instructions on how to build our skills in the most effective way. Like, what do good practice habits actually look like? How many repetitions is enough? How long should each practice session be? What are we supposed to do when something doesn't get better no matter how many times we repeat it over and over?

And then there are the other tricky challenges that every musician puzzles over at some point or another. Such as, how can we play things correctly the first time, instead of on the second or third try? How can we memorize music so that it's truly reliable under pressure? How can we unlearn bad habits that only reemerge at the worst possible times? How can we maintain a steady rhythmic pulse and avoid rushing or dragging when the nerves kick in and we no longer have a metronome to rely on?

The book that you're holding in your hands is that missing handbook. If you've ever wondered if there were a better way to practice, a more efficient, effective, engaging, gratifying, and *fun* way, the answer is yes—and you're about to learn exactly how.

Molly Gebrian has a rare talent for distilling complex, nuanced research across multiple disciplines into clear guidelines and concrete action steps. When she told me that she was writing a book on the science of effective practice, I couldn't wait to read it. And it was well worth the wait!

I've been teaching classes on performance psychology at Juilliard for over a decade, and have worked with musicians at all levels, from international competition prizewinners and principal players in major orchestras, to students and learners ranging in age from 12 to 80+, to university and conservatory faculty, K–12 educators, and private studio teachers.

I explain to each musician I work with that the ability to perform confidently and freely under pressure begins with habits that are cultivated in the practice room on a daily basis, not with weird tricks or quick-fix hacks that we can apply on a moment's notice. I also emphasize that just like playing in tune, producing a beautiful sound, and crafting a convincing musical phrase, practicing itself is very much a skill. One that improves, with practice.

Of course, in the same way that it helps to have a guide when exploring a new city, it can be invaluable to have a guide on your practice journey as well. Especially since many of the most effective learning strategies and techniques are not necessarily intuitive! It could take years of trial and error or blind luck before you might stumble upon some of the most impactful approaches to skill development—if ever!

FOREWORD xiii

Yet, as you read through the pages of this book, you'll find that everything makes so much sense! Especially once you learn the underlying science and rationale. You may find yourself nodding along, thinking "Of course! How did I never think of that before?" Or even, "I can't wait to go practice and try this!"

Whether you're new to your instrument, returning to music after years away, or have been practicing for years and performing professionally for decades, I'm certain that if you apply the concepts in *Learn Faster, Perform Better: A Musician's Guide to the Neuroscience of Practicing*, your experience in the practice room—and on stage—will be changed forever!

Noa Kageyama, MM, PhD
Performance psychologist
Faculty, The Juilliard School
bulletproofmusician.com

Acknowledgments

This book would not have been possible without the help and support of many people over many years. First and foremost, I would like to thank my parents, Robin and Jeffrey Gebrian, for always supporting me in all of my different endeavors. This book and my life as a musician simply would not have been possible without them.

I also give my deepest gratitude to all of my major teachers not only for teaching me viola and making me a better musician but also for teaching me how to practice. David Einfeldt, Kathy Almquist, Peter Slowik, Carol Rodland, James Dunham, and Garth Knox made me who I am as a musician and violist more than anyone else, and I will be forever grateful for what I learned from them (and continue to learn from them).

That being said, I also wouldn't be who I am without the outstanding education and support I received at Oberlin, New England Conservatory, and Rice. These institutions and the amazing individuals who work and teach at them not only supported me in my dual passions of music and neuroscience, but they encouraged me to pursue them. Thank you.

A huge thank you to everyone who read early drafts of this book and provided feedback: Tony Brandt, Melinda Daetsch, Michelle Gott, Danny Holt, Michael Kimber, Anne Slovin, Jan Stirm, Jeffrey Sykes, Anne Timberlake, Beth Wenstrom, and both of my parents. I especially thank Jeffrey Sykes not only for reading the entire book in draft form but also for giving me extremely detailed and thoughtful feedback. His suggestions and ideas have made this book immeasurably better.

I also thank David Bynog, Christine Goodner, and Ivo van der Werff for talking to me in the very early stages of this project to help me understand the world of book publishing from their perspective as authors. I had no idea what I was doing and their input helped enormously.

The graphs and other figures in this book would not have been possible without the graphic design wizardry of Sonny Oram. Having clear graphics makes a huge difference in understanding and appreciating the findings of many of these studies, so a big thank you to him for making all the figures look so nice!

xvi ACKNOWLEDGMENTS

When Noa Kageyama agreed to write the Foreword for this book, I was over the moon. Noa's work has been a huge inspiration to me for many years and I am a superfan of his website BulletproofMusician.com. If you don't know about his website, podcast, courses, or the many other resources he offers online, remedy that right now by visiting his website. Nobody does it better than Noa, and I have learned a tremendous amount from him over the years. I am so honored and grateful to include his Foreword as part of this book.

Thank you also to Michelle Chen, my wonderful editor at Oxford University Press. Your support and guidance through this entire process, answering all of my incessant questions, and enthusiasm for this project from the very beginning made the whole thing possible. Thank you for helping bring this book into the world.

And finally: thank you to all of the musicians I have met and interacted with at conferences, presentations, and online over the years. Your interest in learning about the science of practicing as well as your questions and conversations have helped me refine my thinking and clarify how I bring this information to our community. This book is for you.

The excerpt from the Bartók Viola Concerto in Chapter 16 is used with permission by Boosey & Hawkes.

Viola Concerto, Sz. 120 by Béla Bartók© 1950 By Boosey & Hawkes, Inc. Boosey & Hawkes, Agent for Rental. Copyright Secured. Reprinted by Permission.

Introduction

My Musical Journey

It's a Sunday afternoon in the fall of my sophomore year in college. I'm alone in a classroom trying to figure out how to improve the Prelude to the second Bach Cello Suite before my upcoming lesson in a few days. My usual method of practicing hasn't been working very well because I'm just not able to play anything the way I want. It's so frustrating to feel like I spend endless hours in the practice room with very little to show for it. I'm tired of feeling this way all the time, so today, I've decided to try something different.

I play a phrase, record it, and then listen back. I hear aspects of the timing, sound, and intonation that I'm not happy with. I try to fix these things, then record again.

> *Okay, the sound and intonation are better, but the timing is still off. Maybe I should slow down more at the end of the phrase . . . ?*

I record again.

> *No, the slowing down sounds terrible. Maybe I should move forward through the end of the phrase instead . . . ?*

I record. Listen.

> *Yes, that's better.*

I try it again to see if I can recreate it. Record. Listen.

> *Yep, that's what I want now.*

I spend the entire afternoon working through the Prelude in this way. It's exhausting but rewarding work. I've never been this focused while practicing before. When I leave to go to dinner, I feel much better about how I sound (for a change).

The next day, I review the Prelude again. Usually overnight, I lose about half of what I practiced the previous day, so I typically have to redo a big chunk of my work. Today, I'm astounded: almost all the practicing I did the day before stuck. What is this magic practice method I stumbled upon?

Learn Faster, Perform Better. Molly Gebrian, Oxford University Press. © Oxford University Press 2024.
DOI: 10.1093/oso/9780197680063.003.0001

2   INTRODUCTION

As musicians, we spend a large portion of our lives practicing, doing our best to improve our technique and musicianship, trying to close the gap between what we can imagine and what we actually hear coming out of our instruments. But often, we are given very little (if any) instruction by our teachers on *how* to accomplish this effectively. We are just told, "This needs more work," or "Spend more time working on intonation here," but the *how* is left out of the discussion. Some of us were lucky enough to have teachers who *did* teach us how to practice effectively, but often the *why* behind the specific practice method was neglected. We are largely left to our own devices, which often results in choosing practice methods that are less than optimal.

The "magic" practice method I stumbled onto that fall afternoon is known as deliberate practice, first described by Anders Ericsson in his 1993 research study on the topic.[1] Deliberate practice means working on a skill specifically to improve your weaknesses and to overcome errors and mistakes, exactly as I was doing that day. Dr. Ericsson also emphasizes that ideally this should be directed by a qualified teacher who has achieved expertise in the field.[2] But how exactly are you supposed to go about deliberate practice? What are the most effective ways to work on your weaknesses and overcome your mistakes? How can you make sure all your careful work is there when it counts, like in a concert? And what does scientific research have to say about the best ways to practice?

That is the topic of this book.

My interest in the science of practicing began as an undergraduate at Oberlin College and Conservatory, long before I ever heard the words "deliberate practice," and well before that day practicing Bach. When I arrived at Oberlin, I knew I wanted to be a double major in viola performance and something else, but I didn't know what the "something else" would be yet. Then I took a freshman seminar on neuroscience and I was instantly hooked. After the first week of class, I knew it was the most intriguing subject I had ever encountered and I wanted to learn as much as I possibly could.

Despite being a double-degree student in viola performance and neuroscience (officially called "biopsychology" in those days), I never intended to pursue my PhD in neuroscience or to become a scientific researcher. I studied neuroscience because I thought brains were endlessly fascinating, but it was purely for my own interest. After Oberlin, I went to New England Conservatory for my master's degree in viola performance, thinking I had left neuroscience behind. But soon after arriving in Boston, I began to feel unbalanced in a way I couldn't quite put my finger on. Partway through the fall semester, my roommate participated in a study at Harvard comparing the brains of musicians and nonmusicians. When she came home from the study and told me about it, I was excited to discuss brains again. I suddenly knew what I was missing: I needed to continue with neuroscience somehow.

Since NEC is a conservatory, it does not offer classes in neuroscience or psychology. Although they have partnerships with other universities in Boston, logistically it wasn't going to work for me to take classes elsewhere. However, I was fortunate that NEC allowed me to do several independent studies looking into aspects of music and the brain that I had started exploring at Oberlin. My neuroscience and psychology classes at Oberlin were not specific to music, but I had begun to see parallels between what I was learning in my neuroscience classes and what I was learning in my lessons about effective practice techniques. For my first independent study at NEC, I took an in-depth look at the research on learning, reading stacks of original research papers on what happens in the brain when we learn new things. As my final project for that independent study, I wrote a paper summarizing what I had learned and explained how to apply that research to practicing. In many ways, that first paper was the seed that made this book possible.

After NEC, I attended Rice University for my doctorate in viola performance. Now that I was back at a university, there was the possibility of taking neuroscience classes again. When I got to campus, I contacted the professor for a cognitive neuroscience class I wanted to take that semester, and after explaining my background, she let me into her class. For most of the three years I was working on my music coursework, I took neuroscience classes with graduate students working toward their PhDs in neuroscience and psychology. I also worked in a lab that specialized in language perception and production, and taught a class on music and the brain. I am forever grateful to Rice for these opportunities and for allowing me to continue to pursue my interest in neuroscience while I worked toward my DMA in viola performance.

The more I learned about how the brain absorbs and retains new information, the more I wanted to share this with fellow musicians. I felt that if more musicians had access to the information that cognitive scientists were discovering in their research, they would practice more effectively, find greater enjoyment from this work, and would perform with greater ease and confidence. Once I started teaching at the collegiate level, I began writing and presenting more on these topics at conferences, universities, and schools around the country to bring this information to more people. When the

4 INTRODUCTION

pandemic hit in early 2020, I converted my presentations into a series of YouTube videos, which have reached musicians of all ages and backgrounds around the world. Finally, everything I had learned about how the brain works was reaching fellow musicians on a broader scale and improving their practicing and performing.

This book is the next step in helping musicians practice and perform better by understanding how the brain works. We tend to think that practicing is about training our bodies: which finger to put down when, how to precisely calibrate our embouchure to control the sound, the exact moment to move our foot so the pedal releases how we want. But practicing is all about training our brains. Our bodies don't do anything without our brains, and if we reframe practicing as brain training it can change how we approach things.

Throughout this book, I will describe what scientists have discovered about the ways in which we learn best, accompanied by practical, actionable methods you can apply immediately to your practice sessions. You will learn what's going on when you can play it perfectly at home, but then it's a disaster in your lesson. We will explore why your work one day seems to evaporate the next—and what to do about it. You will learn about how to fix bad habits quickly and permanently. We'll discuss the power of sleep for learning and the surprising role of mental practice in helping us improve. We'll also talk about specific challenges, like playing from memory or working up a fast passage. And we'll look at optimal practice schedules in terms of how much and how often you should practice, as well as that finicky practice partner: motivation (or lack thereof). In the back of the book (Appendix A), you'll find a complete list of all the practice methods discussed in each chapter. You can also download this list as a PDF from my website (www.mollygebrian.com) to keep with you while you're practicing. On my website, you will also find many other free resources (videos, podcasts, articles, and PDFs) to help you practice more effectively.

My hope is that musicians—of all levels and from a variety of backgrounds—will find useful, practical information in this book to help them achieve their musical goals. Many of the practice strategies we'll discuss come from research on training athletes, surgeons, and other experts, as well as studying for academic tests or performing everyday physical skills. As such, most of the information in this book is broadly applicable to anything you are working to improve. However, because I was trained as a violist in the tradition of Western classical art music, that is the perspective I bring to this work. I make the assumption that most of the students, teachers, and performers reading this book come from that tradition as well, although I intend for it to be more universally helpful. Throughout, I use the word "playing" (as opposed to "playing and/or singing") as a generic term for making music, so I hope singers don't feel left out by this terminology. Because I have zero training and little experience with improvisation, I purposely do not discuss that topic in this book. I don't have the practical performance expertise to discuss improvisation skills knowledgeably and in a way that would be helpful. I also don't discuss research specific to neurodivergent learners, again because it falls outside my area of expertise. Despite this, I hope that readers who were hoping to find information in these areas will still find something of value in these pages.

This research has been transformative to my own personal practice and that of my students, and it has resulted in more satisfying, expressive, and consistent performances as a result. My hope is that this book will demystify some of the challenges around practicing, give you many new ideas to try, and help you overcome the frustration we can often experience when things just aren't improving. I believe that when we understand how our brains work and learn best, we can make smarter choices in the practice room and therefore give more confident, convincing, enjoyable performances.

Let's get started.

SECTION I
BRAIN BASICS

Understanding the basics of how the brain works will set the stage for the topics covered in the rest of this book. In this section, we will look at how the brain learns in general, what sets top performers apart from everyone else in terms of how they practice, and the important role of errors in learning.

1

Good Practicing and How It Changes the Brain

Growing up, I hated to practice. I thought it was a frustrating waste of time that didn't accomplish much of anything. I did it because I was a diligent student and I knew it was expected of me, but I didn't quite see the point. My practice in those days consisted of getting out my instrument, playing through the music a few times that my teacher had assigned, and then calling it a day. When I messed up, I'd start over, trying to play without the mistake. Or sometimes I'd repeat the spot where I had tripped up once or twice to correct the mistake, and then I'd just go on. Anything that wasn't immediately made better by these two methods was essentially ignored. *Maybe my teacher won't notice that I can't really play that part*, I thought.

Good practice habits

As a kid, I didn't realize that I wasn't actually practicing. I was just playing things through, which *isn't* practicing. I think this misunderstanding is true for many musicians, especially when we're growing up. So before we start delving into the world of brains and scientific research, let's talk about what good practicing should look like.

Good practicing is problem solving. Good practice focuses on weaknesses, not strengths. Throughout the chapters of this book, you'll learn many different possible solutions to a variety of practicing and performing challenges. The wonderful (and sometimes frustrating!) thing about practicing is that there's no one-size-fits-all solution. I wish I could lay out a detailed step-by-step practicing guide that you could follow for any piece of music you wanted to learn. Unfortunately, it doesn't work that way. In much the same way that there isn't a step-by-step guide for raising kids—because every child is different, with their own strengths and weaknesses—good practicing is dynamic. It is assessing in the moment the challenges *you* are struggling with

Learn Faster, Perform Better. Molly Gebrian, Oxford University Press. © Oxford University Press 2024.
DOI: 10.1093/oso/9780197680063.003.0002

10   BRAIN BASICS

and figuring out how to fix them. What you'll learn in this book are the scientific principles behind a variety of practice methods so you can choose the ones that will work best for the specific issues you are trying to solve.

Broadly speaking, however, this is what good practicing should look like: identify problem spots, hypothesize solutions, try out those solutions, solidify the solution that works best, then move on to the next issue. This process could take as little as a few minutes, or it might take many weeks or months. I often liken practicing well to being a good doctor. When you go to the doctor with a health concern, they ask questions to find out what's going on, perform a physical exam, and maybe run some tests. Once they've gathered all the data they need, they provide a diagnosis and give you a treatment. Sometimes the treatment is a progressive series of steps, like getting surgery followed by physical therapy. Hopefully the treatment plan works, but if it doesn't, your doctor will start the process over again to figure out what they missed.

We need to do the same thing while practicing. We need to identify the exact location of our problem spots and then try to figure out what's causing the issue. You may not know right away, and that's fine. Come up with an idea as to the cause of your mistake and a possible solution, just as I was trying to do that fall day working on Bach (" . . . *the timing is still off. Maybe I should slow down more at the end of the phrase . . . ?*"). Try it out and see if it gets you closer to solving the problem. If your solution makes things worse, that's still valuable information. If it makes it better but it's still not quite right, at least you know you're on the right track. Keep repeating this problem-solving process until you've figured it out and fixed your mistake.

Practice habits to avoid

Before we start getting into brain research, I also think it's important to talk briefly about what practice should *not* look like. Here are a few common examples:

- Running through from beginning to end to start your practice session (with two exceptions, which will be discussed in Chapter 2)
- Starting from the beginning, playing until you make a mistake, fixing that mistake, and then continuing on until the next mistake (repeating this process until you get tired or bored and then stopping)

GOOD PRACTICING AND HOW IT CHANGES THE BRAIN   11

- Starting from the beginning, playing until you make a mistake, and then starting over again and trying to do it again without your mistake (repeating this process until you get tired or bored and then stopping)
- Putting on the metronome at a slow tempo and playing through the whole piece or big sections at that tempo, stopping here and there to correct small problems
- Playing through everything you can already play well over and over again
- Doing endless repetitions of something that doesn't sound good without stopping to assess what's *causing* the issues, hoping they will magically get better

My guess is, if you're like most people, you recognize yourself in at least one of these. The first three were definitely how I practiced as a young music student. As you read through the different chapters of this book, it will become clearer why these practice strategies are either useless or detrimental. I wish someone had told me this as a kid; I had no idea that the way I was "practicing" wasn't actually practice. I didn't realize I was supposed to be actively problem-solving.

Once I started to learn what good practice *should* look like, not only did I start to make rapid improvements in my playing, but I started to enjoy practicing much more.

Now that we've talked a bit about what good practice should look like and which common practice habits are harmful, it's time to start discussing brains and the details of how to practice.

Brain basics

Let's start with how our brains are structured. Our brains are composed of billions of neurons*—86 billion neurons on average—that are in constant communication with each other. The way neurons talk to each other is largely through synapses, tiny gaps between individual neurons. When one neuron wants to send a message to a neighboring neuron, it releases

---

* All terms are also defined in a glossary at the back of the book in case you need a reminder at any point.

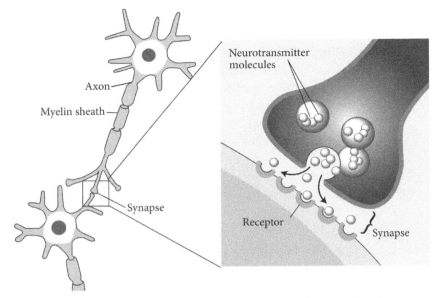

Figure 1.1 The structure of a neuron, with the synapse shown in detail on the right.
Illustration by Sonny Oram.

neurotransmitter (a chemical signal) into the synapse. Dopamine, serotonin, and adrenaline are all examples of neurotransmitters. There are many others, but these are some you may have heard of before.

Once the neurotransmitter is released into the synapse, it travels toward the neuron on the other side. If that neighboring neuron has receptors that are the right shape and size, the neurotransmitter will bind to those receptors (see Figure 1.1), causing an electrical change in the second neuron. Often the analogy used to describe this process is that of a lock and a key: the neurotransmitter is the key and the receptor is the lock. If the key is the right shape and size, it will fit in the lock (bind to the receptor) and allow the lock to be opened (the electrical change that occurs).

After the neurotransmitter binds to the receptors and causes an electrical change, this pulse of electricity travels down the long arm of the neuron, called the axon. Once it reaches the end of the axon, it stimulates the release of neurotransmitter once again and the cycle repeats itself. So all of the communication in our brains is a chemical signal that gets translated into an electrical signal, back into a chemical signal, and so on.

GOOD PRACTICING AND HOW IT CHANGES THE BRAIN   13

When we practice, we want to strengthen the synapses relaying information on how to play something correctly, while weakening those that send erroneous or irrelevant messages. To understand how this works, think of an old, leaky garden hose that has many holes in it. Some of the water will go through the hose and out the nozzle, but a lot of it will leak out the holes. This is what your brain is like when you first start to learn something: the water running out the holes is all the erroneous and irrelevant information your brain is sending to your fingers, lips, feet, etc. Once you plug the holes in the hose, all the water goes then out the nozzle; in your brain, this is analogous to the synapses relaying the correct messages being much stronger than those sending incorrect messages. The brain accomplishes this through changing the structure of the synapse to make it easier for the correct neurons to communicate. A common phrase in neuroscience is "neurons that fire together wire together," meaning neurons that communicate with each other often (fire together) change their structure to make that communication even easier (wire together).

This means that every time you practice or learn something new, you're actually changing your brain. If you learn something incorrectly, to use the hose analogy, it would be as if you made one of the holes so big that most of the water was going out of the hole, rather than the nozzle. To correct the issue, you would have to close the hole before you could get the water moving in the right direction. In brain terms, you would have to strengthen one group of synapses while *also* weakening another, rather than just strengthening one group. That's twice as much work!

These changes are just the beginning, and since they occur at such a microscopic level, they are relatively easily undone. As you continue working, not only do the synapses involved get strengthened, but new synapses are formed between neurons that weren't connected before. At the same time as this is happening, groups of neurons—called *neuronal ensembles*—become more and more streamlined in their behavior. At first, as an ensemble, they send a lot of random messages and do strange things. It's a lot like a youth orchestra rehearsing a newly composed piece for the first time—there are many individual mistakes, and it sort of sounds like the piece, but not really. As the neuronal ensemble gets better at working together, just like an orchestra, individual mistakes may still happen here and there, but what comes out is much more cohesive and intelligible. In fact, if a neuroscientist looks at the activity of a refined neuronal ensemble, she can predict relatively accurately which physical movement in the body will result before it even happens.[1]

14 BRAIN BASICS

Another common phrase used in neuroscience is *neural pathway*, which describes the connections formed between different areas of the brain. The word "pathway" is useful for understanding what happens when we get good at something—or have a bad habit we're trying to get rid of—because it leads to another helpful analogy. Imagine you are standing in front of a giant field of snow, so big that you can't see what's on the other side. You are trying to visit your friend's new house for the first time, but they didn't give you any directions other than to tell you, "It's across the big snowy field." When you arrive at the field, you see a nice clear path cutting through the snow, so you reason that by following the path, it will take you to your friend's house. But if you follow this path and it leads you to the town dump instead, you probably won't be very happy.

In brain terms, a path to the town dump would be like having a neural pathway established in your brain that results in some sort of bad habit or mistake (you always tense up when singing high, for instance). But if this is the only neural pathway you have, you don't really have a choice: that error in performance is going to happen because that's the only neural communication that's set up. Your brain literally doesn't know any better, just like you didn't when you followed the path to the dump.

Now imagine that the only available pathway delivers you to your friend's front door. Success! In brain and music terms, this is like everything coming out exactly how you want it to. If it's a well-trodden pathway, it's easy to follow. Likewise, when we have good habits established, playing well feels effortless. This is also why great performers can make things look so easy: they have the right neural pathways in place so they aren't fighting against a bunch of bad habits.

Lastly, imagine that when you approach the snowy field, there are two pathways going in opposite directions, looking identical. Both are nice and wide and cleared of snow. Which one are you going to take? Well, you're going to have to guess, which means you have a 50/50 chance of making it to your friend's house. In brain and music performance terms, having two essentially equal pathways for the same skill—some days your embouchure feels great, other days you revert back to old habits—means you have a 50/50 shot of it going the way you want it to. For most musicians, getting up on stage with only a 50% chance of success doesn't feel good at all. That feels incredibly risky and anxiety-provoking.

How can we give ourselves better than a 50% chance at success? If your friend wanted to ensure nobody would take the wrong pathway, they could get out their shovel and cover over the incorrect pathway with snow. As long as nobody used that path and packed down the snow with footprints, the pathway to the dump would disappear. The process is similar in our brains: our brains can distinguish important pathways from unwanted ones and will strengthen those that are the most valuable to us while we sleep.[2] If you repeatedly reinforce the incorrect pathway inadvertently, your brain will think it's important and strengthen it, rather than allowing it to disappear like an unused pathway through the snow.

Pathways and practicing

Now that you understand a bit more about what's happening in the brain when you are trying to improve, let's return to those unproductive practice habits I mentioned earlier. Think about the methods I relied on as a kid: I would play until I made a mistake, and then either fix the mistake and go on, or start over again and try to do it a second time without my mistake. The reason these methods are so ineffective is because even though I knew I'd made a mistake, I had inadvertently reinforced the incorrect pathway; I had just walked down and therefore reinforced the pathway to the town dump. And so naturally, my brain thought that pathway was important and kept it around. Again, neurons that fire together wire together, whether you want them to or not. What you repeat is what is preserved and reinforced in the brain. More than anything else, practicing is brain training, so we have to make sure we are training our brains well.

A much better way to practice is to start directly at the spots that are challenging for you. Even if you think, "Well, I don't know where those are," think harder. You *do* know. They are the spots you worry about when you play in front of your teacher or another listener. Maybe it's just a single measure where the rhythm trips you up. Start right there and try to figure out *why* you have trouble at that spot. Maybe you don't understand how the rhythm goes. Or maybe you understand the rhythm, but you can't do both the rhythm and the notes at the same time. Or maybe you can do the rhythm fine by itself, but coming from the previous bar makes it confusing. Or maybe there's some other reason. There can be a whole host of reasons why something is difficult for you. Try to determine the *exact* reason because the more precise you can be in your diagnosis, the easier it will be to find a good solution.

16 BRAIN BASICS

Once you've identified the specific problem, figure out how to break down the problem into smaller, more manageable parts. If you don't understand the rhythm, can you write in where the main beats fall? Can you clap the rhythm? Count it out loud? Once you can do that, can you play the rhythm on your instrument on just a single note? Then try it with the printed notes, but slowly. Finally, use your metronome to help get it up to tempo. Start at a slow tempo that feels easy and gradually increase the speed until you reach your goal tempo (more on this in Chapter 16). By breaking down problems in this way, the solution is more likely to stick because you have made the correct pathway very strong and the bad pathway hasn't gotten any reinforcement.

So now that you've identified the precise problem, broken it down into manageable parts, and fixed the issue, what's next? Most people just move on to the next problem spot, but that's a mistake. You have to *solidify* your solution so the problem stays solved. To do this, students are often advised to play something 10 times correctly, or some variant of that advice. At some point growing up, I heard this advice and it made sense to me. Finally, a practicing strategy to actually make things better!

However, there is a potential danger in how this advice is often followed.

Imagine little me in the practice room: I'd play the measure my teacher said needed work and maybe it was perfect on the first try. Hooray! Maybe the second try was also great. But on my third try, I was distracted by something, so that time wasn't very good. Okay, that one doesn't count. Fourth time: also not great. Doesn't count. Fifth time: good! Now I have three correct, two incorrect. I would continue like that until I had 10 correct ones.

You can imagine, though, that by the time I did 10 correct repetitions, I probably also did 10 (or more!) incorrect repetitions that didn't count. In that case, I had accomplished literally and precisely nothing (except wasting my time) because I had reinforced the correct pathway 10 times, but also the incorrect pathway 10 times. I still had two completely equal pathways, and therefore only a 50% chance of it going well. And when it inevitably *didn't* go well in my lesson, I would think, "I can't play this correctly! No matter how much I practice it, I can never do it right!"

Sound familiar?

We need to ensure that the correct pathway gets reinforced many more times than the incorrect pathway. Again, neurons that fire together wire together. To accomplish this, it's important to have a consequence for an incorrect repetition. To make this happen, add the words "in a row" to the number

GOOD PRACTICING AND HOW IT CHANGES THE BRAIN   17

of correct repetitions you plan to do: 10 times correctly *in a row*. This means if you get it wrong on the third repetition, you have to start over again at zero. When faced with the consequence of having to start all over again, you will focus much more, and you will focus on exactly what you need to do to get it right. They won't be mindless repetitions. And this information—how do I ensure that I get it right?—is exactly what you need to know to perform it correctly in front of your teacher or in a concert.

But why 10? Why is that the magic number of repetitions?

It's not, actually.

The number of correct repetitions depends on how many *incorrect* repetitions you did before finally getting it right. This is called *overlearning*, which seems to be necessary for something to stick long-term. According to research on overlearning, the minimum number of correct repetitions is half the number of tries it took before you got it right the first time (50% overlearning). So, if it took you 10 tries before you got it right, you'd want to do five more in a row to solidify it. Even better than 50% overlearning is 100% overlearning: if it took you 10 tries to get it right, you'd want to do 10 more correct ones in a row to solidify it.[3] This research on overlearning is also incentive to try to get it right as early as possible in the process, without too many incorrect repetitions first. The more times you do it wrong, the more times you will have to do it right to ensure the correct pathway is getting reinforced many more times than the incorrect one.

If you get it right on the first try, I've found that doing it at least five times in a row is necessary for it to really stick (unless it was very easy). Three times seems to be too few. It is also necessary to actually count your repetitions. Don't just play many times in a row and assume it was at least five (or that you've achieved 50% or 100% overlearning). Chances are, you will drastically underestimate the number of correct repetitions in a row you've done. If you don't believe me, video record yourself practicing and watch it back—you'll find that your assessment of the number of correct repetitions in the moment was not at all accurate. Remember, if you mess up, the count starts over from zero.

The other benefit to counting repetitions is that it creates psychological pressure to get it right. Coping with that pressure of "You have to play it correctly right now!" is a skill we all need to learn in order to perform well. In Chapter 4 we'll also discuss another method of doing repetitions that builds in breaks to further enhance learning and consistency, and in Chapter 8 we'll discuss the power of varied repetitions, so stay tuned for that.

18 BRAIN BASICS

Why is it necessary to do repetitions in the first place? Why isn't it enough to do it correctly once and then move on? After all, you've proven to yourself that you can play it the way you want to. Think again about that snowy field. Pretend there are no pathways at all. You would have to arbitrarily start walking. Chances are, your first guess would be incorrect, so you would try again and again until you found your way to your friend's house. The snowy field would then be covered with crisscrossing pathways in the snow, all made from your individual footsteps. None of them would be clear or well-worn. How in the world would you (or someone else) ever be able to find the correct pathway in the future? You would probably remember that you started by veering to the right instead of the left, for instance, but beyond that, it would be hard to retrace the correct pathway again without mistakes. The correct pathway just isn't clear enough or differentiated enough from the other footprint paths you created. It's the same thing in practicing: often along the way to playing something correctly and fixing a problem, we do it incorrectly many times. That's fine—and as we'll talk about in the next chapter, necessary—it's part of the learning process. But once you *do* find the solution, you need to make sure *that* pathway sticks out from all the incorrect ones. You need to repeat the correct solution to make sure *that* pathway is the clearest, strongest one.

Myelination

The other benefit to repetitions is the additional reconstruction the brain does when a pathway gets used very frequently. In our analogy of the snowy field, this would be like the city coming in and paving the road to your friend's house, putting up a big sign saying, "Friend's house: this way!" There would be no question which way to go. Earlier, we talked about how synapses get strengthened when you learn something new. This process is called *long-term potentiation*, something we'll return to later. That's the first step in the process. The next step is called *myelination* and this is really when things start to feel easy and automatic.

Remember that when a neurotransmitter binds to a receptor, it causes an electrical change in the receiving neuron. That sends an electrical pulse flying down the axon, the long arm of the neuron. When an electrical signal repeatedly moves through an axon like that, the axon gets wrapped up in something called *myelin*, which is essentially just a layer of fat. The myelin allows the electrical signal to move more rapidly down the axon, similar to when you insulate an electrical wire: it allows the electricity to move more efficiently, rather than the energy being lost to the surrounding air.

When a pathway has been well-myelinated, that skill, action, or thought pattern feels automatic to you. For anyone reading this book, writing your name is automatic. You don't have to think about how to spell your name or how to make the individual letters. You can write your name easily even while talking to someone else. But when you were a little kid, that process wasn't so easy. Probably you had to really concentrate to write your name (and even so, you may have drawn some of the letters backward). That's because when you were little, that pathway wasn't myelinated yet.

When we're just starting to learn something, we often feel clumsy and uncoordinated. This is because the axons haven't been myelinated, so the various signals coming in from different parts of the brain aren't well synchronized yet. They are arriving slightly too early or slightly too late because the myelin isn't there to speed and smooth the electrical transmission of information. You experience this as clumsiness. Playing an instrument is immensely complicated and we need to coordinate very intricate actions with extremely precise timing. If the timing of the signals in our brains is just a little bit off, it will come out sounding messy.

So how do you get your brain to produce more myelin? Nothing is more frustrating than learning a new technique on your instrument, understanding how it's supposed to sound and what you're supposed to do, but having it come out all wrong every time you try it. Fortunately, it's the electrical signals themselves that also tell the surrounding brain tissue to put a wrap of myelin around the axons involved in the skill. The more times a signal passes through, the more wraps of myelin are put on, making the skill feel easier and easier. Things that feel effortless and automatic have many wraps of myelin, which is another reason repetitions are important: they increase myelin wraps. When something isn't working, it's easy to get frustrated and give up, saying "I just can't do it." But if you keep trying, the brain will continue to myelinate those pathways. If you just give up, the myelination stops, too.

When I'm practicing, I like to picture the little Minion characters furiously rushing around inside my brain, trying to connect new synapses and myelinate axons. They're working as fast as they can, even if it doesn't feel like it on the outside. And for them do their work, they need input from me. If I stop giving them input—because I give up out of frustration, saying "I'll

20 BRAIN BASICS

never be able to do this!"—they just stand there looking dejected because they don't know what to do next. But if I stick with it, they rush around as fast as they can myelinating everything, and eventually I can feel the improvement and greater ease on the outside.

The flip side to myelin is bad habits: those little Minions will myelinate whatever you are reinforcing, whatever you are repeating in your practice. Our brains don't know bad habits from good habits—they just know what we've done repeatedly. Again, neurons that fire together wire together. And this is why bad habits can feel so hard to break: they are supported by a very well-myelinated pathway and so they feel automatic. They can feel "normal" and "comfortable" even if we understand intellectually that the bad habit is hindering our progress. The conventional wisdom has been that myelin only wraps, it doesn't unwrap; there is no mechanism in the brain to remove myelin that you don't want anymore. More recent, cutting-edge research has suggested that the thickness of the myelin sheath can be thinned to allow for more precise communication between neurons. Unfortunately, there isn't much information yet on how this thinning process works, but it will be exciting to watch this area of research develop in the next few years.[4]

Despite these new findings, there is no evidence that in healthy people myelin breaks down if you stop using a given pathway. If you are trying to get rid of a bad habit, you need to make sure you never allow yourself to do your old habit mindlessly (although in the next chapter we'll discuss doing things wrong on purpose to correct bad habits). If you are a string player trying to change something in your bow hold, for instance, you need to use your new bow hold even when you are tuning, sightreading, or messing around on your instrument. It's not going to feel good because it's going to require much more attention than you are used to, but it will ensure you are building a new pathway and not allowing yourself to use or reinforce the old pathway at all. Myelinating the new pathway is at the root of developing habits you want to keep.

Are you reinforcing the right pathway?

One question that goes a long way toward promoting better practice habits is to constantly ask yourself, "Which pathway am I reinforcing right now by how I'm practicing?" Often, when we are frustrated and just not seeing improvement even after a lot of practice, it's because we have been inadvertently reinforcing the incorrect pathway.

Several years ago, a cellist came to have a lesson with me because she was struggling with intonation, an issue her teacher felt was caused by how she was practicing. When I asked her how she worked on intonation, she explained that she would play very slowly and then if she was out of tune, she would adjust. The minute she said that, I knew exactly what her problem was. She was reinforcing the adjusting pathway, rather than the play-in-tune pathway. By adjusting, she thought she was practicing well, but she was actually teaching her finger it could go down in approximately the right place and then get in tune after the fact, rather than going down in exactly the right place the first time. In performance, this constant adjusting just sounded like she was playing out of tune. A much better way to work on intonation is to stop on the note in question and if it's out of tune, *don't* adjust it. Listen to it and figure out if it's flat or sharp. Then back up a note or two and try again. Stop on the note in question—again don't adjust if it's out of tune—and figure out what's wrong with it. Continue this process until you can land on the note perfectly in tune with no adjusting. Keep track of how many tries it took before you got it right and then aim for at least 50% overlearning to solidify what you've learned.

Looking back, my biggest practicing mistake as a kid was not reinforcing the right pathways. I was either inadvertently reinforcing the wrong pathway (like the cellist), or I was making so many footprint tracks in the snow that when I got to my lesson, my brain had to just choose randomly which path to follow. Sometimes I got lucky and the path was the right one (or close enough). But just as often, my brain chose the wrong path. I thought I had prepared for my lesson because I had picked up my violin and played through all my songs each day. But the "practicing" I had done didn't seem to make much difference, so why was I wasting my time practicing? Now I know: I *wasn't* practicing. I wasn't problem-solving and I wasn't reinforcing any correct pathways. I was just playing mindlessly.

Again, our brains only know what we reinforce. If we reinforce the wrong thing, the brain will think it's right. If we don't reinforce anything, the brain will just have to guess the next time we come to a particular note or passage. By figuring out how to do something correctly and then reinforcing that, we cause actual physical changes in our brains, making it much more likely we will play the way we want the next time around. Learning means

22 BRAIN BASICS

making physical changes in the brain. Without physical changes in the brain, no learning has occurred.

Despite all this, errors are a necessary part of how we learn, even though they are incredibly frustrating. In the next chapter, we'll discuss how top musicians deal with mistakes and how they practice differently from those who don't perform as well. It's easy to think they just don't make as many mistakes in the first place, but that's not what the research shows. It's all in how they handle their mistakes, and it's a skill anyone can learn.

2

Practice Like a Pro

As frustrating as it may be, we can't learn without making mistakes. Despite all the discussion in the last chapter about good and bad pathways and the importance of reinforcing the correct pathway, errors are necessary for learning. If there is no mismatch between what the brain expects and what actually happens, there is no reason for the brain to change. It can feel frustrating when your body won't do what you know needs to happen, but that just means the necessary connections haven't been formed yet in your brain. If you can reframe that feeling of frustration as, "Oh, my brain is changing now! This is what learning feels like," it's easier to stick with it. And you don't have to get it right immediately or all at once. Clumsiness and mistakes are inevitable and a normal part of the learning process. As you continue to try different things, the brain will refine its connections and get you closer to your goal. So when you feel frustrated, don't stop. Keep going. It's how you learn. The Minions need you so they can do their jobs.

In the next two chapters, we'll look at two types of aggravating situations that just about every musician has experienced. First we'll discuss what to do when you just can't seem to make that one passage sound better, despite all of your best efforts. We'll look at what the research says about how best to chip away at mistakes, to make what we hear in our heads align with what actually comes out. And then, in Chapter 3, we'll look at persistent bad habits and the best methods to overcome them.

The role of mistakes

Before I started teaching at the collegiate level, I was a Suzuki teacher for many years, teaching kids as young as four years old. Often, I would demonstrate a very basic skill to one of my little students—like slurring two notes together—and they would say in awe, "Miss Molly, you're *so* good at violin. How do you *do* that?" It was cute and funny, but it wasn't much different from how I looked at the older students when I was a first-year in college. *How do*

Learn Faster, Perform Better. Molly Gebrian, Oxford University Press. © Oxford University Press 2024.
DOI: 10.1093/oso/9780197680063.003.0003

24 BRAIN BASICS

they play so well and make everything look so easy? I would wonder. *I have to work so hard all the time and I can never get it to sound that good.* It felt unfair and discouraging at times.

I think it's natural to assume that people whose playing we admire can just *do it.* We think it's easier for them, that they make fewer mistakes and have fewer struggles than we do. But is this really true?

A lot of the research we'll discuss in this book was not done on musicians, but there was an instructive study done on pianists to look at this question.[1] In this experiment, there were 17 piano-performance majors from the same school, ranging from junior and senior undergraduates all the way up through students getting their doctorate in piano performance. All of them had to learn a short excerpt from a Shostakovich concerto in one practice session. They were given unlimited time and were told to practice however they wanted until they were confident that they could perform it at tempo. The next day, they were given 15 tries to perform the excerpt, and their performances were rated by a panel of expert judges. Based on their performances, they were then ranked from best to worst. The top three players were all graduate students (two doctoral students and one master's student), but interestingly, the bottom two performers were also graduate students (a doctoral student and a master's student). Most of the undergrads were in the middle of the pack.

When the researchers analyzed how the pianists had practiced, they found two very interesting results. It wasn't that the top performers were just better than everyone else. They spent roughly the same amount of time practicing and made the same number of mistakes in the initial stages of learning as everyone else. What they did differently was how they *handled* their mistakes. They made sure to locate precisely where the mistake was, they slowed down to make sure they could play the passage correctly, only gradually bringing it back to tempo, and most critically, they made sure to play it many more times correctly than incorrectly. They were reinforcing the correct pathway much more than the incorrect one, just as we discussed in the previous chapter. The bottom performers didn't do this.

Interestingly, the top performer and the bottom performer initially made the same number of mistakes while practicing. However, the top performer went on to play 93% of their practice run-throughs and 100% of their performance run-throughs perfectly or nearly so. The bottom performer, on the other hand, was only able to play 54% of their practice run-throughs near-perfectly, and none perfectly. Not a single one of their performance run-throughs was perfect or nearly so. This is a pretty stark difference, especially from two people who started out in the same place in terms of errors. It highlights the importance of isolating errors and reinforcing the correct way to play something.

Of the other pianists in the experiment, only three used some of these critical practice strategies, namely identifying the precise location of the error and making sure they did more correct repetitions than incorrect ones. Not surprisingly, these pianists were also among the top ranked.

This study is backed up by a large body of research on both athletes and musicians looking at the differences in how higher-performing individuals practice versus those who don't perform as well. For instance, in a classic experiment looking at high school varsity basketball players, researchers wanted to see how the highest-scoring players practiced differently from those who didn't do as well.[2] Throughout a practice session focused on free-throw shooting, the basketball players were asked different questions to try to probe what they were thinking about while practicing.

Before they started practicing, the experimenters asked the players, "Do you have a goal when practicing these free throws? If so, what is it?" If they said yes, they were asked, "What do you need to do to accomplish that goal?" If they missed two shots in a row, they were asked, "What do you need to do to make the next shot?" and "Why do you think you missed those last two shots?" After two successful free-throws in a row, they were asked, "Why do you think you made those last two shots?"[3]

Their answers to these questions illuminated how the high-scoring players and the lower-scoring players went about practicing differently. To the question about goals, the higher-scoring players gave much more specific answers, like "to make 10 out of 10 shots" or "to keep [my] eye on the rim of the basket," whereas the lower-scoring players would say something more general, like "to make baskets" or "to concentrate more." When asked about their strategies for accomplishing their goals or what they needed to do to make the next shot after they had missed a couple, the higher-scoring players again were much more specific. They said things like, "[I need to] keep my elbows in" or "focus on the back of the rim," whereas the lower-scoring players were again more vague, saying things like, "[I just need to do] my normal routine" or "focus."[4] When they missed shots, the higher-scoring players were also much more likely to attribute this to a specific issue with their technique, unlike the lower-scoring players, who were more likely to point to something general again, like lack of practice or lack of focus.

26 BRAIN BASICS

These results have been replicated many times in a variety of sports, in individuals at a variety of ages and ability levels. One study that looked at elite athletes competing at either the international or national level found that those who competed internationally were again much more likely to have specific goals, specific ways to achieve those goals, and specific reasons for their mistakes in the event of a failure.[5] This has also been found repeatedly in musicians across a variety of instruments. Researchers emphasize over and over that you cannot achieve a high level of performance by practicing mindlessly without specific goals and specific solutions.[6]

One of the leaders in this area of research, Dr. Barry Zimmerman, has put forth a three-step model for effective practice, which should be used in a constant cycle while practicing:[7]

Step 1: The Forethought Phase: Goal-Setting
Set specific goals for the practice session and choose specific practice strategies to achieve those goals.

Step 2: The Performance Phase: Self-Monitoring
Put the chosen strategies into practice and monitor closely how you're doing.

Step 3: Self-Reflection Phase
Evaluate how you did and precisely why things went well or didn't go well.

This model captures how the highest-performing musicians and athletes practice, and can be used by anyone, regardless of skill or years of experience.

Can effective practice skills be learned?

A frequent question about both musicians and athletes is whether their abilities are innate or acquired through practice. Maybe the people who are better at making specific goals, choosing specific strategies, and evaluating exactly why things didn't go well when they make mistakes are just better at those skills in the first place. And because they are better at those skills, they get better at their instrument or sport as a result.

Let's look at two studies that aimed to answer this question, one on athletes and one on musicians. In the study on athletes, researchers recruited college students who had never played basketball with the goal of helping them improve their free-throw shots.[8] Some of the students practiced free-throw shooting without any input on how to practice (the control group). The other students were taught about the three-part model developed by Dr. Zimmerman. Some of these students were only instructed in goal setting, some in both goal setting and self-monitoring while practicing, and some in all three parts (goal setting, self-monitoring, and self-reflection).

As you might guess, the groups who used the three-part model made much more improvement than the students who practiced however they wanted. Interestingly, the group that was only instructed in goal setting didn't do much better than the control group. The researchers also noted that the group who used the full three-step model focused the most on the process, rather than the outcome. And it was this focus on the *process* of improvement that allowed them to achieve more progress than the others.

This is a key point: focusing on the *process* will allow you to achieve a better outcome than only focusing on the outcome itself.

From this study it seems like teaching people to set specific goals, use specific practice strategies, monitor progress, and then reflect on exactly how things went seems to improve performance. It's a skill that can be learned.

But these were novice basketball players. What about more advanced musicians?

In an experiment looking at collegiate classical guitar students, the guitarists were given ten 20-minute practice sessions over about two weeks to learn a new piece of music.[9] Every practice session was video-recorded. After every other practice session, the guitarists performed whatever they had been working on (not necessarily the whole piece) as a way to measure their progress over the 10 practice sessions. After each of these "performances," everyone had to evaluate themselves. Half of the guitarists were shown the video of their performance before they did this self-evaluation.

In this study, the researchers were most interested in whether there was any change in the guitarists' ability to self-evaluate. The guitarists who watched their performance videos became much more precise and specific in their self-evaluations over the course of the experiment. Their comments became increasingly geared toward solving specific problems rather than more general comments about how satisfied (or not) they were with their playing. This focus on specific problem-solving goals was especially evident in the highest-performing guitarists, which further reinforces the other studies we've looked at.

28 BRAIN BASICS

It seems from these studies that this type of practicing—with a focus on specific goals, self-evaluation, and self-reflection—not only produces better performances, but is something that can be learned. Video-recording practice sessions and run-throughs and watching them with the intention of figuring out precisely what needs work is an especially helpful way to develop these skills. The benefit of video recording is reinforced by an interesting tidbit in another study that looked at different practicing strategies in pianists.[10] In that study, the top performing pianist was the only one who video recorded herself during practice and watched it back to assess how she was doing. Recording yourself and listening or watching back may be painful, but it's one of the most effective ways to improve.

Common practice mistakes and what to do instead

Now that we've discussed what good practicing looks like and why, let's return to some of those common bad practice habits I mentioned in Chapter 1 to look at what to do instead.

Common practicing mistake #1: Running through from beginning to end to start your practice session or starting from the beginning and stopping when you make a mistake (to either fix it or start over)

As you now know, simply playing through an entire song, piece, or movement is not practicing, it's just *playing*. You didn't set any specific goals before you started and as we've learned, this method will only solidify your mistakes, making them that much harder to fix later. "But how am I supposed to know what needs work if I don't run through it first?" you ask. My answer to that question is: if you were to do a run-through right now in front of your teacher, which spots would you worry about? That's where you should start. If your answer is, "I don't know," then you haven't been paying specific enough attention in your practicing up until now. Try recording yourself if you struggle with this. Even when a piece of music is brand new, you should have an idea of what's going to be hard for you based on past experience.

Try to be extremely specific about what needs work. Saying "everything sounds bad" is neither true nor helpful. It's critically important to be able to say very specifically, "The E on beat two of measure three is sharp" or "I'm rushing the 16th notes in beats three to four in bar 13," rather than just saying, "I'm out of tune" or "I'm rushing." It's only when you can be precise in this way that you can set specific goals and choose targeted strategies to address the issues that need attention.

In Chapter 1, I mentioned that there are two instances when running through is okay. The first is when a piece is brand new. On the *very first day* you start working on something, playing it through for the purpose of figuring out fingerings, bowings, where to breathe, and other fundamental matters of technique is fine. But in this case, you're not playing through from beginning to end. You're stopping to write in your fingerings, bowings, etc. While you're doing this, you should make a note of the sections you think will be the most difficult. Once you've finished putting in fingerings, etc., get right to work on those spots that you marked as the most challenging.

The other instance when running through is helpful is when you are getting ready to perform. Two to three weeks out from a performance (at least), your music should be completely learned so that you have time to practice performing (we'll discuss this more in Chapter 7 on interleaved practice). In that case, you *should* start each practice with a recorded run-through to assess how performance-ready you are. Your specific goal should be something along the lines of "Give a complete and compelling performance free from hesitations or stopping if I mess up" or "Concentrate all the way through and make all of my musical shapes and phrasing intentions convincing and clear." These are specific enough that you can evaluate exactly how you did afterward. Then listen to the recording of the run-through with your music to see whether you achieved your goals. Use your practice journal (which we'll talk about more in the final chapter) to write down everything that didn't go well, and then get to work on those spots.

Running through your piece should be a last step, never a first step. It may be months before you do your first full run-through. You shouldn't be running through the entire piece until you have solved all the problems and can play each section well. Then you have to work on joining the sections together. Once you've done that, now you're ready for a run-through. Often students feel they need to run through a piece repeatedly to "get a feel for it" or to "figure out how it goes." These were exactly the kinds of comments made by musicians in the studies we discussed at the beginning of the chapter who had the lowest rankings in terms of performance. These are too vague to be helpful goals or to direct you in using specific practice strategies.

30 BRAIN BASICS

If you do feel like you need to get a better feel for a piece before you can start to practice it, there are much more effective methods to accomplish this than running through. Listen to recordings, the more the better. Listen to see what different performers do in terms of timing, tempo, articulation, sound quality, vibrato, dynamics, phrasing, etc. Make notes of what you like and what you don't like. Again, be specific. When you hear something you like—or don't like—try to figure out *how* the performer is doing it.* Use mental practice to familiarize yourself with the piece (something we'll discuss in detail in Chapters 9 and 10). You can do an awful lot of work on phrasing, sound, expression, pacing, etc., before you even pick up your instrument. Study the score, particularly if it's something you will eventually play with other musicians. How does your part fit with the other part(s)? What's the structure of the piece? How do the different motives interact with each other? All this work can and should be done away from the instrument and will give you far more information than just playing it through repeatedly.

When you truly don't know where to start and everything seems to need an equal amount of work, the following two strategies can be very helpful:

1. Divide the piece into sections. Make sure these make musical sense—don't just do it by the line or the page. Look at each section and designate it as a Red, Yellow, or Green section. Red sections are the ones in the worst shape. These are your emergencies. Yellow sections are those that don't sound great, but aren't an emergency. Green sections sound fine. Maybe they're not perfect, but they're acceptable for now. Then start by working on your Red sections.

2. Work backward. Start from the final phrase (or final line, or final measure) and work on that until you're happy with it. Then back up a phrase/line/measure and work on that until you're happy with it. Put the two last phrases together to make sure you can go from one to the other smoothly. Keep working backward in this way until you're either

---

* I know many teachers discourage their students from listening to recordings of the piece they are working on for fear that the student will not develop their own interpretation. My opinion is that it depends on the level and sophistication of the student. Certainly, listening to only one recording over and over will be detrimental to developing a unique and flexible interpretation. But especially for undergraduates (and younger students), listening to the specific choices other artists have made in the pieces they are working on is a necessary part of their education to open their ears and imaginations to the possibilities that exist. To my mind, telling a student not to listen to recordings is akin to never demonstrating in a lesson. Students can't develop their interpretative skills if they have no models to draw from.

out of time or you make it to the beginning. This can help clarify which areas need work because doing it in reverse order will feel less familiar. When it's less familiar, your weak spots will be highlighted, which is exactly what you want in order to improve. You should be able to start literally anywhere in the piece and play it the way you want to. If your teacher has ever suggested starting from a certain measure and you've said, "Oh, I can't play it from there. I need to start the line before," this will be an especially valuable practice method for you.

Common practicing mistake #2: Putting on the metronome and playing through your piece slowly

I often hear students practice this way and I think they believe they are practicing well. After all, everyone is always saying to practice slowly, right? The purpose of practicing slowly is so you can feel and hear more clearly what the issues are, and so you can correct them with good form and technique. Going slowly helps you problem-solve more easily. But if you are just playing through big sections (or the whole piece) slowly, you're not accomplishing anything because there is no problem solving going on—you're just playing. Again, playing through is not practicing, it's just playing.

Maybe you think you're getting a feel for the piece this way and locking in good habits because you're going slowly and minimizing errors. But this is a very general goal and a very general practice strategy, not the kind of specific, targeted strategy that has been shown to work much better. Think of it this way: if you had to learn 100 vocabulary words in a second language, would it be effective to read each word and its translation, slowly one after the other, until you got through the whole list? Of course not. By the time you got to the end of the list, you'd probably remember maybe four words total—the first two and the last two, most likely. It would be much more effective to make flashcards and then divide them into three piles: words you already know, words that seem familiar (but you don't know), and words that are completely unfamiliar. Then, you would start studying the completely unfamiliar pile in small batches. The same thing is true with practicing: if you play through big sections slowly, you're going to retain next to nothing. Better to figure out where the hardest spots are (as described in the previous section) and get to work.

32   BRAIN BASICS

Common practicing mistake #3: Playing through your best spots over and over

It feels good to play well. We all like to play well. But the purpose of practicing is to improve your weaknesses. When you play music you can already play over and over again, you aren't accomplishing anything. What's your specific goal when you do this? As we've discussed, mistakes are necessary to learn. If you're not making mistakes, there's nothing to correct, and so nothing to learn. Leave the playing through of your best sections until the end, as a reward for all the hard work you did in the rest of your practice session.

Common practicing mistake #4: Doing mindless repetitions

Repetitions in and of themselves are not going to do anything. If you hear something that doesn't sound good and you play it over and over without stopping to figure out *why* it doesn't sound good and exactly how to fix it, all you are going to do is solidify the problem. You may be setting a specific goal (fix the shift in bar five) and using a specific strategy (do repetitions), but you aren't doing the self-reflection piece: *why* are you failing to nail that shift each time? Every time you play something, it should take you closer and closer to your goal. If you are making the same mistake in the same way each time, you haven't identified clearly or precisely enough what is causing that mistake. Take a step back and try as many different things as you can come up with to solve the problem. If nothing works, make a note to talk to your teacher about it.

Here is another tidbit from one of the studies on practice strategies: in a study with volleyball players, the highest performing athletes were much more likely to say they would seek out help from their coach when they missed their serves repeatedly.[11] I think students are often scared to tell their teachers that they are struggling with something, but it's literally our job as teachers to help you solve the problems you can't solve on your own. The very best lessons are the ones where students come in with a list of things they need help with, rather than trying to hide their weaknesses from me as their teacher.

Nobody likes making mistakes. They're frustrating, especially when we want to just *play*. But they're necessary and inevitable. The difference between great players and merely good players is how those great players *respond* to their mistakes. Having specific goals, specific strategies, and precise self-reflection makes all the difference.

But what if there were a way to make mistakes *on purpose* to speed up learning? That's the topic of our next chapter.

3

Use Errors to Your Advantage

Samantha arrived for her first lesson with me and I noticed immediately that her bow hold was getting in her way. Her pinky and thumb were straight—rather than curved, with springy flexibility—and her hand was contorted at an awkward angle. We worked hard in that lesson to start fixing her bow hold, and she seemed like an attentive and diligent student, so I was hopeful that she would be able to correct the problems relatively quickly. When she left that day, it was already looking better.

The next week when she arrived, I asked how her practicing had gone.

"Good, I think . . . ?" she told me with a shrug.

She started to play, but her bow hold looked exactly the same as the week before. No improvement.

"So, do you remember that last week in your lesson, we talked a lot about your bow hold?" I asked her.

"Yeah."

"Did you work on that at home this week?"

"Um . . . I didn't really think about it that much, actually."

Okay, I thought, she doesn't know how to work on it. No wonder! So I proceeded to talk to her about good practice techniques.

The next week, it was the same issue. And the week after that. And the week after that. In fact, after a whole year, nothing much had changed. When I reminded her to pay attention to her bow hold, she could do it just fine. But she never seemed to hold it correctly without my prompting. I was a relatively new teacher at the time, and I was frustrated by her lack of progress. Did she just not care? Or was she not really paying attention? Or maybe I just wasn't explaining it clearly enough.

It turns out, it was none of these things.

Learn Faster, Perform Better. Molly Gebrian, Oxford University Press. © Oxford University Press 2024.
DOI: 10.1093/oso/9780197680063.003.0004

36 BRAIN BASICS

Why bad habits are so persistent

In many ways, the brain is a prediction machine. When there is a mismatch between what you predict and what actually happens, your brain registers that discrepancy. In fact, something that comes as a surprise causes a larger reaction in the brain than when everything goes according to plan.[1] We also learn more quickly when we are surprised by something than when our predictions are correct. Think about the experience of playing loudly in a rest because the conductor takes more time than you expected. You only need to do that once to make sure you are looking up at the conductor at that spot so you don't fall into the same trap twice.

It's the same when we are practicing: our brains register the mistake *if we are aware we've made one.* If we don't do anything to try to change that mistake, that's when the wrong pathway starts to get reinforced, as we discussed in the first chapter. But what if you don't even realize you've made an error? Or what if you don't realize you have a bad habit, you just know things aren't working? How can you fix something you're not even aware of?

Enter two powerful techniques for getting rid of bad habits: amplification of error and old way/new way.

Before we discuss either of these methods, though, we need to understand why bad habits are so hard to correct beyond the fact that they are well-myelinated pathways (as discussed in Chapter 1). The inventor of old way/new way is Harry Lyndon, a teacher who worked in Australia. He explained that something called "proactive inhibition" is trying to protect the bad habit from going away.[2] Proactive inhibition—or interference, as it is most commonly known these days—is a well-documented phenomenon in the brain where old knowledge can prevent us from learning new knowledge if that new knowledge conflicts with the old knowledge. For instance, if you were erroneously taught that an F major scale has no sharps or flats, just like C major, it will be hard to remember to play a B-flat in the F major scale. The new knowledge (F major has one flat) conflicts with the old knowledge (F major has no sharps or flats), even though that old knowledge is incorrect.

The old knowledge actually makes us forget the new knowledge more quickly that we normally would. We have no control over this—it's just a feature of how the brain works. When it comes to bad habits, the teacher can clearly see the issue, but the student can't really feel the problem because they are so used to playing that way. This is exactly what was going on with Samantha and her bow hold: it was simply outside of her conscious awareness, even though I had pointed it out repeatedly and it was very obvious to me as her teacher. Some people have much higher levels of proactive interference than others, which makes it even harder for them to correct bad habits. So part of the reason bad habits are so stubborn is that our brains are *protecting* them. And since they are outside of our conscious awareness, we do them automatically without realizing it, even if they have been pointed out repeatedly.

Harry Lyndon reasoned that if you could bring the bad habit into conscious awareness, then you could override the proactive interference and correct the bad habit. This principle of bringing automatic habits back into conscious awareness is why amplification of error and old way/new way work so well.

Amplification of error

Now that you understand this, let's discuss amplification of error first. I should note that both methods we'll discuss ideally require you to have a (good) teacher to help you through this process.*

In amplification of error, the teacher should identify the main cause of the bad habit. There may be many different reasons for the bad habit, but you want to try to identify the primary issue that's causing other elements of the bad habit. As an example, maybe a viola player's left wrist is bent too much so the heel of the hand is touching the neck of the instrument, as shown in Figure 3.1b. This is known as a "pizza wrist" to many violin and viola teachers. Often, a pizza wrist is caused by the instrument being unstable on the player's shoulder, so they are trying to hold it in place more securely with the hand and wrist. A pizza wrist will help secure the instrument, but it won't allow you to play very well. In this case, the primary issue is the security of the instrument on the shoulder, not the wrist itself.

Once you've identified the main error, the next step is to exaggerate the error. In the example of the pizza wrist, maybe the violin doesn't feel secure on the player's shoulder because they are pushing their shoulder up and

---

* If you are trying to correct bad habits on your own without a teacher to help guide you, I would encourage you to watch many videos of great players to see the exact physical motions they make. Then video yourself from many different angles until you can pinpoint the precise differences between how you play and how great musicians play. Even better, though: take a lesson with someone, even if it's just a single session over the internet. That could save you hundreds of hours of frustration.

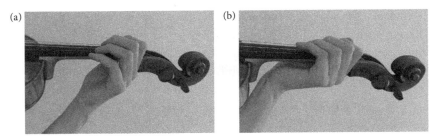

Figure 3.1 a. Proper left-hand shape. b. Incorrect left-hand shape, known as a "pizza wrist."

forward. In that case, the player should push it up and forward even more. By exaggerating the bad habit, it makes the student more aware of it, and then they can feel more clearly why it's a problem. In one study looking at this teaching method in golfers, researchers found that a group of golfers who were taught to exaggerate their bad habit self-corrected the issue without their coach having to get involved. In contrast, the group who were given explicit instruction on the correct way to hit the ball showed the same lack of improvement as the control group who weren't given any feedback at all.[3]

This all comes with an important caveat, however. When someone's initial skill level is relatively high, amplifying the error seems to work quite well to help correct the issue. But when someone's skill level is lower, they already have so much variability in what they are doing, amplifying the error can make things worse. In that case, what's known as "haptic guidance"—helping show someone what it feels like to do it correctly—is more helpful. This is what parents do when they hold the back of a kid's bike who is learning to ride without training wheels for the first time, or when a dad stands behind his daughter learning to swing a baseball bat and puts his hands over her hands, guiding her in how to swing.[4] So if you're already pretty skilled at something and you're trying to refine that skill, amplifying the error can help you figure out a better solution. But if you have a lower skill level, amplifying the error can be like flailing around randomly—it probably won't help that much.

Old way/new way

The second technique, old way/new way, is also designed to rapidly correct a bad habit by bringing it into conscious awareness. Again, this is best done under the guidance of a good teacher. Amazingly, old way/new way works so well that in a *single session* people can go from doing something correctly 0% of the time to doing it correctly at least 80% of the time. Even better, this change seems to be permanent.

Before we get into the steps for old way/new way, I should mention that all the steps are necessary—so, no cutting corners—and the student must be motivated to change their bad habit.

With those preconditions met, here's how it works:

Step 1: The student and the teacher should gather video evidence of the bad habit in action, as well as video of the good habit, performed by either the student themself, the teacher, or another professional. They should watch these videos together to make sure the student can clearly see the difference between the old way (the bad habit) and the new way (the good habit they are trying to learn). The student should describe the differences between the two as clearly as they can. They may need the teacher's help for this, which is why this step should be done together.

Step 2: The student should perform the action the old way, doing their bad habit on purpose. They should then describe in as much detail as possible what the old habit feels like. This may take a while because what the student is feeling may be pretty vague at first. But it's critically important that they can describe clearly and concretely what it feels like because this will bring the habit back into conscious awareness. Again, the teacher likely needs to help with this step. (It may also help for the student to close their eyes to feel what they are doing more clearly.) Like the error amplification method described above, this step should focus on the primary error that is causing other issues. Once the student can describe the old way clearly, they need to repeat the old way several times to make sure they can do it on purpose reliably. Again, the point of this step is to bring the old way into conscious awareness.

Step 3: The student needs to figure out how to do the new way (the new habit they are trying to learn). Again, they will probably need the teacher's help for this. Once the student can do the new way correctly, they should describe what it feels like in as much detail as possible. Like describing the old way, this also needs to be as concrete as possible.

Step 4: The student then alternates between the old way and the new way. They should do the old way and describe in detail what it feels like. Then they should do the new way and describe what that feels like. Go

40 BRAIN BASICS

back and forth between the old way and the new way like this five times. Even though it can be a bit annoying, it's extremely important not to skip the step of describing what it feels like each time because the verbal descriptions are what bring the habit back into conscious awareness.

Step 5: Do only the new way several times (studies on this method have differing numbers of repetitions of the new way, but most do six repetitions).

And that's it. The error should be corrected. No need to repeat this process at the next lesson or the next day as a review.

The studies that have looked at this method in athletes have some very encouraging results. One study looked at two Olympic athletes—a javelin thrower and a sprinter—who were clearly great athletes, but they both had stubborn bad habits that were having a negative effect on their ability in competitions.[5] For the javelin thrower, the day after the old way/new way intervention, she did 100% of her throws correctly in practice and continued to throw accurately in the weeks following. The sprinter had similar results. And in competition, both athletes performed correctly 85%–90% of the time. The numbers in Figure 3.2 speak for themselves.

Another study looked at a swimmer who did an old way/new way intervention only three days (!) before the national championships.[6] That may seem risky, but it paid off for the swimmer. Before doing old way/new way, he started races—diving into the water and then starting to swim—incorrectly about half the time, both in practice and in competition. This really cost him time. Again, the numbers in Figure 3.3 speak for themselves, but look especially at the percentage of correct starts in the national championships: 85% of the starts were correct in an extremely high-pressure situation just *three days* after making the change. Anyone who has ever tried to correct a bad habit the usual way will appreciate how amazing that is.

		Before Old Way/New Way		After Old Way/New Way	
		Incorrect Tries	Correct Tries	Incorrect Tries	Correct Tries
Javelin thrower	Practice	90%	10%	15%–20%	80%–85%
	Competition	100%	0%	10%	90%
Sprinter	Practice	100%	0%	13%	87%
	Competition	100%	0%	15%	85%

Figure 3.2 Percentage of incorrect and correct tries for each athlete before and after the old way/new way intervention.

Before Old Way/New Way		
	Incorrect Tries	*Correct Tries*
Practice	60%	40%
Competition	50%	50%
After Old Way/New Way		
	Incorrect Tries	*Correct Tries*
Practice 2 days later	0%	100%
Nationals 3 days later	15%	85%
Practice 2 weeks later	17%	83%
World Championships 1 month later	0%	100%
Practice 8 months later	6%	94%

Figure 3.3 Percentage of incorrect and correct tries before the old way/new way intervention compared to after the intervention in a variety of different events.

This approach has also been used in vocational training—people learning to be hairdressers or carpenters or plumbers—with great success.[7] In an experiment using old way/new way in these kinds of settings, researchers compared the traditional way of getting rid of an old habit—the teacher shows the student the right way and has them do many repetitions—with old way/new way. At the beginning of the study, all the students were doing the skill incorrectly 100% of the time. After the different training methods, the old way/new way students were getting it right up to 94% of the time. In contrast, the students corrected in the traditional way were able to do the new way, at best, 35.9% of the time. Figure 3.4 shows a graphic representation of these statistics.

Old way/new way seems to have additional benefits beyond just technical correction: in a study looking at this method with a tennis player, researchers also measured the effect this intervention had on psychological skills, namely anxiety control, concentration, self-confidence, and motivation.[8] They found that in addition to fixing the tennis player's bad habit, all the psychological measures improved as well, as shown in Figure 3.5. These sorts of psychological skills are obviously of critical importance in performing well, so any method that can correct a long-ingrained bad habit and can also improve psychological performance skills is well worth trying.

42 BRAIN BASICS

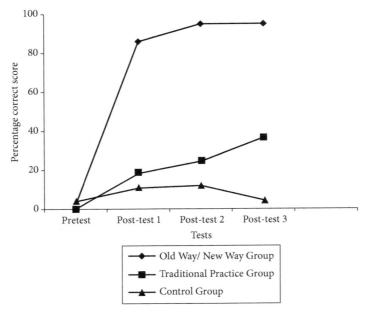

Figure 3.4 Performance of each group on a series of three skills tests given after the old way/new way intervention.

Reproduced with permission from Baxter, P., et al. (2004). Less pain, more gain: rapid skill development using old way new way. *Journal of Vocational Education and Training.* 56(1): 21–50. ©The Vocational Aspect of Education Ltd, reprinted by permission of Taylor & Francis Ltd, http://www.tandfonline.com on behalf of The Vocational Aspect of Education Ltd.

	Before Old Way/New Way	After Old Way/New Way
Anxiety Control	13%	58%
Concentration	29%	63%
Self-confidence	50%	86%
Motivation	64%	89%

Figure 3.5 The athlete's scores (out of a possible 100%) on each psychological measure, both before and after the old way/new way intervention.

Although most of these studies were done with a small number of participants, the fact that the results were replicated across a wide variety of sports and skills gives confidence that this method works. From my own teaching, I can attest to the effectiveness of old way/new way. No longer do my students persist in their bad habits for weeks and months as they used to.

The role of feedback

Both methods of error correction described in this chapter serve to bring detrimental habits into conscious awareness so the student can self-correct. This aligns well with other research on the best *time* for teachers to give feedback to students. Students who are given immediate feedback do far worse in performance tests than students who are asked to self-evaluate before receiving feedback.[9] It seems that when students are given immediate feedback, they are not allowed to develop their own error detection abilities, and instead rely solely on the feedback of their teacher.[10]

This is directly related to the common advice of practicing in front of a mirror. Often string players and singers in particular are told to do this in order to become more aware of what they are doing. This can be beneficial at first, but it doesn't solve the problem long-term. The most obvious example of this for string players is learning to play with a straight bow (keeping the bow parallel to the bridge). This is a difficult skill to learn for two reasons: on violin and viola, when you move your arm in what feels like a straight line, the bow will go crooked relative to the bridge; plus, what looks straight from the player's perspective often is an optical illusion caused by the curvature of the bridge and the fingerboard.

Violinists and violists are commonly told to practice in front of a mirror to straighten out their bow. Many of us (myself included) spend years and years practicing in front of a mirror to no avail. We can play with a perfectly straight bow when we are looking in the mirror, but as soon as we are without that feedback—like in a lesson or concert—we can't keep our bows straight. The reason is that the mirror prevents us from forming a clear kinesthetic image of what a straight bow *feels* like—we are unable to tell by feel if our bows are straight when we don't have the visual feedback of the mirror. In this case, a much better way to work on straight bow is to video yourself playing a short passage—and don't look at the screen while playing—while trying to keep a straight bow. Then watch it back to see how you did. You will be able to match your memory of what it felt like to what you see on the video, which is much more beneficial in helping develop the kinesthetic awareness of what a straight bow feels like. This principle can be applied to anything you would normally practice in front of a mirror. The mirror is a great tool to get started, but then the simultaneous feedback needs to be removed so you can develop a clear sense of what something feels like when it's correct. A mirror will hinder you in that pursuit.

44 BRAIN BASICS

I had many more students like Samantha over the years, with bad habits that just didn't seem to go away despite my (and their) best efforts. Now I use old way/new way and amplification of error instead, and I can vouch for their effectiveness. Old way/new way usually takes an entire hour-long lesson, but it seems to me to be a good use of time, especially compared to how long it used to take—months or years or sometimes never! Learning about these techniques strongly reinforced for me the power of errors in learning. Rather than being scared of mistakes and trying to avoid them at all costs, we can harness our errors to work for us rather than against us if we are strategic in how we use them.

SECTION II
USING YOUR TIME WELL

As musicians, we are always looking for ways to maximize our time in the practice room, to learn faster and more efficiently. In this section, we'll look at what the research has to say about how to best utilize our time for maximum benefit by discussing the importance of taking breaks, the power of interleaved practice, and the benefits of including variability in your practice sessions.

4

The Fastest Way to Learn Music: Take More Breaks

When I started giving presentations on the neuroscience of practicing, people often approached me afterward to ask a variant of the same question. It would go something like: "So once, I got really sick a few weeks before my recital and I had to stop practicing for a whole week. When I started practicing again, I could play my music *better* and more easily than before I was sick, even though I hadn't practiced for a whole week. What's that about?" Or: "Once I tried to learn how to double tongue and I could not do it at all, so I just gave up. But then I tried again a few months later and it was really easy. How did that happen?"

Most of us have had strange experiences like this that seem too good to be true. Despite that, taking breaks on purpose as a practice strategy just seems wildly irresponsible. After all, if you're not practicing, you're not improving. Right?

Maybe not.

The power of breaks

One of the most common misconceptions about practicing (especially in classical music) is that it's necessary to practice many hours every day, tackling everything all at once for as much time as possible, and to practice each individual piece, passage, or skill for a long time before moving on to something else. It's not unusual for students in top music schools to practice six to eight hours a day (or more) and for students to believe this is required to become a "serious" musician. These same students often practice for two to three hours (or more) at a time without a break (or with only minimal breaks). And it's common for students to get fixated on one section or passage for an hour or more at a time. Students are using their time in this way

Learn Faster, Perform Better. Molly Gebrian, Oxford University Press. © Oxford University Press 2024.
DOI: 10.1093/oso/9780197680063.003.0005

48 USING YOUR TIME WELL

because they believe—or have been told by their teachers—that this sort of punishing schedule is the only way to succeed.

It's not.

In fact, research going back to the 1880s shows that this sort of schedule is the *least* effective for learning something both quickly and durably. Yes, this schedule will eventually lead to improvement and performance success, but there's a *much* easier, much less time-consuming way that works significantly better. Taking breaks is one of the most powerful practice strategies we have. It sounds too good to be true, but it's not. It's a general principle of how all living things learn.

Take more breaks and learn faster.

To understand what's going on here, we need to start with a German psychologist by the name of Hermann Ebbinghaus. He is credited with discovering the power of breaks, something researchers now call spaced practice. He published his findings in 1885 in a book entitled *Über das Gedächtnis. Untersuchungen zur experimentellen Psychologie* (published in English as *Memory: A Contribution to Experimental Psychology*), and his discoveries have continued to be studied and tested ever since.[1] Today, it is well established and universally accepted by scientists that taking breaks is more effective than doing one big block of practicing all at once. Unfortunately, this counterintuitive idea has not made it into mainstream culture or the culture of music practicing.

There are countless studies that have found that spacing out practice sessions by taking breaks is the most effective way to learn. Much of the research examines how people study for academic tests. But more recently, researchers have extended this question to tasks requiring a combination of complex motor and cognitive skills, like playing music. The best studies looking at the power of breaks when it comes to combining these skills were done with surgeons. If you think about it, surgical skills provide a good parallel to musical skills: surgeons are required to learn extremely precise, challenging motor skills that are performed in high-pressure, cognitively demanding situations. What has been found in surgeons can therefore be applied to musicians. Let's take a trip to medical school to see what we can learn.

In one experiment, medical students were divided into two groups to learn a set of surgical skills. The first group practiced these skills for three hours straight without a break, something known as massed practice.[2] I'll call this group Team Massed. A second group practiced for 40 minutes and then took a 20-minute walk. I'll call them Team Breaks. When they came back, they

THE FASTEST WAY TO LEARN MUSIC: TAKE MORE BREAKS   49

practiced for another 40 minutes and then took another 20-minute walk. After their second walk, they practiced once more for 40 minutes. Note that Team Breaks only practiced for two hours total, a full hour less than Team Massed. However, when they were tested at the end of the training, Team Breaks did significantly better. Not only did Team Breaks get to take two nice walks, they practiced for a full hour less than Team Massed, and yet they did better on the skills test.

Interesting for sure. But there's more.

In another study, researchers focused on how surgical skills taught in the lab transfer to real-life situations.[3] Again, there were two groups. In this case, Team Massed did four training sessions all in one day for a total of five and a half hours of training. Team Breaks had one training session per week for four consecutive weeks (every Monday for a month, for instance) until they had also done a total of five and a half hours of training.

Like the first experiment we discussed, Team Breaks did better when tested on their skills. But they also vastly outperformed Team Massed when it came to transferring the skills to a more real-life situation. In fact, for some of the skills, Team Massed scored the same on the transfer test as they had on the pretest before they had done any training at all. That's not good! They made literally no measurable improvement that transferred after five and a half hours of practice! In contrast, Team Breaks did significantly better in the real-life transfer situation versus their score on the pretest.

This is critical information for us as musicians. When our skills transfer to new situations more effectively, we save time because we don't have to work on those basic skills in every new context. We hope that what we learn in one context (scales, etudes, etc.) will be there for us in a piece of music so we can focus more on the *music* and less on the technical aspects of what we're playing. We also don't want to feel like we have to start each new piece from zero. Hopefully the skills we just acquired working on that last concerto will transfer to our new sonata movement, for instance.

So far, we've seen that medical students who spend less time practicing and take walks instead perform better in the end, and we've seen that practicing something just once a week—versus five and a half hours all at once—results in better transfer to other situations, also saving time. But an important question to ask is whether this applies at different skill levels. Maybe the absolute skill level of both groups isn't very high. Maybe the spaced groups are doing better, but overall nobody is very good at the skills they're learning. As musicians, we want our practicing to be effective, but we also want to play

50   USING YOUR TIME WELL

at the highest level possible. The idea of taking breaks is only worth doing if you're not going to sacrifice quality, and maybe long practice sessions are what it takes to reach that level of ability. It's a good question, and it's relevant to surgeons, too. After all, you want your surgeon to be highly competent and precise!

To look at this question, a team of researchers decided to measure the percentage of students who reached *proficiency* on a given surgical task.[4] That's a much higher bar. Again, there were two groups of students. In this study, Team Massed had three blocks of training all in one day, back-to-back. Each training session was 75 minutes long. Team Breaks also had three total training blocks of 75 minutes each, but they had one training per week for three weeks (e.g., every Monday for three weeks).

In the end, the differences between the groups were astounding—and worrisome if massed practice is the way surgeons are typically trained. On one skill, only 11% (!) of Team Massed reached proficiency, while 70% of Team Breaks reached proficiency. On another skill, only 39% of Team Massed reached proficiency, compared to 90% of Team Breaks. In fact, for every skill tested, Team Breaks did significantly better by at least 33 percentage points or more, as shown in Figure 4.1.

So far, spaced practice is looking pretty good: higher skill level in less time with better transfer. But what about how long it sticks with you? That's important, too, if you are trying to maximize your time. Intuitively, we're aware that cramming doesn't work well to remember something long-term. Think about those all-night cram sessions before an exam: you might remember just enough to get through the exam, but if someone asks you about that material a year later (sometimes even a week later!) you can't remember any of it. But maybe it's just because you were studying in the middle of the night and

	Team Massed % at proficiency	Team Breaks % at proficiency
Elastic band	39%	90%
Pipe cleaner	11%	70%
Beads	11%	50%
Cutting circle	22%	60%
Suturing	22%	55%

Figure 4.1 The percentage of surgical students who reached proficiency in each group after training on each skill.

THE FASTEST WAY TO LEARN MUSIC: TAKE MORE BREAKS   51

you were tired; maybe it has nothing to do with spacing out your studying over a longer period of time.

An experiment on mice shows otherwise.[*]

In this experiment, the mice were trained to run through a maze.[5] In this case, Team Massed trained for an hour all at once. In contrast, Team Breaks trained for 15 minutes at a time with an hour break in between each training session until they had also done an hour total. By the end of the training, both groups of mice were doing great at the maze. None of the mice received any additional training, but each day, they were tested to see how well they could remember the maze. After 15 days, Team Massed were basically back to where they started—they had forgotten how to run the maze. In contrast, Team Breaks could still remember how to run the maze 60 days later! Again, both groups got the same amount of training, but Team Breaks remembered how to run the maze for significantly longer.

Here's what we've learned so far: when we take more breaks between practice sessions, we perform better, our skills transfer better to new situations, we reach a much higher level of proficiency, and we remember what we learned for far longer. It seems like magic, doesn't it? Now the question is *why*: why does taking breaks work so much better? To answer this question, we need to look at what is happening inside the brain.

What happens in the brain during breaks?

In the summer of 2021, a fascinating study came out that captured the attention of the scientific community.[6] It looked at brain activity during so-called microbreaks. In this experiment, researchers asked people to learn a key-press sequence on a computer keyboard. The goal was to perform this sequence as quickly and accurately as possible. Participants were given 10 seconds to practice, followed by a 10-second microbreak, during which they just sat and did nothing. They continued through multiple rounds of this while the experimenters measured not only their performance but also their brain activity.

Amazingly, researchers found that the majority of the performance improvements happened during the *breaks*. You can see this in Figure 4.2. In

---

[*] I know mice aren't humans, but spaced practice is a basic principle of how all living things learn most effectively, so it's worth looking at what this research can teach us.

52 USING YOUR TIME WELL

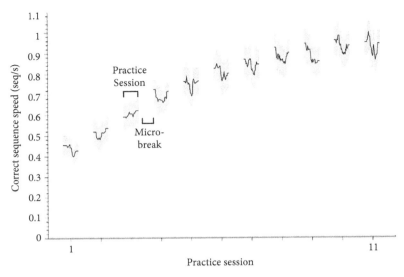

Figure 4.2 Performance while practicing interspersed with microbreaks, from practice session #1 (left side) to practice session #11 (right side).
Modified from Buch, E., et al. (2021). Consolidation of human skill linked to waking hippocampo-neocortical replay. *Cell Reports.* 35(10): 109193. © Elsevier 2021.

this graph, the little squiggles show the participants' performance while they were practicing. The spaces between the squiggles are the breaks. The left side of the graph shows the first practice session, progressing to the final practice session on the right. You can see that after each break, the participants performed at a higher level than at the end of the previous practice session.

More interestingly, the researchers discovered that during the breaks, the brain replayed the key-press sequence 20 times faster (and backward). The brain was continuing to practice in a super fast-forward manner while participants were taking their breaks.

The implications of this study are enormously important. Breaks aren't wasted time: they are the *most important time* for skill improvement.

Based on this research, I now do my repetitions a bit differently than I used to (as discussed in Chapter 1). I used to do all my correct repetitions—say, five times in a row—in one block without a break. Now I do three correct repetitions in a row, take a 10–15 second break, and then do three more in a row. The same rules apply (discussed in Chapter 1) about going back to zero if you mess up and trying to achieve at least 50% overlearning. There are just breaks built in now. I find that I can solidify my work faster this way and it sticks with me better over time (like those mice in the maze).

Is anything else going on in the brain when we take breaks?

Long-term potentiation

In Chapter 1, we touched on the idea of long-term potentiation (LTP), the process by which synapses strengthen themselves when you learn something new. Long-term potentiation essentially makes it easier for the neurons involved to talk to each other, facilitated by structural changes to the synapse. It's a little bit like upgrading your modem and the speed of your wifi: when you have faster internet speed and better equipment, it is much easier to communicate during a video call because it doesn't freeze or distort every two seconds.

Long-term potentiation is the first step in learning something new or improving. Scientists study what happens to neurons undergoing LTP to understand what may be happening in the initial stages of learning. Researchers can simulate LTP in the lab by zapping a neuronal ensemble with an electrical pulse, which mimics the electrical signal that travels down the axon, discussed in Chapter 1. Scientists have found that when you activate a neuronal ensemble in this way, some of the neurons undergo LTP, but not all of them.[7] If you zap them again 10 minutes later, nothing happens—no more neurons undergo LTP. But if you wait for an hour and give them another zap, then many more neurons undergo LTP. In fact, you double the amount of LTP by waiting an hour.

Why? Why wait for an hour?

As mentioned earlier, LTP involves structural changes at the synapse to make communication between neurons easier. Those structural changes require building materials. If those materials are sitting there waiting, the neuron can take advantage of the electrical stimulation right away and undergo LTP. But if the building materials aren't there, the neuron needs time to move them to the cell wall. Researchers have found that apparently an hour is the amount of time needed. If another round of electrical stimulation is given 10 minutes (or even 30 minutes) after the first one, it won't do anything—the building materials aren't there yet. Think of it like a construction site that is waiting on more wood and paint to arrive: telling the construction site to

54 USING YOUR TIME WELL

hurry up won't do any good. The wood and paint have a commute that takes an hour, and so everybody just has to wait.

Since LTP is the first step in learning something new, once neurons have made this change, they are at a higher level of readiness for further practicing or studying. Because neurons that have undergone LTP can communicate more easily, the skill supported by those neurons will feel easier. Scientists think this is one of the mechanisms underlying the efficacy of spaced practice. But can't you just keep practicing that same skill during the hour that the neurons are moving the building materials to the cell wall rather than taking a break? Unfortunately, no. The brain doesn't start doing any necessary construction (or reconstruction) while you are actively using the neurons involved. Consider a city road as an analogy: during significant construction, workers need to shut down the road for paving and other improvements. You can't have cars driving on the road while it's being fixed. The same thing is true for your brain: it can only do the necessary construction when you are taking a break.

What does this mean for practicing?

In practical terms, this research means that particularly when you are working on something new, practice it for a little bit and then leave it. Come back to that passage later in the day and work on it a bit more. Then leave it alone and come back to it once more at the end of the day. But don't overdo it—from the study on LTP we were just discussing, it seems that three times is enough: additional rounds of stimulation after the third had no effect.

What should you do during your break?

Should you abstain from all practicing during the break, or is it okay to practice different music while you're taking a break from one passage? After all, it's not very practical for most musicians to work on one small passage and then stop practicing completely for an hour or two—we just have too much music to learn. A group of researchers realized the same thing was true of students learning surgical skills: they have very intensive training schedules and need to learn many different skills quickly. In an experiment designed to test this, there were five different groups:[8]

- Team Massed practiced without breaks
- Team Similar practiced a very similar skill during the break

THE FASTEST WAY TO LEARN MUSIC: TAKE MORE BREAKS   55

- Team Different practiced a very different skill during the break
- Team Observation observed expert surgeons performing the skill they were learning during the break
- Team Break took an actual break and did nothing.

At the end of the experiment, all the groups were tested on the skill they had practiced. As I'm sure you can guess, Team Massed did the worst. Team Similar did just as badly. Interestingly, Team Different did as well as Team Break. In fact, the final three groups—Team Different, Team Observation, and Team Break—all did about the same. Therefore, as long as you are practicing something that's different enough, you can continue to practice during your break from the first passage you were working on. As an example, if you were working on a fast, flashy passage and now you're taking a break from that, maybe working on something slow and lyrical would be a good contrast for your brain. For multi-instrumentalists or percussionists who play many different instruments, switching to a different instrument for a while would also be a good way to take a break and let your brain do the necessary reconstruction.

Retroactive interference

In addition to the brain activity during breaks that we've already discussed, the brain also appears to do more large-scale reorganization during the breaks, especially when something is brand new. When we start learning something new, an area of the brain called the prefrontal cortex is heavily involved. This area of the brain, right behind your forehead, is typically involved at the early stages of learning when the new skill feels effortful and we aren't very good at it yet. The new skill usually feels unstable as well. In one study looking at brain activation for a new skill versus that skill after a break, researchers found that when participants practiced a skill for the first time, the prefrontal cortex was indeed highly active. But when the participants returned five and a half hours later for a second practice session, the prefrontal cortex was no longer activated.[9] This time, it was areas further back in the brain that were activated: the premotor area, the parietal lobe, and the cerebellum. These areas are associated with more stable storage of the skill, meaning it will feel easier and more automatic.

This longer-term reorganization is related to something called *retroactive interference*, which is also mitigated by taking breaks. In Chapter 3, we discussed something called *proactive* interference, which is when old knowledge makes it much harder to learn something new (as in the case of bad habits). *Retroactive* interference is the opposite: new knowledge hampers the performance of old knowledge.

Confused? I don't blame you. And also, how can you ever learn anything if the interference goes both ways?

Retroactive interference is typically only seen under special conditions: if you learn two brand new things back-to-back that are very similar, the second one will get in the way of the first one, making the first one harder to remember or perform. In this case the "old" knowledge isn't actually old, it's just what you learned first when you learned two brand new things. Let's clarify this with a musical example. Let's say you are a kid learning Bach's *Minuet in G* for the first time. The main melody has two different endings, as shown in Figure 4.3. If you work on Ending A and then work on Ending B immediately after, you're going to have a harder time playing Ending A when you come back to it the next day. The two versions are quite similar to each other, and you learned them back-to-back, so they interfere with each other.

According to research, you can avoid this problem by waiting approximately six hours in between practicing Ending A and Ending B. When you take a break of about six hours, this retroactive interference effect disappears, presumably because your brain has time to strengthen Ending A during the break.[10] When material is brand new to the brain, it's fragile and easily disrupted. But when you take a break, this new skill gets strengthened, and so it's less susceptible to interference later. I like to think of new knowledge like a little baby animal that was just born. It's so fragile and small and it needs protection. Breaks provide protection, giving new knowledge a little bit of armor and making it less vulnerable. But again, retroactive interference only seems to show up for things that are very similar to each other. You don't have to worry about this interference happening if you learn the opening to a brand

Figure 4.3 Music for *Minuet in G* (attributed to J.S. Bach) with the two different endings indicated.

new Romantic-era concerto, followed by a brand-new Bach Allemande. This material is very different, so it is not likely to trigger retroactive interference in the brain.

Our brains are doing a lot when we're taking a break. Rather than being wasted time when we should be practicing, breaks are critical if we want to learn effectively and improve as quickly as possible. So far, we've only looked at what's going on in the brain during short breaks within one day. What about those surgical studies where they took a week off in between practice sessions? Or musicians who take a week off by accident and suddenly can play much better once they come back? What's the brain doing over longer breaks?

To answer these questions, we need to talk about the role of sleep, the biggest and most important break of all.

5

Can You Learn Music in Your Sleep?

If you're like most people—and especially most conservatory students—you probably think sleep is a waste of time. Given the choice between practicing more or getting enough sleep, I think most musicians would choose practicing. Or at least that's what they feel they have to do. There just aren't enough hours in the day to get everything done, so sleep is the first thing to go. I mean, do you really need to spend eight hours out of every day lying in bed doing nothing? It seems so unproductive . . . .

However, sleep is critical for learning, and the influence of sleep—and sleep deprivation—on learning is astounding. I know it's hard to get enough sleep, especially when you're in school, but I hope by the end of this chapter you'll reconsider your sleep-deprived lifestyle. If you prioritize sleep, you will be more productive and retain more of what you've practiced. Suddenly, you'll realize you have more time each day: when you're well rested, you can get everything done in a lot less time.

The magic of sleep

To begin our discussion on the importance of sleep, I'd like to introduce you to the work of Dr. Matthew Walker, one of the leading neuroscientists on the study of sleep. He has done research on sleep and learning for decades, and his findings are directly applicable to musicians. In a series of studies from the early 2000s, Dr. Walker asked research participants to perform a button-press sequence as quickly and accurately as possible. His control group (Group 1) practiced 12 times (the initial training) and then were retested every four hours for the rest of the day.[1] Think of these retests as mini performances. Not surprisingly, as the participants practiced, they got a little better every time in a linear way that the scientists could predict. They also got a little better at each mini performance, again in a linear way that was predictable. No surprises there—this was just to demonstrate that people

Learn Faster, Perform Better. Molly Gebrian, Oxford University Press. © Oxford University Press 2024.
DOI: 10.1093/oso/9780197680063.003.0006

60 USING YOUR TIME WELL

continue to get better as they practice and that repeated performances within a day continue this predictable trend.

What *was* surprising were the results the next day, when the participants returned after a full night's sleep. Suddenly they performed the tasks much faster and more accurately than the day before. This also wasn't a linear increase, it was a huge jump, as you can see in Figure 5.1. In these graphs, the black bars show performance on Day 1, whereas the white bars show performance on Day 2. The top graph shows speed, the bottom graph shows number of mistakes. There is a clear jump in performance (faster with fewer mistakes) on Day 2, following a night of sleep.

To probe this surprising finding, a second group of people (Group 2) also completed the initial 12 training trials, but they didn't have any mini performances at all until Day 2. Despite less practice on Day 1, they also showed a huge jump in performance on Day 2. Group 2's first mini performance was at a significantly higher level than at the end of training on Day 1 and far outpaced Group 1's first mini performance.

But maybe it has nothing to do sleep per se, maybe it's just the passage of time that matters. In the last chapter, we saw several different examples of how the brain continues to work during breaks, resulting in better performance after the break. Maybe for the effect Dr. Walker found, 12 hours has to pass and sleep has nothing to do with it.

To test this, Dr. Walker recruited two new groups of people (Groups 3 and 4). Group 3 practiced first at 10 am, followed by a retest at 10 pm. There was some improvement, but not a huge jump, even though 12 hours had passed. However, at the second retest at 10 am the next day, the participants *did* show a large boost in performance; they were faster and more accurate following a night of sleep. Group 4, on the other hand, had their first practice at 10 pm followed by a retest the next day at 10 am. This is also a 12-hour window of time, but critically, these 12 hours include a night of sleep. If sleep is what matters—and not just the mere passage of time—Group 4 would be expected to show the large jump in performance at their first retest the next day. In fact, this is exactly what was found. Further, Group 4's second retest at 10 pm on Day 2 showed some improvement, but again not that much. In both Groups 3 and 4, the jump in performance only happened following a night of sleep.

Figure 5.2 shows these findings. As in Figure 5.1, the black bars are performance on Day 1, whereas the white bars are performance on Day 2. The top graphs show speed, whereas the bottom ones show number of mistakes. The graphs on the left show Group 3, the graphs on the right show Group 4.

CAN YOU LEARN MUSIC IN YOUR SLEEP? 61

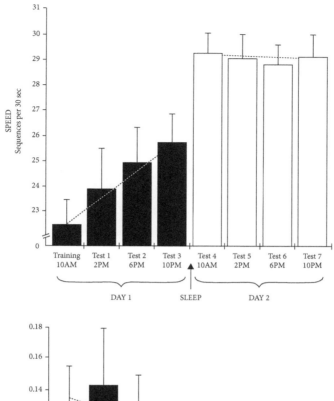

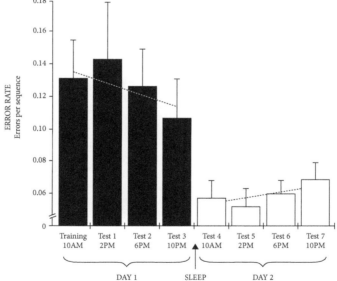

Figure 5.1 Graphs showing performance on Day 1 (black bars) versus Day 2 (white bars) for both speed (top) and number of mistakes (bottom).

Reproduced with permission from Walker, M., et al. (2002). Practice with sleep makes perfect: Sleep-dependent motor skill learning. *Neuron*. 35(1): 205–211.
© Cold Spring Harbor Laboratory Press.

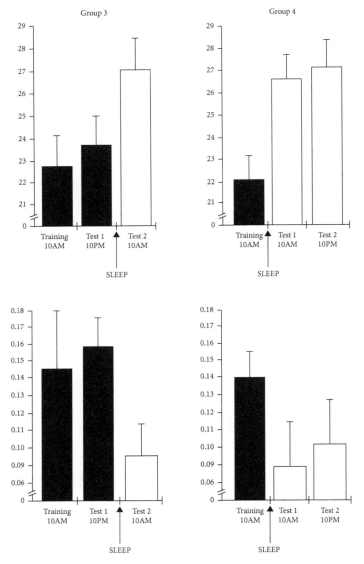

Figure 5.2 Graphs showing the performance of Groups 3 and 4, and the role of sleep in boosting performance.

Reproduced with permission from Walker, M., et al. (2002). Practice with sleep makes perfect: sleep-dependent motor skill learning. *Neuron.* 35(1): 205–211.
© Cold Spring Harbor Laboratory Press.

Notice that the jump in performance always follows a night of sleep and is not merely due to the simple passage of time.

In fact, all the different parameters tested showed the same thing: practice within a day yields minor increases in ability, whereas after a full night of sleep, there is a significant jump in ability, both in terms of speed and accuracy. One group was even assigned double training—so they practiced 24 times instead of just 12—but that didn't seem to make much difference in ability over the course of the day.[2] In fact, the group with double training was no more accurate at the end of the day than the people who practiced half as much. And their overnight improvement was essentially the same as the other groups. They spent twice as much time for no measurable gain! In a nutshell, this research shows that if you practice far less and get a full night's sleep, you will suddenly be *much* better the next day without any additional effort.

Hopefully you are starting to see the critical role of sleep in making the best use of your time. But again, the question is *why*. What happens when we're asleep to produce this amazing result?

To answer this question, Dr. Walker and his colleagues asked participants to sleep over in the lab to monitor their sleep. Through this monitoring, they found there was a strong correlation between the amount of improvement people made the next day and the amount of time they spent in something called Stage 2 NREM sleep in the fourth quarter of the night. Let's break down what that means.

Many people have heard of REM sleep (rapid eye movement sleep)—that's when we are dreaming and our eyes are moving quickly behind our eyelids. The opposite of REM sleep is non-REM sleep, or NREM sleep.

Sleep scientists also divide sleep into four different stages to describe how deeply someone is sleeping. Stage 1 sleep is very light sleep when it's easy to wake someone up. At the other extreme, stage 4 sleep is very deep sleep—the kind of sleep that causes you to sleep through your alarm. Stage 2 sleep, therefore, is on the lighter side, but not the lightest kind of sleep.

Lastly, sleep scientists consider a full night's sleep for adults to be eight hours on average. This is divided into four quarters of approximately two hours each, so the fourth quarter is the final two hours in an eight-hour night of sleep.

To reiterate, the amount of improvement seen the next day is strongly correlated with the amount of time people spend in Stage 2 NREM sleep in the fourth quarter of the night. But again: WHY? What's so special about Stage 2 NREM sleep in the fourth quarter of the night? Plus, this is a correlation. Scientists are always quick to point out that correlation is not causation: just because two things are related, you can't necessarily say one causes the other. However, based on other sleep research, we know there is a special kind of brain activity—called sleep spindles— which peaks during Stage 2 sleep, particularly in the fourth quarter of the night. Sleep spindles cause changes at the synapse, and in Chapter 1 we discussed the fact that changes at the synapse are necessary for learning. Scientists also know that for motor tasks that are not terribly complex, NREM sleep appears to be critical for consolidating, strengthening, and stabilizing a new skill. Basically, the more time people spend in Stage 2 NREM sleep in the fourth quarter of the night, the more opportunity their brains have to make the necessary changes that support learning. This is thought to be the reason behind the major performance improvements the next day.

A reasonable question at this juncture is whether anyone has looked at this in musicians or in people learning complex, real-world skills generally. As it turns out, there *was* a study done on musicians to answer this question. In this experiment, nonpianist musicians had to learn a short two-bar melody at the keyboard (shown in Figure 5.3). Just like the people Dr. Walker tested, musicians made small gains during the day as they continued to practice, but after a night's sleep they got a significant boost in their performance.[3] To make sure it was sleep that was making the difference, the researchers tested a variety of groups, all with different practice and sleep schedules. In every case, the jump in performance ability was only seen after a full night of sleep. This is also backed up by an experiment that used the video game *DanceStage* for PlayStation 2 to test complex motor skill learning. Researchers found the same thing: the boost in performance ability only happened following a night of sleep.[4]

Figure 5.3 The short two-bar melody participants learned at the piano.

Sleep deprivation

If all of this is true, then you would expect to see impairments in performance due to sleep deprivation. Is this what studies have found?

In one experiment, participants learned a difficult motor task and then their sleep was disrupted in a variety of ways (except the control group, who got to sleep normally).[5] Figure 5.4 shows the different experimental groups and how their sleep was disrupted.

Everyone was then tested a week later so that nobody would be sleep-deprived at the test itself. All the groups performed approximately the same except for one: the group that was kept up all night immediately after learning the task (Group 1). This group performed substantially worse than every other group, even though it was a week later and they had caught up on sleep. From this study, we can infer that the first night of sleep after you've learned something new is critical in preserving the learning you've done during the day.

To look more carefully at that first night of sleep, the researchers recruited more volunteers and subjected them to different types of sleep disruption.[6] One group was woken up every time they went into REM sleep. Another group was *only* allowed to get REM sleep, so they were woken up whenever they left REM sleep. A third group was kept up all night. The final group was allowed to sleep for four hours and then they were kept up after that. Again, everyone was tested a week later.

The results are fascinating and not what you'd expect. The group that wasn't allowed to get any REM sleep performed as well as the control group. The group that wasn't allowed to get any NREM sleep did not do nearly as well, which supports the findings we discussed earlier. However, the two

---

Sleep Groups:
Group 1: No sleep on Night 1
Group 2: Kept up 3 hours past bedtime on Night 1
Group 3: No sleep on Night 2
Group 4: Kept up 3 hours past bedtime on Night 2
Group 5: No sleep on Night 3
Group 6: Kept up 3 hours past bedtime on Night 3
Group 7: No sleep on Night 4
Group 8: Kept up 3 hours past bedtime on Night 4

Figure 5.4 The eight different experimental groups and how their sleep was disrupted.

66   USING YOUR TIME WELL

groups that did the worst by far were the group kept up all night and the group that was only allowed to sleep for four hours. That last result is really surprising: getting only four hours of sleep was as bad as getting no sleep at all, at least in this study.

That's sobering.

This doesn't mean that if you can get only four hours of sleep you might as well stay up all night. Sleep has many benefits, and something is always better than nothing. But getting only four hours of sleep, especially chronically, is not going to help you retain what you're trying to learn.

What is the point of REM sleep then? Why didn't the people deprived of REM sleep show any detriment to their performance? This was a motor learning study, and scientists have found that motor skills and cognitive skills work differently in the brain when it comes to REM versus NREM sleep. To look at cognitive skills, researchers did an experiment with similar sleep deprivation conditions—total sleep deprivation, partial REM deprivation, and NREM deprivation—but this time the participants were practicing a difficult puzzle-solving task.[7] In this study, researchers found that NREM-sleep deprivation didn't have much of an effect, but REM-sleep deprivation was *worse* than total sleep deprivation. In fact, the people who were not allowed to get enough REM sleep were worse than before they were trained, even a week later.*

Given that playing an instrument is both a motor skill and a cognitive skill, getting a full night's sleep is as beneficial as practicing itself. The NREM and REM sleep we get toward the end of the night seems especially important to solidify learning. If we only sleep for four to five hours, we deprive our brains of those critical final hours and we run the risk of losing the work we put in the day before. On the other hand, when we do get enough sleep, we get a significant boost in our ability the next day, starting out at a higher level than where we left things the day before.

If you take nothing else away from this book, take this: sleep is absolutely essential for learning and if you want to maximize the results of your practicing, you have to prioritize sleep.

This research also explains why cramming doesn't work particularly well. When you cram, you only get the boost in performance from one or two nights of sleep versus several nights. Practicing just 10 minutes each day is

---

* Interestingly, in this study, they only deprived people of the last two periods of REM sleep, not all REM sleep, but that was enough to seriously disrupt learning.

much more beneficial than practicing 70 minutes once a week. Doing a little each day will give you seven sleep-boosts versus just one sleep-boost after one day of 70 minutes.

Hopefully the previous chapter convinced you of the power of taking breaks. Since sleep is the most important break of all, it's critical to prioritize it. As we discussed in Chapter 4, most of our improvement is made during breaks. Said another way, most of our *learning* happens when we are taking a break, if you define learning as changes in the brain. I realize this is extremely counterintuitive. It feels like you're working hard and (hopefully) making lots of improvement when you're practicing. But this is an illusion. When you're practicing, you're giving your brain the input it needs to make the necessary physical changes to support a higher level of skill. It's only during breaks that those physical changes can be made. And as we've discussed previously, if there are no changes in the brain, no learning has happened.

Naps

Whenever I discuss the science of sleep, the first question I'm always asked is, "Well, what about naps?" It stands to reason that if our brains are doing so much reorganization at night while we're asleep, then taking a nap during the day should also have a benefit.

In fact, there are all sorts of amazing benefits to taking a nap during the day. There are many studies that find a 60- to 90-minute nap after learning— across a wide variety of skills—boosts performance on a retest after waking up from the nap.[8] Figure 5.5 shows the results of one of these studies.[9] The critical information in this figure is the difference between performance at the end of training (the post-training bar) and on the retest. When there was a nap between the end of training and the retest, people performed at a much higher level on the retest.

This improvement was also highly correlated with the amount of time people spent in stage 2 NREM sleep during their nap. This supports what was found in the overnight sleep studies. Researchers also found the same connection to sleep spindles we discussed in those overnight studies: the more sleep spindle activity seen during a nap, the larger the improvement after the nap. There was even one person who was a huge outlier in terms of sleep spindle activity and amount of time in stage 2 NREM sleep. This person made *much* more improvement than the other participants—to the point

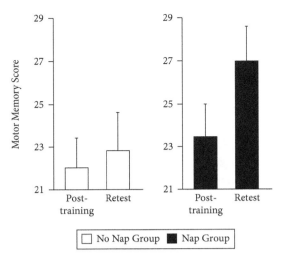

Figure 5.5 Graphs showing performance at the end of training (post-training) and on the final test (retest) for the nap versus the no-nap group.
Reproduced from Nishida, M., et al. (2007). Daytime naps, motor memory consolidation and regionally specific sleep spindles. *PloS ONE.* 2(4): e341. © 2007 Nishida, Walker.

that the researchers had to exclude them from the data analysis because it would skew the results too much.

There are other interesting benefits to naps as well. One study on juggling found that not only did a daytime nap significantly boost performance, but a nap during the day followed later by a full night's sleep resulted in an *even greater* enhancement in performance ability on that second day versus not taking a nap.[10]

Naps also seem to block retroactive interference, which we discussed in the last chapter. Just as a quick recap: retroactive interference happens when you learn two similar things back-to-back, like Ending A versus Ending B in Bach's *Minuet in G*. Whichever one you learn second is going to interfere with the one you learned first. In the previous chapter, we saw that if you take a six-hour break between learning two similar things, retroactive interference is no longer a problem.

When we first discussed retroactive interference, I didn't tell you the whole story because you didn't know about the power of sleep yet. Now that you do, we can talk about it in more detail. When you learn two brand-new things that are similar to each other without a long enough break in between, the boost in ability after a night of sleep *disappears*. I know this is surprising, but it just demonstrates how powerful retroactive interference can be. Naps, however, can help overcome this issue. If the break between learning similar things is only two hours—which *should* cause retroactive interference—but you take a nap during that two-hour break, retroactive interference doesn't happen.[11] You still get that boost in performance the next day after a full night's sleep. Yet another reason to nap.

Maybe you're saying to yourself right now, "That's nice and everything, but I don't really have time for a 60- to 90-minute nap every time after I practice!" Me neither. If you don't have time for a nice long nap, is there any benefit to taking a shorter nap instead?

Yes, there is.

One study found that even just a six-minute nap was beneficial in boosting cognitive performance. (A longer nap was better, but a six-minute nap was better than nothing.)[12] Another experiment looked at people who got only five hours of sleep the night before. Researchers found that a 10-minute nap was nearly as good as a 30-minute nap and didn't have the downside of making people groggy afterward (which happened with the 30-minute nap).[13] One caveat about these two studies: by six minutes or ten minutes, they mean six or ten minutes of actual sleep. I don't know about you, but I don't fall asleep immediately and it's hard to know how long I actually slept when I take a nap.

There's one more study, however, that seems to suggest that falling asleep isn't completely necessary. This experiment looked at two people who are paralyzed and have microelectrodes permanently implanted in their brains.[14] This microelectrode implant is part of a clinical trial to develop a brain-computer interface, allowing people who are paralyzed to control computers with their brain waves. In this study, the participants practiced playing a game in which a circle made up of four different colored quadrants was displayed on a computer screen. The four colored quadrants lit up in a particular order (e.g., green, yellow, red, blue) and the participants had to use their brain waves to tell the computer to click on the colored quadrants in the same order. There was one color pattern that kept coming back repeatedly with other random patterns interspersed in between. The researchers were interested in measuring two things: the participants' improvement on the pattern that kept coming back, and the exact firing patterns of the neurons involved when they controlled the computer cursor with their brains.

After the participants played the game for about 20 minutes, they got a 20- to 30-minute break. During the break, they were asked to sit quietly with their eyes closed, napping if they wanted to. Because the two people had microelectrodes implanted directly into their brains, the scientists were able to see the precise neural activity both when they were playing the game and when they were resting afterward.

Similar to the microbreaks study discussed in Chapter 4, the researchers found that the pattern of brain activity during the 20-minute rest break matched the brain activity seen when they were practicing the pattern that returned repeatedly. As in the microbreaks experiment, the brain was continuing to practice during the 20-minute break, and this could be seen directly in their brain activity.

In this case, both people did nap at least a little bit during the break, but not for the whole 20 minutes. There was also a lot of variation between the two people and across the five separate sessions of this experiment. It seems, at least from this study, that just 20 minutes of rest following your practice session is beneficial, whether or not you actually sleep. You can just rest with your eyes closed and your brain will continue to work on what you've just learned.

Decades of research makes it clear how powerful sleep is for learning. And as we have seen, this is true for both extended overnight rest and shorter naps during the day. In my ideal future music school, there will be napping rooms that students can sign out like practice rooms for use after a practice or study session. But in the meantime, we can each try to change the culture of music education and study by prioritizing sleep in our own lives. And maybe someday, musicians will be just as serious about getting enough sleep as they currently are about their practice routines.

6

What's the Perfect Schedule of Breaks?

All the research we've looked at in the last two chapters demonstrates that taking breaks, getting enough sleep, and spreading practice sessions out over multiple days are all extremely beneficial. But it can also feel scary to start taking breaks as a practice strategy, especially since it goes against what we are commonly taught about good practicing.

So what's the perfect practice schedule?

Unfortunately, there's no perfect, one-size-fits-all schedule because it depends on what you're trying to learn, how hard it is for you, when the performance is, and many other factors. But in this chapter, we'll discuss some principles you can apply to help craft a schedule that will work for you.

The forgetting curve

Testing out different spaced practice schedules was a COVID-19 pandemic project/experiment I did on myself in the spring and summer of 2020. I had known about this research for years, but I was always too scared to really try it. If taking breaks *didn't* work and then I wasn't prepared for a concert, that would not be good. I knew my usual method of trying to practice everything every day and never taking breaks worked well enough, so why mess with it? But then the world shut down in March 2020, all concerts were canceled, and it seemed like the perfect opportunity to experiment with this idea. After all, if it didn't work like the research said it should, it didn't matter because I had no concerts anyway. Spoiler alert: it worked so well that I'm never going back to how I used to practice. I not only learn music *much* faster now, but the music also feels a lot more secure, and I can learn significantly more music because of all the extra time I have while taking breaks from other pieces.

At the end of the chapter, I'll tell you the results of my self-experiment and the practicing schedule I use now as a result, but first, let's talk about the various principles of optimal spaced practice so you can understand how I made my decisions.

Learn Faster, Perform Better. Molly Gebrian, Oxford University Press. © Oxford University Press 2024.
DOI: 10.1093/oso/9780197680063.003.0007

72 USING YOUR TIME WELL

To start, it's a delicate balance between breaks that are too short and breaks that are too long. If the break is too short, your brain doesn't have the time to do the necessary reconstruction to get you to a higher level of readiness for further learning. But if the break is too long, the memory trace disappears entirely and you're back to square one. However, research indicates there is more of a penalty for breaks that are too short than breaks that are too long, so err on the side of longer breaks. You want to hit the sweet spot of almost forgetting, but not quite.

Ebbinghaus, the scientist who discovered spaced learning in the 1880s, came up with a principle called *the forgetting curve*. This principle shows that over time, you gradually forget information if you don't attempt to maintain it through further study or practice. He came up with a complicated equation to explain the decay of memory over time, but essentially when something is brand new, we tend to forget it relatively quickly, whereas when we've worked on something for longer, we tend to remember it longer as well. Therefore, the length of breaks between practice or study sessions depends in part on how new the material is. The newer something is, the shorter the break should be. The more you've worked on it, the more time off you should take.

Ebbinghaus found that when we are reminded of something we've *almost* forgotten, we tend to remember it better than if we're reminded when it's still fresh in our minds. Take a party where you've met many new people as an example. Someone introduces themselves to you and you promptly forget their name the minute they walk away. (We all do it!) Later in the party, you realize you've forgotten their name and you feel embarrassed. It's on the tip of your tongue, but you can't quite remember. Was it Mary or Marsha? Maybe Melanie? Then you hear someone come up to them and say, "Hey Margaret! It's so great to see you!" Phew, crisis averted. And now you definitely won't forget their name. However, if you were introduced and then immediately afterward someone came up to them and said, "Hey Margaret! It's so great to see you!" that's probably not going to cement their name in your brain in the same way.

Let's look at another example: working on a skill. Imagine the kid next door is learning the order of operations in math. They ask you for a math problem so they can practice. You write down $2(5+3) - 7(4-3) = ?$ After figuring out the answer is 9, they ask you for another math problem, but you're tired, so you just give them the same one again. Since it's fresh in their mind, they can just tell you the answer is 9; they don't have to solve it again. Because of that, they don't get more practice on the order of operations. But if they come back a week later and you give them that same math problem, they will probably have forgotten the correct answer, so they'll have to solve it again, getting more practice with the order of operations.

To take an example from music, a common strategy to work on memorization is to look at the music, then look away and try it without the music (we'll discuss memorization more in Chapters 12 and 13). After going back and forth this way a few times, students often feel like they have it memorized, only to discover in their lesson the next day that they can't remember it at all. That's because the passage wasn't actually memorized. During the practice session, they had *just* looked at the music, so their brain didn't have a chance to forget a bit—it's like hearing "Margaret" too soon at the party. When the material is fresh in your mind, it's going to be a lot easier to play the passage "from memory." But the real test comes after a break, after you have given your brain a chance to forget a bit.

This is why it's better to err on the side a break that is too long rather than too short. And the better we know something, the longer the break should be because it takes us longer to forget. Think days or weeks versus minutes or hours.

Crafting a practice schedule

This leads to a discussion of expanding, contracting, and fixed schedules of spacing your practice. In an expanding schedule, the breaks between practice sessions get longer and longer as you get better at something. A contracting schedule is the opposite: breaks get shorter over time. In the middle is a fixed schedule: breaks last the same amount of time no matter what. The research on this is mixed, but most show that either fixed or expanding schedules are best for solidifying learning. Some show an advantage for expanding schedules, but some show no difference between an expanding versus a fixed schedule. However, none shows that an expanding schedule is *detrimental*. Contracting schedules (the breaks get shorter) seem to be the best option only when the time between the very first practice session and the final performance is a week apart or less.[1] For musicians, we typically have more than a week to learn something from scratch before we perform it, although not always. So keep contracting schedules in mind if you need to learn something very quickly. But it seems that for musicians, expanding schedules—or fixed schedules—are the best most of the time.

74 USING YOUR TIME WELL

Group 1 Schedule

Monday	Tuesday	Wednesday	Thursday	Friday	Saturday	Sunday
Training 1	Training 2	Training 3				
		Training 4				
		Final Test				

Group 2 Schedule

Monday	Tuesday	Wednesday	Thursday	Friday	Saturday	Sunday
Training 1	Training 2	Training 3				
		Final Test				

Figure 6.1 Training schedule for the two groups of surgical students.

Like the research on spaced practice in general, much of the research on expanding versus contracting schedules was done on people studying for tests, but there is evidence from surgical training (again) that supports this for complex motor skills as well. In one experiment, everyone trained three days in a row.[2] (So, spaced training for everyone; none of the surgeons had to do all three trainings back-to-back all in one day.) Group 1 had an additional practice session one week after the initial training. Group 2 got no additional practice. Then, two weeks after the initial three-day training, all the surgeons were tested on their skills. Group 1, therefore, was using an expanding schedule: three days in a row for their initial training, a week off, then one more training, then another week off, followed by the test. Figure 6.1 shows the schedule for each group.

Not surprisingly, Group 1 did better in the final test given they received extra training. But the details of how the two groups differed are what's interesting about this study. Figure 6.2 shows the results. The graph on the top shows how quickly each group could perform the skills, with lower scores indicating better performance. You can see that in the practice session one week after training, Group 1 is faster than at the end of training, and even faster still in the performance at the two-week mark. Group 2 was slower in the final performance test after a two-week break, indicating that the break was too long for them to retain their skills. The graph on the bottom shows the number of mistakes (again, lower scores are better). Group 1 maintained their performance level between Training 3 and the practice session one week later, and were even more accurate at the final performance. Group 2, however, was much worse in final the

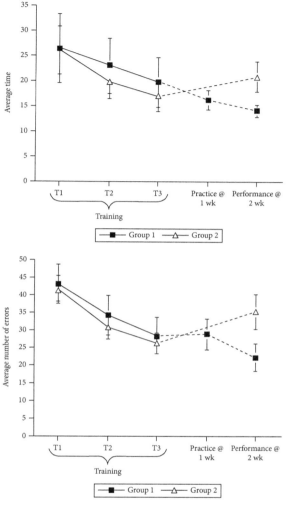

Figure 6.2 Graphs showing the performance of Groups 1 and 2 for speed (top) and number of errors (bottom) at different points in time.

Reproduced with permission from Gallagher, A., et al. (2012). Prospective, randomized assessment of the acquisition, maintenance, and loss of laparoscopic skills. *Annals of Surgery*. 256(2): 387–393. https://journals.lww.com/annalsofsurgery/pages/default.aspx

performance, again indicating that a two-week break was too long and their skills degraded.

How can you use this information to craft the optimal schedule of practicing and breaks? First, as we discussed in Chapter 4, when something

76 USING YOUR TIME WELL

is brand new, don't just practice it once in the day and leave it until the next day. When skills are new, we forget quickly, so the breaks need to be shorter. Start with the microbreaks method we discussed in Chapter 4. Then, come back to that passage or skill two or three times over the course of the day (with breaks in between). Once you can play something well, leave it alone and don't practice it for at least a few days to allow your brain to forget. When you come back to it, if it still feels good, leave it alone for longer.

The better you get at a particular passage or section, the longer the breaks should get. Every time you come back to the passage, not only will it feel more secure, but you will cement it in memory precisely because it's not fresh in your mind anymore.

The flip side of this is also true: sometimes when you are so frustrated with something that you want to smash your instrument against the wall—we've all been there! —the best thing you can do is take a break. It may be that your brain needs you to rest so it can stabilize your progress and do some (re) construction. Taking a day or a week off can make a huge difference. When you come back to it, it will feel much easier. You may also gain some insights into how you could practice it differently during the time away, which will help you approach it with fresh eyes when you return. Remember, though, that frustration is necessary for learning. Don't just take a break from a given passage at the first sign of trouble. Keep at it and try to work through the frustration. But if you really feel like you've hit a roadblock you just can't get past, then try taking a break from the passage.

Sample schedule

Now that you understand these principles, let's return to my spaced practice pandemic project. For about three months, I experimented with different length breaks and ways of organizing my time. Based on the research, I decided to try a variety of different expanding schedules. I've come to a schedule that works well for me, but I encourage you to experiment yourself. After a few months of trying different schedules, Figure 6.3 shows how I practice now.

When I start something brand new, I pick a passage and work on it two to three times that first day (Practice 1 in Figure 6.3). Usually I start with the hardest section in the piece because I know it's going to take the most time to learn. The length of the passage depends on how much time I have and

WHAT'S THE PERFECT SCHEDULE OF BREAKS? 77

Monday	Tuesday	Wednesday	Thursday	Friday	Saturday	Sunday
Practice 1	Practice 2	Practice 3		Practice 4		Practice 5
	Practice 6					
	Practice 7	Practice 8	Practice 9			
			Practice 10	Practice 11	Practice 12	

Figure 6.3 My spaced practice calendar.

how difficult the passage is, but I usually err on the side of less music. The most I ever do is a page of music if it's not terribly hard. Other times, it's as short as a single measure if that measure is very difficult. Typically, though, it's around 8 to 16 bars. For three days in a row, I work on that passage, usually doing it two to three separate times in a given day.

Then I take a day off from that passage—but not from practicing completely. I use my extra time on the day off to work on other music or to start something else new. After the day off, I practice the passage every other day, usually three times during the week: e.g., Friday, Sunday, Tuesday (practice sessions 4–6 in the calendar). Sometimes I do a little less (just Friday and Sunday) or sometimes a little more (Friday, Sunday, Tuesday, Thursday) depending on how it feels, but usually three days is good.

Then I take a week off (again, just from that passage). When I come back to it after a weeklong break, it's amazing how good it feels. I generally practice it for three days in a row again—practice sessions 7–9 in the calendar—but sometimes only two days in a row, again depending on how it feels. I've never had to do four days, but if I needed to, I would.

Then, I take two weeks off from that passage. When I come back to it after two weeks, it feels solid and secure.*

At this point, the material is usually ready to be integrated into the larger framework of the piece, although I've also been doing that integration all along when adjacent passages are on the schedule to be practiced on the

---

* If I have to miss a day or my schedule gets disrupted because I'm too busy to stick to my schedule, it doesn't matter. Again, there's more of a penalty for breaks that are too short than breaks that are too long. If I miss a day, I just push everything one day forward in the calendar. It looks much more rigid on paper than how it actually works out in practice.

same day. I'm also ready to start using interleaved practice to get the section performance-ready, which is the subject of the next chapter. If I add up all the individual practice days for a given passage using this schedule, it's about 9 to 12 days total. That's not very much, and yet the passage feels very secure. Even better, during all the days off from that passage, I have lots of time to practice other music.

I keep track of everything using my Google calendar. The system is quick and simple; if you're curious to know how it works, there is a video on my website that demonstrates this process. In Appendix B, I've also included a few sample calendars showing how this schedule plays out over time with multiple different passages.

As I said, this has forever changed how I practice. It can be scary to take long breaks like this, but every musician I've worked with who has tried it agrees: they are never going back to how they used to practice. Taking strategic breaks just works so much better to learn music quickly and securely than the traditional approach of hammering away at the same thing day after day. Experiment and find out what works for you. My schedule of breaks works well for me but is just one possibility.

Hopefully this research on spaced practice and sleep will free you from the guilt we often feel whenever we take breaks or opt to sleep instead of getting that extra hour of practice in. Your body and your brain will thank you for giving them the rest they need.

7

Be More Consistent in Performance

Evan unpacked his viola while we chatted about how his week was going. Once he was tuned and ready to play, I asked to hear the Bach we had been working for his end-of-semester performance jury in about three weeks. We had worked hard together to get this movement in good shape and we both expected a nearly polished performance.

That's not what happened.

"Oh my gosh, I'm so sorry. That was horrible!" he said, embarrassed, after he finished. "I have no idea what happened. It sounded so much better yesterday when I was practicing!"

After working together for a few minutes to address the problems, he assured me that he understood how he needed to practice in the week ahead.

"I'll be much more prepared next week, I promise," he told me.

When he arrived for his lesson the following week, we once again started with his Bach. And again, it was not very good.

"I'm so sorry!" he said, distraught. "I promise, I could play it so much better yesterday at home! I don't know what's going on."

We started to work on the issues again, but almost immediately he sounded remarkably better. When that happened, I understood what the problem was and exactly which practice strategy he needed.

Interleaved versus blocked practice

Many musicians struggle with getting their practice to stick, especially in performance or lesson situations. Each of us has likely had Evan's experience of feeling very prepared for a lesson, only to play terribly in front of our teacher. This mortifying, frustrating situation seems to be a universal experience. But it's also bewildering: we practiced so hard and so well, why can't we play it when it counts?

Learn Faster, Perform Better. Molly Gebrian, Oxford University Press. © Oxford University Press 2024.
DOI: 10.1093/oso/9780197680063.003.0008

But step back and think about what you did while practicing to reach the point where your music was feeling good. You probably broke it down into smaller sections, did repetitions to solidify the harder parts, played it at a slower tempo, and then used various practice methods to work it up to speed. Then you gradually put it back together, and by the end of your practice session, it was feeling solid.

Now think about what a lesson often looks like: you have to perform your piece in front of your teacher without stopping, trying to get it right on the first try. That is a very different thing you are asking of your brain than when you were at home practicing. It's also a much more difficult thing to do. Plus, you're doing it for the first time in a high-pressure situation—in front of your teacher! No wonder it doesn't go the way you want it to. You are asking your poor brain to do something it never got to practice, for the very first time, in front of someone who intimidates you (at least a little bit). It would be miraculous if it *did* go well, quite frankly!

How can we practice to improve our ability to perform the way we want to under pressure? The short answer is that we need to practice what our brains are going to have to do in a *performance* situation. Again, practicing is brain training more than anything else, so our practicing should hone the skills our brains will need while performing. This is where something called interleaved practice comes in.

Interleaved (or random) practice is a form of spaced practice (discussed in Chapter 4). It's designed to train your brain to be nimble and adept at switching what it's doing, and at reconstructing from scratch exactly how to play well on the first try. The opposite of interleaved practice is known as blocked (or massed) practice. This is how we practice most of the time: we focus on one thing for a block of time before moving on to something else.

To illustrate the difference between these two methods of practicing, let's take a few examples. If you were working on orchestral excerpts and you practiced *Don Juan* for 30 minutes, then worked on Mendelssohn *Scherzo* for 30 minutes, and then finally Beethoven 5 for 30 minutes, that would be an example of blocked practice. If, on the other hand, you switched between the three excerpts every five minutes in a random order until you had done 30 minutes total on each one, that would be an example of interleaved practice. (As we'll see, there are an infinite number of ways to use the principle of interleaved practice, so switching every five minutes is just one possibility.)

At first glance, interleaved practicing seems like an extremely chaotic, unfocused method of practicing, unlikely to yield good results. But the research says otherwise, particularly if you want to perform well.

Skeptical? I don't blame you. But hopefully a look at the research will persuade you.

Let's start with a study that was done on baseball players.[1] In this experiment, the goal was to improve the players' batting average (how many balls they could hit). The baseball players were divided into two groups: the blocked practice group and the interleaved practice group. The blocked practice group was pitched 15 fast balls, then 15 curve balls, then 15 change-up pitches and they had to hit as many as possible. The interleaved practice group was also given 45 total pitches, but they never knew which kind of pitch to expect, so they might get a fast ball, then two change-up pitches, then another fast ball, then a curve ball, etc. They also had to try to hit as many as possible.

While they were practicing, it looked like the blocked practice group was doing better. This makes sense: they knew what was coming and they just had to hit the same kind of pitch over and over. The interleaved group, on the other hand, had no clue what they were going to get, and so they had to adjust in the moment. However, when the researchers brought the baseball players back for a performance test two days later, they found that the blocked practice group had made a 25% improvement in their batting average, whereas the interleaved group had made a 57% improvement. That's a pretty big difference. You can see this in Figure 7.1: during the practice sessions, the blocked practice group was doing better, but in the performances, the interleaved group came out on top.

But why is this?

For one thing, in a baseball game, the batter doesn't know what kind of pitch is going to be thrown at them, so the interleaved group got more real-world practice. Another reason is because of something called *contextual interference*. Basically, the same skills (hitting baseballs) in different combinations (the different pitches) "interfere" with each other in the brain. This makes it harder for the brain because it must switch rapidly between slightly different skills—hitting a fast ball versus hitting a curve ball—and it must remember how to execute the different skills correctly in the moment. That's much more difficult than just doing the same thing over and over, but this is exactly what our brains have to do when we perform. If we want to perform well, our brains need to be adept at switching quickly between different skills and mindsets.

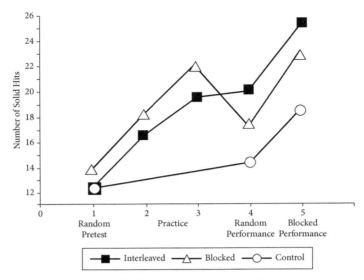

Figure 7.1 Graph showing the blocked and interleaved practice groups in the baseball study.

Adapted from Hall, K., et al. (1994). Contextual interference effects with skilled baseball players. *Perceptual and Motor Skills.* 78(3): 835–841. © 1994 by SAGE Publications. Reprinted by permission of SAGE Publications, Ltd.

We don't get a chance to try things out first and remind ourselves how to do them. Interleaved practice helps us develop this mental nimbleness.*

Much of the research on interleaved practicing comes from athletes, like the baseball study, but does this also apply to practicing music? Fortunately, researchers are also testing this out in musicians to see whether they will find the same results.

One experiment took a group of pianists and invited them into the lab to learn a series of short pieces that were composed specifically for the experiment, so nobody could've known them already.[2] These were pieces that were too hard to sightread, but not so hard that they required months of practice to get them to an acceptable level. All the pianists learned all the pieces, but they learned some using a blocked practice method and others using an interleaved practice method.

---

* You maybe be wondering how this idea connects to retroactive interference, discussed first in Chapter 4. When two similar things are brand new, interleaved practice probably won't work very well because the learning is too new and fragile. But once they are more well-learned, interleaved practice is essential to help you keep similar passages straight. We have all had the experience of playing the first-time version the second time by accident and getting stuck in an endless loop. Interleaved practice is a great way to prevent this from happening.

While they were practicing, it looked like the blocked practice method was working better than the interleaved method, just as in the study with the baseball players. Two days later, the pianists returned to give a concert of the pieces they had learned. Again, just like the baseball players, the pianists performed the pieces they had learned using the interleaved method much more successfully. This result is also backed up by the work of clarinetist and cognitive science researcher Christine Carter, who has found the same result with clarinetists learning a concerto exposition: those who practiced in an interleaved manner performed much better.[3]

My favorite part of the experiment on pianists is what happened after the concert. The experimenters interviewed the performers and asked them whether they thought blocked or interleaved practice was better. The pianists all agreed: blocked practice was better.

No, that's not a typo.

The pianists thought blocked practice was better, even though they could see for themselves that the interleaved practice method produced a better performance. In fact, this mistaken belief in the superiority of blocked practice is so common that psychologists have given it a name. It's called the "illusion of mastery." Robert Bjork, one of the leading researchers on interleaved practice, has pointed out that we tend to use our performance during a *practice session* (rather than in a performance or lesson) as evidence for how much improvement we have made. This leads us to overestimate how well we can play a given passage and also to use practice methods that are not optimal, like blocked practice.[4]

Here is an uncomfortable truth: the measure of how well you practiced isn't how it sounds at the end of your practice session. It's how good it sounds the next day when you come back to it. I know that is extremely counterintuitive. When we sound fantastic during practice only to play terribly in a lesson, we have fallen victim to the illusion of mastery. When we decide to do a run-through and then stop on the first or second line a few times before making it through, convincing ourselves that those first few poor tries were just because we're "not warmed up yet" or "not in the groove yet," we are falling victim to the illusion of mastery. A distinction that is not clear to many musicians—and certainly was not to me—is that just because you can *play* something does not necessarily mean you can also *perform* it. We tend to think that if we can play it, we can automatically perform it, but that isn't always true. We have to practice differently to ensure that we will be able to perform well under pressure. When Evan came to his lesson that second time, with his seemingly unprepared Bach that got better very quickly once we started to work on it, I realized he could *play* it just fine, he just couldn't *perform* it yet.

The solution was interleaved practice.

One of the most powerful illustrations of the power of interleaved practice comes from what is likely the very first study on this method of practicing.[5] In this experiment, not only were there blocked and interleaved practice groups, there were also blocked and interleaved *performance* groups. (For musicians, an interleaved performance situation is what we do every time we perform: perfect on the first try, no second tries. A blocked performance would be like getting up on stage, trying it out a few times in front of the audience until it's sounding good and then saying to the audience, "Okay, you can pay attention now. This time will be good." If only!)

When the researchers compared different combinations of blocked and interleaved practice and performance, by far the worst combination for performing well was blocked practice followed by an interleaved performance, as seen in Figure 7.2. The left-hand side of this graph shows the performance of the two groups during practice. The critical part of this graph is

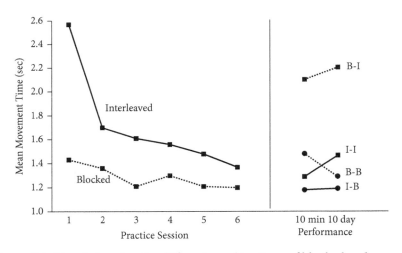

Figure 7.2 Graph showing the different combinations of blocked and interleaved practice and performance, and the effect of each combination on performance.

Adapted from Sonderstrom, N., et al. (2015). Learning versus performance: An integrative review. *Perspectives on Psychological Science.* 10(2): 176–199. © 2015 by SAGE Publications. Reprinted by permission of SAGE Publications, Ltd.

the right-hand side; this shows the result of the four different combinations of practice and performance. B stands for "blocked" and I stands for "interleaved," with the first letter in each pair indicating the type of practice and the second indicating the type of performance. Lower scores are better. By far the worst combination is blocked practice, interleaved performance (the "B-I" group).

Before learning about interleaved practice, this is exactly what I would do in the practice room. I did lots of repetitions, focusing on one thing for a long time before moving on to something else: blocked practice. Then I would get on stage (or to my lesson) and somehow expect my brain to know how to perform perfectly on the first try: interleaved performance. No wonder I was often disappointed.

This idea of switching often between different sections or passages goes against how many of us were taught to practice. After all, in Chapter 1 we were talking about the importance of making well-worn pathways through the snow, about correct repetitions and overlearning. These ideas seem to be contradictory and raise the question: does blocked practice have any place at all? Maybe we should only be doing interleaved practice . . . ?

To answer this question, let's look at an experiment that was done with basketball players.[6] In this study, there were three groups: a blocked practice group, an interleaved practice group, and a group that had an increasingly interleaved practice schedule. To illustrate what this third group did, I'm going to return to my example of practicing orchestra excerpts from earlier. An increasingly random schedule would start with blocked practice (so 30 minutes of each excerpt before moving on to the next). The next step is something called serial practice. With the orchestra excerpt example, you would do each one for five minutes before moving onto the next, but in a predictable order (*Don Juan*, Mendelssohn, Beethoven, *Don Juan*, Mendelssohn, Beethoven, *Don Juan*, Mendelssohn, Beethoven, etc.). Your brain gets practice switching gears, but it can predict the switching. The final step in this process would then be interleaved practice, five minutes of each piece in a random order.*

---

* Musicians often ask what the point is to the last step. Why not just stop at serial practice? After all, it's not like we're ever going to perform our music in a random order. My first answer to this is that unexpected things happen in concerts all the time. We all have stories about the time the power went out or our instrument malfunctioned or there were fire trucks going by outside the entire time. We want to be able to play our best no matter what is going on in the concert hall, and interleaved practice ensures that we can do that. Second, interleaved practice is more taxing on the brain, leading to a more durable yet flexible skill set, which is exactly what we want when performing.

86 USING YOUR TIME WELL

Getting back to the basketball players, the experimenters found that the group with the increasingly interleaved schedule did the best of all. The researchers speculated that first you have to solidify the skill using blocked practice, then you have to increase the level of difficulty by moving on to serial practice, and finally, you need to test whether you can perform well no matter what by doing interleaved practice. In my experience, this is definitely true. If I can't play something five times in a row the way I want, I won't be able to reliably perform it perfectly on the first try. It's just not solid enough yet. I have to do blocked practice first to learn and solidify the basic skill. It's also important to consider retroactive interference, too, if new skills are similar (discussed in Chapters 4 and 5). Doing interleaved practice too soon will increase retroactive interference, which will slow down learning. In this case, it will be more beneficial to use interleaved practice later in the learning process.

Brain activation

What is going on in the brain during interleaved versus blocked practice? Is there evidence that interleaved practice makes the brain work harder in a way that benefits performance, or does it just *feel* harder? To answer this question, researchers put people in an fMRI machine, which shows which areas of the brain are active when someone is doing a particular task.[7] In this experiment, participants were asked to practice a variety of complex button-press sequences using both blocked and interleaved practice methods. After a break, the participants had to perform the button press sequences as best they could while still in the scanner.

While the participants were doing interleaved practice, the experimenters found that the participants' brains were very highly activated and working hard. In comparison, the brain wasn't doing nearly as much when the participants were doing blocked practice. So yes, blocked practice is easier for the brain. There's that illusion of mastery again: the brain doesn't have to work as hard, so you have the illusion that you have it down cold.

You can see this in the graphs on the left-hand side of Figure 7.3, labeled "practice." This series of graphs is showing the brain activation in three areas of the brain (areas a, b, and c), which are involved in higher-order thinking skills. Larger bars indicate that the brain is working harder. In the graphs on the left, you can see that the brain is not working as hard during blocked practice as during interleaved practice.

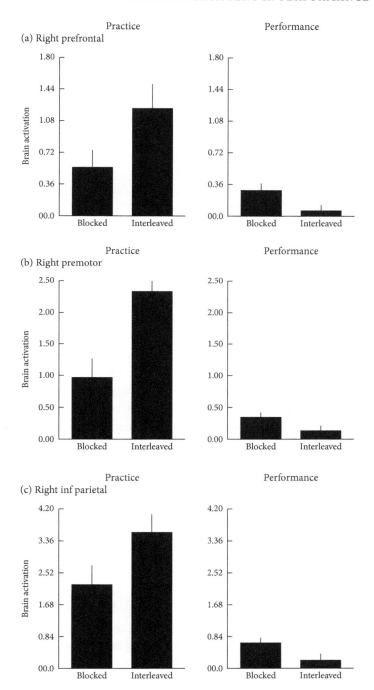

Figure 7.3 Graphs showing brain activation during practice and performance for blocked versus interleaved practice.

Modified from Lin, J., et al. (2011). Brain–behavior correlates of optimizing learning through interleaved practice. *Neuroimage*. 56(3): 1758–1772. © Elsevier 2011.

88   USING YOUR TIME WELL

The fascinating result is what the researchers saw in the performance situation. When the participants performed the sequences they had learned using interleaved practice, their brains were barely doing anything at all.

Read that again: their brains were barely doing anything at all *in a performance*. Minimal brain activation means it's easy for the brain, so doing interleaved practice makes performing feel effortless.

In contrast, the participants' brains were doing significantly more when they were performing the sequences they had learned using blocked practice. You can see this in Figure 7.3 as well, in the graphs on the right-hand side. The interleaved bars in this case are tiny compared to the blocked practice bars, meaning minimal brain activation when performing something learned using interleaved practice.

Taken together, this means that interleaved practice makes the brain work very hard while practicing, which then makes it much easier on the brain in a performance situation. Conversely, if we use blocked methods, it's much easier during practice, but then our brains work harder in performance (and not in a good way).

Many musicians will tell you that their brains feel a bit discombobulated when they get on stage. I certainly experience this. Therefore, we want to make it as easy as possible for our brains when we place them in a performance situation. Plus, if our brains don't have to work so hard to execute the technical demands of our music, we have that much more brain capacity to devote to expression and communicating with our fellow musicians and the audience.

Another interesting finding from this study was that interleaved practice resulted in more efficient motor memory retrieval by the end of the experiment. The researchers measured something called motor cortex excitability, which is a measure of motor cortex activity in the brain as it relates to reaction time. The more excitability there is, the faster the reaction time. Blocked practice had no effect on motor cortex excitability, whereas the excitability was significantly increased as a result of interleaved practice. In other words, interleaved practice improved reaction time. Yet another benefit from practicing in this way.

When exactly should you start doing interleaved practice? The basketball study suggests that at the beginning of learning something new, we should use blocked practice and gradually transition to interleaved practice. A different experiment, however, suggests that doing *some* interleaved practice from the very beginning can be beneficial.[8] In this study, researchers looked at areas of the brain that were communicating with each other one week after learning something new. When participants used blocked practice to learn the new skill, researchers saw communication between the prefrontal cortex and the anterior putamen. This brain activation is typical for something new, so that wasn't surprising.

However, when participants practiced the new skill using interleaved practice, researchers found something unexpected: the sensorimotor cortex and the posterior putamen were communicating with each other, completely different parts of the brain. This is especially surprising because these two areas are associated with the *long-term* storage of a skill. You only expect these two areas to be communicating once you get better at the skill, not when it's still new. Essentially, doing interleaved practice from the beginning jump-starts the learning process and pushes us to a higher level of skill much sooner in the process—at least in terms of the brain areas involved. In fact, in many studies on interleaved practice, people are practicing a brand-new skill, and yet the benefits of this practice method are still seen in performance tests. So although this is an absolutely essential practice method for *performing* well, it's also something we should be using at every stage of the learning process.

Specific practice strategies

Hopefully this chapter has convinced you that interleaved practice is something worth incorporating into your work. A quick caveat before we get into specific ways of using this: if you've never practiced in this way before, it can feel very frustrating at first. Your brain is working much harder than you are used to, and therefore you're no longer getting the illusion of mastery. But there have been studies looking at interleaved versus blocked practice on every sport you can imagine, on every age of person from children to elderly individuals, and for just about every academic subject. They all come to the same conclusion: interleaved practice is better if you want to perform well. You will be absolutely convinced of this once you perform for the first time after incorporating interleaved practice into your regular routine. Your performances will be more reliable and less scary because your brain will be prepared for the specific challenges of performing. Over time, you'll get used to the feeling of your brain working harder and you'll come to associate that sensation with what deep learning feels like. I would never dream of getting on stage without having done interleaved practice now. It feels like getting on stage and sightreading something very difficult, an experience I hope never to have!

90   USING YOUR TIME WELL

Now that you've been forewarned, let's talk about specific practice techniques using these principles. There are an infinite number of ways to use the concept of interleaved practicing, but here are some ideas to get you started.

Serial practice

Make a list of your hard spots. These can be within one piece or movement or across several different ones. You want to have at least five spots but no more than around 15. They can be quite short (just a measure) or slightly longer, but probably no longer than half a page. These should be spots you've practiced and solidified so that now you can test whether they are ready for performance.

Perform your first spot as if it's a concert, no stopping no matter what. If you're happy with it, put a tick mark next to that spot on the list. If not, just go on to the next spot. Perform the next spot as if it's a concert, giving yourself a tick mark if it's good, moving on if it's not. Continue in this way until you've gone through your entire list. Then go back to the beginning and perform the first spot again. If it's good, it gets another tick mark. If it's not good and you had a tick mark there from the first time, you must erase that tick mark and go back to zero for that spot. Continue through the list like this, erasing all the tick marks you've accumulated for any spot that doesn't go well. The goal is five tick marks per spot.

Probably some of your spots will get five tick marks easily and others will be more of a struggle. Once a spot has five tick marks, it drops out of the list. If you get down to fewer than five spots that still don't have five tick marks, start a new list so you have at least five spots. You need to give your brain a chance to forget a little bit in between repetitions of each spot to get the maximum benefit from this method (just like with spaced practice, discussed in Chapters 4–6). If you have too few spots it won't work as well. This method is also very effective for working on orchestra excerpts. Make a list of your excerpts and go through that list in the same way.

Interval timer practice

An interval timer allows you to set a timer to go off repeatedly (say, every five minutes), rather than just once. There are many free interval timer apps. Before you start practicing, pick out one spot that you want to nail in performance. This can be as short as one bar, or as long as half a page or so. Then start practicing something completely different and start your interval timer. Every time the timer goes off, stop whatever you're practicing and perform the spot you picked out, just like it's a concert. No stopping no matter what. Then return to whatever you were practicing when the timer went off. It doesn't really matter what you set your interval timer to as long as it goes off at least three to four times within your practice session. You just want the time between "performances" to be long enough for you to forget a bit and for it to feel fresh when you come back to it. Again, this is very effective for working on orchestra excerpts. You could play the same excerpt each time the timer goes off, or you could play one at random. Both strategies are effective.

Time-constrained practice

This method also uses an interval timer and works well for brand new music as well as music you've been working on for a while. For this one, pick three to five sections that need work. Set your interval timer to go off every two to three minutes (but no more than every five minutes). Whenever the timer goes off, you must switch to a new section. When I do this, I preplan the order of the sections ahead of time so I don't have to decide in the moment what to switch to. I find it most useful if the order is random (rather than just 1 2 3 1 2 3 over and over). You want to visit each section at least three times in total. Since you have extremely limited time to work on a given section, you have to be very focused and quite specific about what you are working on and how you are working on it. This can dramatically increase focus and therefore the effectiveness of your practice. When you return to a section, you will also have to remember quickly what you were working on the last time you visited this section, which will further cement your work in memory. This method is especially beneficial for people who tend to practice mindlessly or zone out when practicing (or who tend to just play through passages over and over). More on focus in the final chapter.

Perform in a random order

Use this when you have practiced everything well for an upcoming concert or audition and want to test it. Divide your music into sections and assign

92 USING YOUR TIME WELL

each section a number. If you have several shorter pieces—no more than a page long—just assign each piece a number. If you have multimovement pieces, probably one movement per practice session will be the best way to do this method. Once each section has a number, either put the numbers into a random number generator or write each number on a separate slip of paper. You can also roll dice to generate the numbers. Draw numbers one at a time and perform that section of the piece. Again, this should be like a concert, so no stopping no matter what. Keep track of which sections went well and which didn't so you have a record of both what's ready to go and what needs more attention.

Brand new music

Most of the interleaved practice methods listed above are for testing whether you are ready for a performance or not. For music that is brand new, it's not ready to be tested in this way. But we saw that doing interleaved practice from the beginning can jump-start learning, so it's worth doing at all stages of preparation. With something brand new, I typically practice the passage several times throughout the same practice session—and throughout the day—interspersed with breaks and other material in between. The first time I practice a given passage in a day is my "main" practice of that section. When I come back to it later, I review the work I did earlier, making sure I still remember a tricky rhythm, or can hear the unusual chromatic harmonies, or remember the hand shapes I drilled in. Usually when I revisit the passage later, it's only for a very short amount of time—less than five minutes—but those short little reminders speed up the learning process enormously.

Bonus: Late night/early morning mock performance

This isn't quite interleaved practice because you're not switching quickly between different tasks, but it does follow the spirit of letting your brain practice what it's going to have to do in performance. Most people's brains don't feel quite normal when they are performing, and it can be hard to concentrate for many reasons. To practice performing well when your brain is not at its best, do a full run-through of your recital or a mock audition at a time when you are at your worst. If you are a morning person, stay up several hours past your bedtime and do this very late at night. If you are a night owl, set your alarm for a very early hour (like 5 or 6 am) and get up and do the run-through then. Warm up as you plan to right before the event and no more. If you're worried you might not have time to warm up, do the mock performance/audition without any warm-up. If you can play well in these extreme mock-performance situations, you'll feel much more comfortable at the actual event.

There are obviously many more ways to use the principles of interleaved practice, but hopefully these suggestions will get you started. The goal is to give your brain a chance to practice the skills it needs in performance. Several of the practice methods described above require you to play through something without stopping even if you make a mistake. Going back to Chapter 1, this suggests a logical question: won't that reinforce the wrong pathway? Shouldn't you stop and fix the problem? There are a few answers to this. First, doing something wrong once isn't going to make a new incorrect pathway in your brain—it would be more like a single line of footprints through the snowy field. Second, most often with these methods, something different goes wrong every time. That means the errors are a matter of focus and failure to think ahead. Every time you return to that spot, you will learn how to focus and think ahead a bit better, which is exactly what you must train your brain to do in a performance situation. And lastly, you need practice coping with mistakes so you know how to handle them and move on without letting them derail you. An absolutely spotless performance with zero mistakes is a myth, and you need practice letting go of errors and staying engaged with the music.

If the same thing *does* go wrong every time, however, that can be a clue that you're not quite ready to use interleaved practice to test performance readiness. Go back and do some additional blocked practice to solidify everything. But what if you go back to this solidification practice and it's completely fine and feels easy? When this happens to me, it's a signal that my issue is psychological, not technical. For some reason, I'm getting anxious or scared or distracted when I use interleaved practice to test out performance readiness. This means interleaved practice is *exactly* what I should be doing to solve whatever psychological issue is getting in my way. It means I need more practice trusting myself so that when I'm on stage, I will have the confidence and focus to play the way I know I can.

That leads to a related question: how do you know when you're ready for interleaved practice methods that test performance readiness? When something feels easy and reliable using blocked practice methods, that means it's time to start testing out whether it's ready for performance. The first time you test a passage in this way, it often doesn't go very well. That can be discouraging, but it's also an accurate representation of how well you can perform it right now. Better to find that out in the privacy of your practice room than on stage in front of an audience! The more you let your brain practice what it's going to have to do in a performance situation, the better you'll get at performance skills, and the more consistent and reliable the passage will feel.

It can be hard to determine when you are ready to test out performance readiness, but over time you should be able to judge this better and better. If you're someone who tends to obsess over all the little details (like me), you should probably start testing performance readiness sooner than feels comfortable. If you are someone who has to restrain yourself from playing through your favorite spots all the time, you probably need to spend longer cleaning up details before you are ready to practice performing.

And how did Evan do at his jury? In his lesson that day, when I realized he needed to be doing interleaved practice, I explained the concept and then set my interval timer to go off every five minutes. We moved on to discuss the other material he had prepared for his lesson, but every five minutes, the timer interrupted us. When that happened, he played me the first phrase of his Bach, and then we returned to our lesson. By the end of the hour, his Bach sounded gorgeous every time. He continued to practice using interleaved practice methods on his own in the weeks following. And at his jury, he gave a performance we were both proud of.

8

Why Exact Repetitions May Not Be the Best Goal

When I was just starting out as a teacher, I struggled with getting my younger students to do correct repetitions to reinforce the new habits they were learning, so I made up a game to make it more fun. Instead of identical repetitions, I would give them small physical challenges each time, like standing on one foot, or walking in a circle, or playing with their eyes closed. Kids *loved* this game and made up all sorts of creative variations themselves, like bending their knees every time they played down-bow, and then going up on their tiptoes every time they played an up-bow.

But I always wondered: was this actually beneficial or was it just fun? Turns out, it's both.

Variable practice

When we're working to perfect something, intuitively it makes sense to figure out exactly how we want it to feel or sound, and then repeat that ideal version many times. But is this really the best way to practice? At a certain point, it can get boring to repeat the same thing over and over, which means it's hard to focus. And if we're not focused, we aren't being effective in our practicing.

Maybe there's a better way.

In a famous study from 1978, researchers asked two groups of kids to practice throwing beanbags to a target on the floor.[1] Group 1 practiced throwing the beanbags to a target three feet away. Group 2—called the variable practice group—practiced throwing the beanbags to targets both two feet and four feet away. Then, all the kids were tested to see how well they could throw the beanbags to the three-foot target. You'd think Group 1, that focused on throwing to the target three feet away, would do better, right? Believe it or not, the opposite was true: Group 2, the variable practice group, was better, even though they had never actually practiced with the

Learn Faster, Perform Better. Molly Gebrian, Oxford University Press. © Oxford University Press 2024.
DOI: 10.1093/oso/9780197680063.003.0009

three-foot distance. Researchers also examined another variation of this—kids throwing beanbags of variable weight to targets at varying distances—and came to the same conclusion: groups with greater variability in practice did better in performance.[2] Same thing with tennis: kids who practiced hitting balls to several different targets did better than kids who just aimed for one target. Remarkably, kids whose training focused exclusively on hitting the test target did *the same* in the performance test as kids trained to simply hit the ball over the net (not aiming at anything), and far worse than kids trained to hit a variety of targets.[3]

These studies are often used as evidence that *variable practice* is more effective than practicing exactly the same thing over and over. Deliberately changing the details and parameters of the skill—like throwing to different targets—enables us to learn the skill in a richer and more flexible way, which we can then generalize to other situations more effectively. When we only practice one version of the skill, our knowledge is narrow and less durable when conditions change. Also, as we discussed previously, our assessment of how well we're doing while practicing is not a valid index of how much we have actually learned. How we sound at the end of a practice session is a measure of the momentary strength of that skill, but how we sound the next day at the start of our practice session is a much more valid index of the underlying strength of that skill. So, doing uniform repetitions can cause a lot of improvement in the moment, but doing varied repetitions will cause those improvements to stick better over time.

However, the story is a bit more complicated than this. A study from 2018 that aimed to replicate the famous beanbag experiment—this time with adults instead of kids—found only small advantages for variable practice that disappeared in a post-test two weeks later.[4] Another study with basketball free-throws found that variable practice was better on the very first try in a performance test after training, but then was no different from uniform practice after that.[5]

This last result is still useful to musicians, though, since we only get one shot on stage. And the difference in performance on the very first free-throw following either varied or uniform practice was dramatic, as seen in Figure 8.1. In this graph, the white square group practiced shooting from the same location each time. The black square group practiced shooting from different locations. During practice, both groups performed essentially the same. In the very first shot during the performance, however, the variable group significantly outperformed the other group.

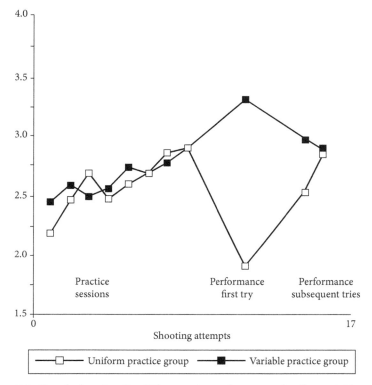

Figure 8.1 Graph showing the difference in performance for the variable versus uniform group in shooting free-throws.

Reproduced with permission from Landin, D., et al. (1993). The effects of variable practice on the performance of a basketball skill. *Research Quarterly for Exercise and Sport.* 64(2): 232–237. © Owned by the Society of Health and Physical Educators, www.shapeamerica.org, reprinted by permission of Taylor & Francis Ltd., http://www.tandfonline.com on behalf of Owned by the Society of Health and Physical Educators, www.shapeamerica.org.

But what's going on here? Why do some studies find a benefit for variable practice, while others don't?

Skill level matters

A few carefully designed studies can give us our answer. In one, kids practiced throwing beanbags of different weights to land on a target, but with a twist.[6] Some of the kids threw the same weight beanbag every time (the constant group). Other kids threw a different weight beanbag each time (the

98 USING YOUR TIME WELL

random group). In the middle between these two extremes were two other groups: one group threw the same weight beanbag six times in a row before moving on to a new weight (the blocked group), whereas the other group threw the same weight three times in a row before switching weights (the variable group). Figure 8.2 summarizes the four different groups so you can keep them straight. In the final test, they found that the variable group, who had the same weight three tries in a row before switching, did the best.

Why would this be? The researchers explain that the constant and blocked versions were too easy, but the random version was too hard. The variable version, on the other hand, was just right. The kids needed a chance to address their errors and reinforce the correct movement, which is why the random version didn't work. However, too many reinforcement throws make it boring, which is why the constant and blocked versions were too easy. The variable group—three times on the same weight—seemed to be the sweet spot of balancing challenge and reinforcement, at least for the kids in this study.

This is supported by an experiment that tested frisbee throwing.[7] Kids and adults practiced throwing a frisbee to different distances and then were given new distances in the final test. Group 1 had to switch distances every time during practice. Group 2 got to practice each distance nine times in a row before switching. On the final test, Group 2 did better. Interestingly, the kids who had to switch every time did much worse than the adults who had to switch every time. Throwing the frisbee was harder for the kids than the adults, and so having to switch distances every throw really degraded the kids' performance on the final test. They clearly needed more practice on each distance before moving on to a new one.

One final study that's especially relevant to musicians tested timing skills in kids. In this experiment, the kids had to press a button to activate a sequence of lights on a track.[8] When the last light in the sequence lit up, they pressed a second button. The goal was to coordinate the second button press precisely with the last light turning on. There was a fast version and a slow version of this light sequence, with the fast version assumed to be easier for the kids based on prior research. The kids were divided into four groups, each with

Constant Group	Blocked Group	Variable Group	Random Group
Same weight every throw	6x on each weight before new weight	3x on each weight before new weight	New weight every throw

Figure 8.2 Practice session structures of the four groups.

Group 1	Group 2	Group 3	Group 4
Slow version only	Fast version only	*New speed each time:* Extra slow, slow, fast, extra fast (random order)	*6x on each speed before switching:* Extra slow, slow, fast, extra fast (random order)

Figure 8.3 The different speeds at which the four groups practiced the light sequence.

a different training schedule (shown in Figure 8.3). Group 1 trained only on the slow version, while Group 2 trained only on the fast version. Group 3 trained with both the slow and fast versions plus an extra slow and an extra fast version, with the speed changing every time. Group 4 trained on the extra slow, slow, fast, and extra fast versions, but they got to do each speed six times in a row before moving on to a new speed. The next day, everyone did a final test on two new speeds—a fast one and a slow one—that nobody had trained on.

Probably at this point you can predict who did the best. The kids who trained on a variety of speeds presented in blocks of six (Group 4) did the best, just like the last few studies we've discussed. They got variety, but they also got to practice each version a bit before moving on to a new speed. Interestingly, the kids in Group 1 (slow version only) also did quite well, better than the kids in Group 2 (fast version only), but also better than Group 3, who switched each time. The slow speed was the hardest for the kids, so it seems that practicing the hardest version was still beneficial even though it was uniform. But switching every time (Group 3) was *too* hard, so it degraded their performance.

Here's what all of this means: whether variability is helpful or not depends on your skill level. If there is already a lot of variability in the movement, like when something is new, adding more may be detrimental. For children and novices, uniform repetitive practice may be more beneficial than introducing additional variability. For someone with a higher level of skill, however, variable practice is better.[9] This aligns with one learning theory that asserts that you learn the most at the *challenge point*, also known as the point at which you have *desirable difficulties*.[10] You want your practicing to be right at the edge of what you are capable of—not too easy and not too hard. Repetitive, consistent, blocked practice may be better at the beginning because the new skill is hard enough. At this level, it will be too difficult to derive any benefit from varied or highly randomized practice. But as you gain skill and

100   USING YOUR TIME WELL

expertise, you also need to increase the level of difficulty. This is where variable practice comes in (as well as interleaved practice, which we discussed in Chapter 7). Variability is an unavoidable feature of how our bodies work. In fact, one study looking at elite discus throwers found that over a one-year period, they never produced exactly the same throw twice![11] But whether introducing more variability will be beneficial depends on where we are in the learning process.

This idea is also backed by a study that has interesting connections to retroactive interference. Recall from Chapter 4 that if there is a break of about six hours in between learning two new and similar skills, retroactive interference doesn't happen. A group of scientists wondered what would happen if people learned a skill (Skill A) and then learned a slightly modified version of that skill (Skill A') six hours later.[12] In this case, Skill A was learning to move a cursor on a computer screen by squeezing a little handheld device. The force with which participants squeezed determined the movement of the cursor. For Skill A', the experimenters manipulated how much they had to squeeze the handheld device, so sometimes they had to squeeze it more, other times less, to get the same result. Skill A' was more variable.

The researchers found that if people practiced Skill A and then six hours later practiced Skill A', they were *much* better at Skill A the next day when they were tested again. If they just practiced Skill A again after the six-hour break, they didn't show nearly as much improvement the next day. You can see this clearly in Figure 8.4 if you compare the group AAA to group AA'A in Session 3 on the line graph. The embedded bar graph shows the amount of change in the skill between the beginning and the end of the experiment, with the group that practiced Skill A' making significantly more improvement.

Interestingly, if the participants practiced Skill A' after only a 30-minute break, they *didn't* show the large gain in performance the next day. This finding aligns with what we saw in Chapter 4 on retroactive interference and the importance of breaks. The researchers also tested to see if practicing Skill A' first, followed by Skill A, or practicing Skill A' twice with a break in between would have the same effect, but neither one did. It seems like practicing the easier, more uniform version first (Skill A) and then the harder, more variable version (Skill A') was the secret for the huge improvement the next day.

To summarize, when a skill is new, the practice should be more uniform to solidify the skill. As you improve, variable practice will be more beneficial.

There's another noteworthy detail from this experiment: at the end of the second practice session, the people who were practicing Skill A again

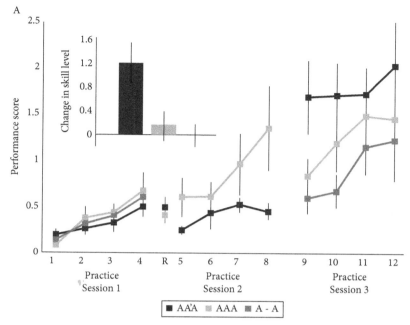

Figure 8.4 Graphs that compare practicing Skill A twice versus Skill A and then Skill A'.

Modified from Wymbs, N., et al. (2016). Motor skills are strengthened through reconsolidation. *Current Biology.* 26(3): 338–343. © Elsevier 2021.

were doing *much* better than the people practicing Skill A'. But at the test the next day, the people who had practiced Skill A' jumped far ahead of the people who had only done additional practice on Skill A. You can see this in Figure 8.4 as well. That's the illusion of mastery again: how well you think you're doing during practice is not a very good measure of how much you have improved. It's when you come back the next day that you really know how much you've learned.

Specific practice strategies

When I had my young students stand on one foot or walk backwards while playing, that was a form of variable practice. I was pleasantly surprised when I learned about this research for the first time; the game I had made up just to hold their attention was actually giving them an added benefit. But is my silly

102 USING YOUR TIME WELL

game the musical equivalent of throwing beanbags or hitting tennis balls to targets at different distances?

Other research has highlighted that the variability needs to relate to the demands of the task at hand.[13] For instance, if a particular passage is fast with tricky coordination demands, the variability should be related to these challenges and not to something unrelated, like the ability to sustain a long note. As an example, one common type of variability in music practice is to play passages in different rhythms and slurring patterns (which we will discuss more in Chapter 16). These methods work well for fast passages because the difficulty in these passages is the precise coordination of movements at the fast tempo. By varying the rhythm, you are changing the coordination parameters, helping your body to create a deeper, more flexible understanding of the necessary movements. Changing the slurring/bowing patterns accomplishes the same thing. However, these methods may not be as effective for slow, lyrical passages because this type of music has different demands. For a singer, these passages may be challenging for breath support, for instance. In that case, practicing them in a wide variety of dynamics might be helpful, or at even slower tempos than written. For any given skill or phrase, you want to think about the specific challenges it presents and create variations based on that.

Here are some general ideas to get you started (with instrument-specific ideas in Appendix C):

- Practice at a variety of tempos, focusing particularly on the tempos that are the most challenging.
- Practice with a variety of different articulations, tone colors, dynamics, and/or vibratos. You can do these one at a time or combine parameters.
- Play with opposite articulations and dynamics. If it says forte, play piano. If it says crescendo, do a diminuendo instead. If it says staccato, play legato. If it's slurred, play staccato.
- Create a "skeleton" version of the music that contains just the essential elements of the phrase. This musical reduction could be just the bass line, just the most important notes of the melody, or just the essential rhythmic elements. Play this version with maximum direction and expression to help clarify what you want musically. You could even record this version and then play as-written along with your recording. This will help you clarify your interpretive decisions.
- Fill in all the note values with subdivided repeated notes (e.g., a half note becomes four repeated eighth notes) not just for the purposes of

rhythmic accuracy, but also for phrasing and direction. This will also help clarify interpretive decisions.

- Practice in a variety of different emotions. This is one of my favorites, which I first learned from Dr. Noa Kageyama. Pick a phrase and play it with the emotional expression you intend. Then, play it again with a different emotion. Try as many versions as you can, even choosing emotions that are the opposite of what would be appropriate for the phrase, trying to make each one as convincing as possible. I often discover that in doing inappropriate emotions—playing happy music as if it were angry, for instance—I find things I really like. It's always surprising to discover that a happy section played angrily sounds better, but often I end up changing how I think about the passage in order to make it come across clearly to a listener.
- Practice playing as if you are impersonating different famous musicians (another idea I learned from Noa). In his classes, Dr. Kageyama has participants play as themselves, and then pretend they are being possessed by the spirit of various famous musicians of their choosing. When someone plays as if they are Yo-Yo Ma or Hilary Hahn or Emmanuel Ax, everything about their playing changes immediately. This is an entertaining game to play in a group—and fun to guess who the person is pretending to be! It's also a great practice method for developing more flexibility and a deeper control over the music (and for discovering new ideas).
- Alternate between physical and mental practice one measure at a time: play one measure, then remove your hands from the instrument and play the next measure mentally, etc. (more on mental practice in the next chapter). This idea, courtesy of pianist Jeffrey Sykes, would be a great memorization challenge as well (more on that in Chapters 12 and 13).
- Practice introducing small physical challenges, like I did with my younger students. These should be things that can be done while playing—and aren't dangerous! Examples include playing with eyes shut, walking around the room (forward and backward), walking in a circle (forward and backward), standing on one foot, crouching down close to the floor, standing on tiptoes, etc. Kids *love* practicing in this way, but it's a nice challenge for adults, too. Particularly for passages where focus may be an issue or where there are already many physical challenges inherent in playing a given phrase, adding an additional level of physical challenge can be beneficial.

In our quest for perfection, it can often feel like we need to do countless exact repetitions of our ideal version for a given passage. But our nervous system is inherently variable, and perfection is simply not possible—although I know that may be a hard pill for many to swallow! By introducing variability into our practice, not only can we make practicing more fun and interesting, but we will come away with stronger skills in the end. And by having more flexibility in how we play something, that will allow us to adjust on stage and respond to our musical partners in a more spontaneous, expressive, and musically convincing way.

SECTION III
THE POWER OF THE MIND

All practicing is about training the brain, but some practice methods feel much more brain-focused than others. In this section, we'll look at research that specifically targets the mental aspects of playing, namely mental practicing, focus, and memorization.

9

The Power of Mental Practice

As we've discussed several times in this book, practicing well is about training our brains. One of the most powerful practice methods for brain training is mental practice: practicing inside our heads without moving or making any sound. It may seem like this couldn't possibly be effective or a good use of time, but hopefully you'll change your mind after reading these next two chapters.

Mental practice changes the brain

I used to be extremely skeptical of mental practice. I had never even heard of it before I was 15, but at the end of my sophomore year in high school, I developed tendonitis in both wrists. I had to take most of that summer off from playing and then resumed practicing extremely slowly in the fall to ensure I didn't reinjure myself. At that time, many teachers often said to me, "Oh, you must do a lot of mental practicing!" I would sort of smile and nod and say something vague, but I would be thinking "Why in the world would I do that? What a waste of time!" Little did I know . . . .

The study that changed my mind asked nonmusicians to learn a simple five-note scale on the piano.[1] The goal was to play the scale up and down in sixteenth notes at quarter note equals 60. The participants, none of whom had any prior musical experience, were divided into three groups: the physical practice group, the mental practice group, and the control group. The physical practice group practiced at a piano, two hours a day for five days. The mental practice group practiced for the same amount of time, but they just *imagined* the feeling of their fingers moving in the correct order. The control group didn't get to practice. At the end of each day, the researchers tested the participants to see how well they were doing. That daily test was the only time the mental practice group and the control group got to actually play a piano.

The results from the control group and the physical practice group were exactly what you would predict: the control group didn't get better, whereas

Learn Faster, Perform Better. Molly Gebrian, Oxford University Press. © Oxford University Press 2024.
DOI: 10.1093/oso/9780197680063.003.0010

the physical practice group could play the scale perfectly at the required tempo by the end of the study. The results from the mental practice group, however, are quite interesting. After five days of practice, the mental practice group had achieved the same level of performance as the physical practice group had after three days, which is pretty impressive. Remember, they had no prior musical experience and they learned the scale just by imagining themselves playing it. After the playing test at the end of the fifth day, the mental practice group was asked to practice physically for two hours. When they came back, they were also perfect.

The mind-blowing part of this study, however, is what the researchers found when they measured something else in this experiment. To understand this "something else" we need to take a brief detour inside the brain.

All of us have a strip of brain called the motor cortex and another strip right next to it called the somatosensory cortex (shown in Figure 9.1), with one of each on both sides of the brain. The motor cortex controls voluntary movements and the somatosensory cortex processes incoming sensory information from your body. The left motor and somatosensory cortices

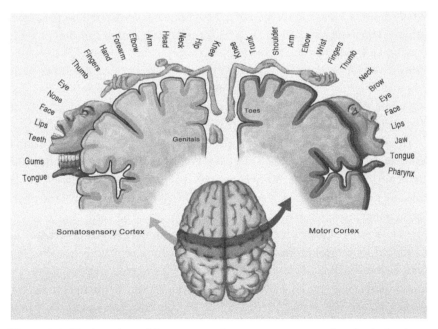

Figure 9.1 The location of the motor and somatosensory cortices in the brain (viewed from the top down), as well as which specific area corresponds to which body part.
Reproduced with permission from Alamy Limited. https://www.alamy.com.

Figure 9.2 The homunculus, or how we would look if our body parts were proportional to the amount of brain area that controls each part.
Reproduced with permission from Alamy Limited. https://www.alamy.com.

communicate with and control the right side of the body, whereas the right motor and somatosensory cortices communicate with and control the left side of the body. There is a specific area of both the motor and somatosensory cortex devoted to each body part, the size of which depends on how much motor control you need over that body part and how sensitive that body part is to sensation. The fingers and the lips, for instance, take up much more brain real estate than, say, the back of your knee. You can see this map of the various body parts laid out in Figure 9.1. The funny looking guy in Figure 9.2 is known as the homunculus, which is what we would look like if our body parts were proportional to how much brain area is devoted to each part. The homunculus has huge lips and hands because much more brain space is devoted to controlling them as compared to our knees and elbows, for instance, which don't need such fine control and therefore don't get as much representation in the brain.

Through a series of studies, scientists have discovered that the area of the motor and somatosensory cortex that controls the left-hand fingers in string players—the hand that plays on the instrument—is bigger than in non–string players.[2] This is a result of the training we undergo and not an innate difference we're born with. For pianists or any musicians who use both hands equally, the finger areas of the somatosensory and motor cortices on both sides are bigger. In fact, when you use any body part intensively the way string players use their left-hand fingers, the brain area controlling that body part gets bigger. If we played instruments with our toes instead of our fingers, the toe areas would enlarge instead of the finger areas.

Now we can return to the mental practice study. In addition to testing playing ability each day, the researchers also measured the size of the area that controlled the fingers, hypothesizing that this part of the motor cortex would get bigger in the physical practice group by the end of the five days. In fact, that's exactly what they found: the physical practice group showed a significant enlargement in that part of the motor cortex by the end of the study. The control group predictably showed no change. The question was whether anything would happen in the brains of the mental practice participants.

Here's the mind-blowing part of this experiment: the change in the motor cortex was almost exactly the same in the mental practice group as in the physical practice group. (See Figure 9.3). That's incredible! Think about what this means: the mental practicers changed the actual physical structure of their brains just by *thinking* about it! You can't change physical matter out in the world like that. You can't just walk into a room and say, "Y'know, I wish this space were a bit bigger," and then have the walls push out and the ceiling shoot up. That would be a superpower! But you can change the actual physical structure of your brain with your own brain. That is absolutely amazing.

Now you can see why I changed my mind about mental practice.

I first learned about this experiment in graduate school while I was studying with Carol Rodland. When I shared this information with her in a lesson, she told me an incredible story about her experience with mental practice. Most of the stories in this book come from my personal experience as a student, teacher, and player, but I'm very grateful that Carol has allowed me to tell her story here to further illustrate the power of mental practice.

When Carol was a student at Juilliard, she got into a taxi accident that prevented her from playing for several months while she recovered. This threatened to make it impossible for her to compete in that year's concerto competition. She especially wanted to enter the competition that year because Dennis Russell Davies, a hero of hers, would be conducting the winner's concert. At Juilliard, everyone had to play the same concerto for the competition, and that year it was *Der Schwanendreher* by Hindemith. This is a standard concerto for violists, but Carol had only ever played the first movement. So there she was: injured, under strict doctor's orders not to play

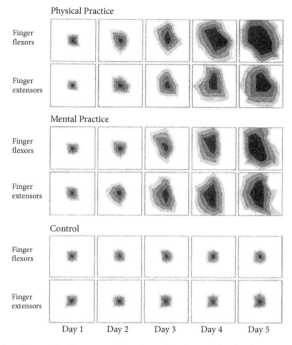

Figure 9.3 A schematic diagram showing the size of the brain area controlling the fingers, from Day 1 through Day 5 of the experiment.

Reproduced with permission from Pascual-Leone, A., et al. (1995). Modulation of muscle responses evoked by transcranial magnetic stimulation during the acquisition of new fine motor skills. *Journal of Neurophysiology.* 7(3): 1037–1045.

or practice, the concerto was a piece she hadn't played in full, and yet one of her heroes was conducting the winner's concert.

She decided she *had* to try for it anyway.

Using a variety of mental practice techniques, she learned (and memorized!) the entire concerto without touching her viola. About two weeks before the competition, she picked up her instrument for the first time in months and started to do some physical practice. She was still under strict doctor's orders, though, so she couldn't play much.

Despite this, not only did she get the concerto ready to perform, but she *won* the competition at Juilliard.

Thanks to extensive mental practice and just two weeks of (limited) physical practice, she got to perform in Avery Fisher Hall under the baton of her hero. If that doesn't convince you mental practice works, nothing will.

What is mental practice?

Now that you're (hopefully) convinced, let's talk about what mental practice looks like. Mental practice is hearing and feeling everything you need to be aware of when you play your instrument, but inside your head without actually doing it. To use string players as an example, we need to feel which finger(s) are playing, the spacing between them, which string(s) they are on, which position we are in, what type of vibrato is being used, where we are going to and coming from for shifts (and what the arm has to do to accomplish this), whether we're playing up bow or down bow, what part of the bow we're in, what string(s) we're on, our contact point, our bow distribution, what the bow stroke is, the feel of the hair on the string, the speed of the bow, the weight of the bow, etc. Not to mention the quality of sound we want, the pitch we are playing, the resonance we want, the timing and phrasing we are going for, and many other aspects of playing and musicality.

I know this can seem overwhelming, and you may have a hard time feeling or hearing things in your head at first. That's fine. That's completely normal (as we'll discuss in the next chapter). With practice, it will get easier and your sense of how things sound and feel inside your head will get clearer. You also don't have to start with everything, especially if mental practice is new to you. If you've never practiced mentally before, it can feel very strange at first to just sit in silence, trying to hear and feel things in your head. But with time, it will get easier.

So you can understand what mental practice feels like in your head, let's take something outside of music as an example. If you want, have someone else read the next several paragraphs out loud so you can close your eyes—it might make the experience easier to imagine.

Pretend you are holding a beautiful, juicy, fresh orange in your hand. Feel the weight of that orange. Run the fingers of your other hand over the rind of the orange and feel its texture. Can you feel the little bumps on the surface? Now gently toss the orange back and forth between your hands. Can you feel the weight shift from one hand to another? Can you feel what it feels like when the orange lands in your hand? Can you hear the sound it makes when it lands in your hand?

Now start to peel the orange. Can you smell the fragrance that comes out? Can you feel the tug of the rind pulling away from the fruit underneath? Does it come off easily or with more difficulty? Are the pieces coming off in little scraps or in one long piece? Keep peeling the orange, feeling the rind

THE POWER OF MENTAL PRACTICE   113

pull away from the fruit as clearly as you can. Can you hear the subtle sound this makes?

Once you have peeled the whole thing, separate the fruit into two halves and place one half on the table in front of you. Now separate a section from the half you are holding and put that section in your mouth. Can you taste it? Can you feel the texture of the fruit and the juice in your mouth?

My guess is you could feel and imagine everything in those last paragraphs pretty clearly. You might have even thought you were actually smelling or tasting an orange. That's what mental practice is like—feeling and hearing all the details of the actual experience of playing, but inside your head without moving or making sound.*

When you are new to mental practice, start with the aspect of playing you find easiest to imagine. If it's your fingers on your instrument, pick a short passage you can already play well and see if you can imagine your fingers moving at the right time and in the right place without actually moving them. If you're a singer, maybe it's hearing the text in your head with good diction. Once that first layer of the music is clear, pick another parameter and try to incorporate that. For string players, maybe you'll try to feel your fingers and the correct bowing. Keep adding more layers until everything is there. If you find that anything is "fuzzy" or hard to imagine, isolate just that layer or small section of music. Try to really concentrate on feeling or hearing it until it's clear. It's okay if this is hard for you, or if you can't hear or feel anything clearly inside your head. That's normal when you're new to mental practice. As you get used to practicing inside your head, you'll find that eventually things will come into better focus. And invariably, the things that are the hardest for us to imagine are also the hardest for us to play as well. If you make it clear in your head, it will be much clearer when you try it on your instrument.

The most obvious application for mental practice is in situations when you can't play your instrument. If you are traveling, you usually can't play your instrument in a plane/train/boat/car/bus. Your fellow passengers probably would not appreciate it. If it's early in the morning or late at night and you want to practice but people are sleeping, you can practice mentally without disturbing them. If you are injured and can't play, you can practice mentally

---

* If you have aphantasia, the inability to see or hear things inside your head, you can still use mental practice as a tool. Aphantasia exists for every sense, and I personally have visual and auditory aphantasia—I cannot see or hear anything inside my head. It's dark and quiet in there. However, I know conceptually what something sounds or looks like, which is how I can "see" or "hear" things inside my head. For me, it's also much easier to imagine how things feel, and so I rely heavily on kinesthetic imagination when I practice mentally. More on developing these abilities in the next chapter.

114 THE POWER OF THE MIND

instead, as Carol did. Many professional musicians (myself included) have practiced countless hours on planes en route to their next engagement.

The combination of mental and physical practice

But what about during a normal practice day? Is there any benefit to doing both mental and physical practice as part of your daily routine? A number of studies have found that the *combination* of mental and physical practice results in better performance than just physical practice alone. One study on golf putting found that when golfers mentally and physically practiced putting, their scores improved much more than golfers who only practiced physically (or only practiced mentally).[3] Another golf experiment found that the combination of mental and physical practice also improved putting *consistency* more than either mental or physical practice alone.[4] Interestingly, this second study also looked at golfers' mental representations of putting—how clearly they understood the sequence of motions involved in the putt and how these motions were related to each other. When mental practice was part of the golfers' training, their mental representations were more elaborate, clearer, better organized, and more functional, as compared to the physical practice-only group (and the control group). Detailed mental representations like this are typically found in people who are highly skilled, so mental practice seems to help us reach this level earlier in our training.

The combination of mental and physical practice has also been shown to be very beneficial for musicians. In one experiment, pianists were asked to learn and memorize two different Scarlatti sonatas.[5] One group got to practice physically for 30 minutes, after which they were tested on their ability to perform the sonata from memory. After that performance test, they got 10 more minutes to practice physically before the final memorized performance. The other group was instructed to practice *mentally* for 30 minutes and after which they also had to perform from memory as best they could. They then were given 10 more minutes to practice, during which they were welcome to practice physically if they wanted to. Then, they also had their final performance test. (Figure 9.4 shows the practice and performance schedule for the two groups.) Even though the second group only practiced physically for 10 minutes, they performed just as well as the group who had practiced at the piano for 40 minutes. This is pretty incredible and also saves a lot of wear and tear on the body.

But this is a very short timeline. We typically practice our music for much longer than 40 minutes total before a concert. Does this still work on a longer

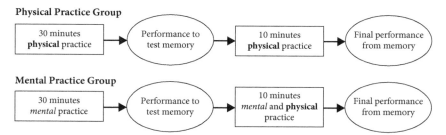

Figure 9.4 Practice and performance schedule for the pianists learning the Scarlatti sonatas.

timescale? In an experiment to answer this question, guitarists were asked to learn and memorize a short Baroque piece.[6] The physical practice group practiced for 30 minutes in the lab and then recorded a performance of the piece to get a baseline sense of where they were in their progress. Then, they were sent home to practice the piece every day for a week, 30 minutes each day. At the end of the week, they came back and performed the piece again. Ten days after that, they performed it one more time, but they weren't allowed to practice between the second performance and the final one. This was to test the durability of their practicing over time.

The mental practice group had an identical schedule. The critical difference in this group was that every 30-minute practice block was split up into 20 minutes of mental practice followed by 10 minutes of physical practice. Figure 9.5 shows the practice and performance schedules of the two groups.

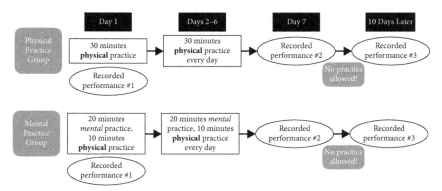

Figure 9.5 Practice and performance schedule for the guitarists learning a short Baroque piece.

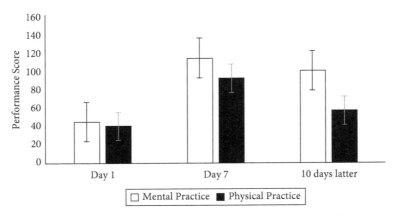

Figure 9.6 Performance scores for the mental practice and physical practice groups on Day 1, after 7 days of practice, and at the follow-up performance 10 days after the final practice session.

Adapted from Iorio, C., et al. (2022). The effect of mental practice on music memorization. *Psychology of Music*. 50(1): 230–244. © 2022 by SAGE Publications. Reprinted by permission of SAGE Publications, Ltd.

On the first day, there was no difference in their performances, as you can see in Figure 9.6. On Day 7, the mental practice group was starting to pull ahead, but the difference was not "statistically significant," as researchers say. The big difference was in final performance on Day 10: here, the mental practice group did much better, meaning the inclusion of mental practice enhanced retention over time. You can see this clearly in Figure 9.6. Like the previous studies we've discussed, it seems that doing just a little physical practice combined with mental practice results in more durable learning.

A few studies have looked more specifically at exactly what musicians are doing when they engage in mental practice. Are they thinking about how it sounds? Or how it feels? Or are they imagining what their movements will look like? One study designed to answer these questions used motion capture while pianists performed short exercises by Brahms.[7] In practicing for the performance, one group was instructed to only use physical practice, while the other group was only allowed to use mental practice, using any mental practice strategy they wanted. After the performance, the mental practice group filled out a questionnaire that probed whether they had mainly relied on how it felt, how it sounded, or how it looked. The researchers found that imagining how it would *feel* to play it was associated with how quickly the pianists moved their hands, whereas imagining how it would *sound* was associated with a better ability to anticipate what they had to play next. Imagining what it would look like to play didn't seem to help at all. From this, imagining how it sounds and feels seems to be much more important than visualizing.

One important note: several researchers have pointed out that if you don't know how to do something *at all* physically, mental practice won't help much.[8] If you're trying to learn a skill that is absolutely brand new, practice physically first before you try to practice it mentally. It seems that the brain needs actual sensory input from the body before mental practice will be beneficial. But if you already know how to play your instrument and you're just learning a new piece of music, you can jump right in with mental practice before you've ever played it. Composer and violist Paul Hindemith was famous for doing this: he would write himself a new piece on the train and then perform it when he arrived at his destination, presumably practicing it mentally while en route.[9]

Taken together, these studies tell us a few things. One: you don't have to spend nearly as much time actually playing your instrument if you are also practicing mentally. This can be extremely helpful to ensure you don't injure or fatigue yourself unnecessarily. In fact, the authors of the motion-capture study said, "As soon as some feedback is provided through minimal physical practice, the learning curve following mental practice shows sudden accelerations, greater than what one would expect from physical practice alone given the little amount of practice."[10]

The second important takeaway: being able to hear and feel the music in your head seems to be especially important, as compared to visualizing. Hearing ahead in particular influences your ability to anticipate the next movement you need to make. This is known as anticipatory auditory imagery, something that also seems to be critically important for good chamber music skills.[11] (Unfortunately, that discussion is beyond the scope of this book, but see the notes at the end for further resources if you're interested in this topic.)

Lastly: mental practice appears to make the learning more durable over time, particularly if you have to play from memory (more on memorization in Chapters 12–13).

118   THE POWER OF THE MIND

Enhancing mental practice

All of these studies make a strong case for including mental practice into your daily routine. Recently, there have been some exciting new discoveries on ways to enhance the benefits of mental practice even further, namely something called AO+MI.

AO+MI (or just AOMI) stands for "action observation and motor imagery." Motor imagery means imagining how something feels (the kinesthetic side of mental practice); action observation means passively watching someone do what you're trying to learn. To understand the power of action observation in this context, we have to take a quick trip to Italy.

In the early 1990s, a group of Italian researchers discovered something surprising by accident.[12] They were investigating which neurons were involved when a monkey would reach to pick up something. One day, the researchers noticed that when *they* went to pick up something, some of those same neurons in the monkey's brain were also active. What was going on? The monkey wasn't reaching for anything, the *researcher* was. And yet the monkey's brain was behaving as if *the monkey* were the one reaching. That led to the discovery of something called mirror neurons, neurons that were active when the monkey watched someone else move. Since then, scientists have learned that watching someone perform a skill will help you improve at that skill because of these mirror neurons. I think this makes intuitive sense to musicians, given how important demonstration is in our training. But it's a different kind of mental practice than we've been discussing thus far because it's largely passive—you're just watching, you're not imagining anything yourself.

What if you combined watching someone else with active mental practice? What if you imagined yourself doing the movements while you watched someone else do them? That's what AOMI is. Recent research has found that this works quite well. Although this is a relatively recent area of inquiry, the consensus seems to be that observing and practicing mentally at the same time is better than either one by itself.[13]

One study looked at people doing either simultaneous observation and mental practice or alternating between the two—watch someone do it, imagine yourself doing it, watch someone, imagine yourself doing it, etc.— and found no difference between the two in terms of their efficacy, so try them both to see which one you like better.[14] As of this writing, there haven't been any studies that look at AOMI plus physical practice compared to only physical practice—or any studies on this with musicians. But since the combination of mental practice plus physical practice appears to be better than just physical practice alone, one would expect that AOMI plus physical practice would give an even greater benefit than just physical practice. There is also evidence that watching a video of *yourself* performing the action is especially powerful, even if you make mistakes—as long as you know they are mistakes.[15] So you can do this at home even if you only have yourself to watch.

In light of this research, I have started to try something new in my teaching. I have asked students to practice small sections mentally in their lessons for many years. Like any teacher, I also demonstrate for my students. Recently, I have started combining the two based on this new research on AOMI. While I demonstrate, I ask the student to watch what I'm doing while they imagine themself doing it along with me (kinesthetic mental practice). I also recommend they do this at home: watch a video of themselves—or me, since I video-record all lessons—and practice mentally along with it. Using AOMI in this way seems to be very beneficial and students have reported that it helps them more than either mental practice or observation alone.

These findings on mental practice are persuasive, and they illustrate how powerful the mind is. But what's going on in the brain when we engage in mental practice? That's the topic of our next chapter.

10

Mental Practice and the Brain

It's clear from the previous chapter that mental practice is extremely benefi-cial. There's an obvious question, though, that we haven't looked at yet: *why*? Why does mental practice work? The research is clear that it *does* work, but what is going on in our brains that causes it to work? And how is it even possible that mental practice can change the actual physical structure of people's brains?

Brain activation

Here's the answer in a nutshell: when we physically play something and when we practice it mentally, very similar areas of the brain are involved. The brain activation is not 100% identical—if it were, we couldn't tell the difference be-tween actually doing something and imagining it!—but it's remarkably sim-ilar. Figure 10.1 shows the areas of the brain that are activated for mental practice, action observation, and physical practice.[1] Figure 10.2 shows the areas in common for each of the different methods. In both figures, the black blobs show which areas are active. You can see that there is a lot of overlap between kinesthetic mental practice, action observation, and actual physical movements.

Let's look at each of these areas individually to understand what they do and their importance in both mental and physical practice.

As you can see in Figure 10.3, the brain has four different lobes: frontal, temporal, parietal, and occipital—one of each on both sides. The four lobes have different specialties and support a variety of functions.

In both mental and physical practice, there is activation in the parietal lobes. For actual physical practice, this activation is in more *anterior* areas (toward the front) that are involved with integrating incoming information from your senses. That makes sense: when you move, your brain compares the movement you intended with the sensory information coming back that tells you the result of your movement. In mental practice, *posterior* areas

Learn Faster, Perform Better. Molly Gebrian, Oxford University Press. © Oxford University Press 2024.
DOI: 10.1093/oso/9780197680063.003.0011

122   THE POWER OF THE MIND

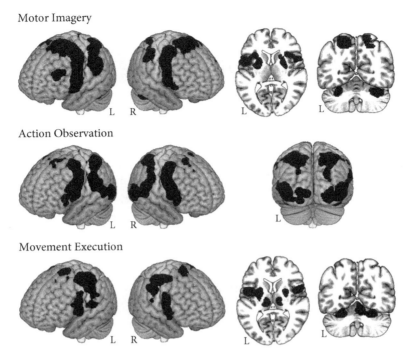

Figure 10.1 Areas of the brain active during mental practice (motor imagery), action observation, and actual physical movement.

Reproduced from Hardwick, R., et al. (2018). Neural correlates of action: Comparing meta-analyses of imagery, observation, and execution. *Neuroscience & Biobehavioral Reviews.* 94: 31–44.

(toward the back) of the parietal lobe are activated. These more posterior areas are involved in generating and storing motor representations, which can be thought of as blueprints for different motions. There is no incoming sensory information when we practice mentally, so it makes sense that the anterior areas wouldn't be involved. In general, many of the differences we see in brain activation between mental and physical practice are due to a lack of incoming sensory information in mental practice.

Communication between the parietal lobes and the frontal lobes also seems to be important for both physical and mental practice. People with brain damage that disrupts this communication have a hard time with both types of practicing. Scientists can create temporary—and safe—brain damage in people using a technology called TMS (transcranial magnetic stimulation). This sends a magnetic pulse into the brain and disrupts communication between different areas. When researchers use TMS on people's

Motor Imagery and Action Observation

Motor Imagery and Movement Execution

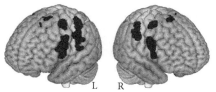

Action Observation and Movement Execution

Motor Imagery and Action Observation and Movement Execution

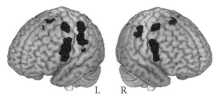

Figure 10.2 Areas of the brain where there is overlapping activation between the different types of practice.

Reproduced from Hardwick, R., et al. (2018). Neural correlates of action: Comparing meta-analyses of imagery, observation, and execution. *Neuroscience & Biobehavioral Reviews*. 94: 31–44.

posterior parietal lobes and therefore disrupt the communication with the frontal lobes, people have a hard time imagining how things feel without moving, modifying actual motions with their bodies, or coordinating their movements.[2] Without this communication between the frontal and parietal lobes, both physical and mental practice would be very difficult, if not impossible.

Two areas in the frontal lobes that are especially important for this communication are the supplementary motor area (SMA) and the premotor

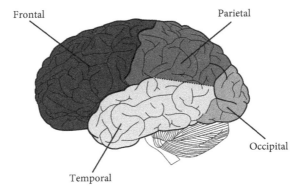

Figure 10.3 The four lobes of the brain.
Illustration by Sonny Oram.

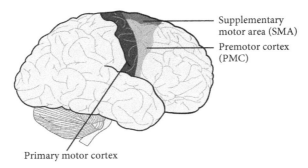

Figure 10.4 The location of the supplementary motor area (SMA) and the premotor cortex (PMC).
Illustration by Sonny Oram.

cortex (PMC), shown in Figure 10.4. The SMA is involved in the control of movements, especially planning complex movements, and is located on the surface of the cerebral cortex, close to the midline (one on each side), and right in front of the primary motor cortex. With actual movement, you see activation in the SMA proper. With mental practice, the activation is in the pre-SMA, which is the very front part of the SMA. The pre-SMA is involved in movement preparation—when you're getting ready to move but not actually moving—so it makes sense that this area would be activated during mental practice. The pre-SMA is also involved in things like conscious action intention, control, and selection as well as the order of movements—all important aspects of playing well.[3]

MENTAL PRACTICE AND THE BRAIN   125

The other critical area in the frontal lobes is the PMC. The PMC is also located on the surface of the brain, right in front of the primary motor cortex. It's just under the SMA if you move from the midline of the brain outward on each side, as you can see in Figure 10.4. The PMC does many different things, one of which is helping you select the correct plan for your movements. It makes sense that the PMC would be involved in both mental and physical practice, since selecting a movement plan is an important part of both methods of practicing.

Two other areas that are active in mental and physical practice are the cerebellum and the putamen, both of which are involved with coordinating movements. Interestingly, the cerebellum is very sensitive to the effects of alcohol, which is why people are clumsy when they've had too much to drink. Activity in the putamen also is associated with controlling the speed of movements, whether you're imagining them or actually doing them.[4] In studies that compare action observation and mental practice, researchers don't find activation in the putamen during action observation, which makes sense since you can't control the speed of what you're watching.

Most research on brain activation while practicing mentally was done with nonmusicians doing nonmusical tasks. Because of this, we haven't discussed any areas of the brain having to do with hearing so far. The primary auditory cortex is the area of the brain that processes incoming sound, so this would be a prime candidate for auditory activation during mental practice. Interestingly, when professional musicians are put into a brain scanner and asked to practice mentally, you *don't* see primary auditory cortex activation, even though the musicians reported hearing music in their heads quite vividly.[5] It seems that when we hear music in our heads, other auditory processing areas of our brains are active, just not the primary auditory cortex.[6] Again, this may reflect the difference between actually hearing something and imagining it.

Experts versus novices

Maybe you've been inspired to try a little mental practice since reading the previous chapter, but you're finding it to be a real challenge. Are you doomed? Researchers have found that people differ quite a bit in their ability to generate vivid mental images, be that visual images, auditory images (hearing

126 THE POWER OF THE MIND

things in your head), or kinesthetic images (feeling things in your head). This makes sense: we all differ in our abilities on all sorts of things. But research has also found that with training, people can improve the vividness of their mental imagery.[7] So if you are having a hard time, don't despair! With practice, you'll get better at it.

There's good reason to work to improve the vividness of your mental imagery. In a study that compared the brain activation of good imagers versus people less skilled at mental imagery, there were a variety of intriguing differences.[8] Good imagers had more focused brain activation in motor areas, which researchers interpreted to mean that they could create a better mental blueprint of the action. Interestingly, when the participants actually performed the motions they had practiced mentally, there were substantial differences in brain activation as well. Even though the physical performance of the two groups didn't differ, their brain activation did. The poor imagers used many more parts of their brain, which is evidence of needing greater brain effort for the same level of skill.

There were also interesting differences in putamen activation, the area of the brain we discussed earlier that's involved with coordination. The poor imagers used the anterior part of the putamen, which is typically activated when a skill is new and not well coordinated yet. The good imagers, on the other hand, activated their posterior putamen, which is associated with later stages of skill acquisition and is involved with retaining the skill long-term. It appears that the good imagers, in both mental and physical practice, were using their brains more efficiently even early on in the learning process. The implication is that if you improve at mental practice, your brain will have an easier time while actually playing, so it's well-worth sticking with mental practice just for that benefit alone.

Additional evidence that mental practice can make us more efficient comes from a different line of research: measuring muscle response when someone is engaging in mental practice. You'd think if you're sitting perfectly still while you imagine doing something, your muscles would not be involved. However, researchers have shown repeatedly that when you imagine yourself moving, there *is* muscle activation in the muscles that would be involved in the actual movement.[9] This muscle response is called a MEP: a motor-evoked potential. Good imagers show larger MEPs when they imagine moving as compared to people not as skilled at kinesthetic mental practice.[10] Interestingly, in good imagers the increase in the MEP is specific to the muscle(s) needed to actually make the motion, whereas in less skilled imagers, the MEP is a more general increase, not localized to the specific muscle(s) that would be involved.[11]

But maybe some people are just better at mental practice to begin with. Where's the evidence that training makes a difference? To answer this question, a group of researchers took expert tennis players and compared them to people who played tennis every once in a while for fun.[12] Everyone was asked to imagine swinging a tennis racket, a table tennis paddle, and a golf club while the researchers measured their MEPs.

In the casual players, there wasn't much difference in the size of the MEPs for the different pieces of equipment, as you can see by comparing the different white bars in Figure 10.5. The tennis experts, on the other hand, showed a much bigger MEP when they imagined swinging a tennis racket than for either the table tennis paddle or the golf club. You can see this clearly in Figure 10.5 as well.

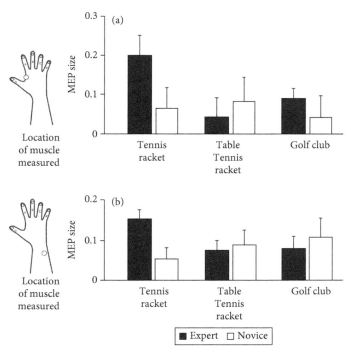

Figure 10.5 The MEP size for tennis pros versus novices while imagining swinging a tennis racket, a table tennis racket, or a golf club.

Reproduced from Fourkas, A., et al. (2008). Kinesthetic imagery and tool-specific modulation of corticospinal representations in expert tennis players. *Cerebral Cortex*. 18(10): 2382–2390.

The tennis experts also reported it was much easier to vividly imagine swinging a tennis racket than either a table tennis paddle or a golf club. In addition, the clarity of their kinesthetic imagery was correlated with the size of the MEP: the more clearly they said they could imagine it, the bigger the MEP.

Because the larger MEP was specific to their area of expertise, this is evidence that the larger MEP is a result of their training, not some innate difference. Nobody would argue that someone goes into tennis because they are better at imagining swinging a tennis racket than they are at anything else. Their tennis training made it easier for them visualize swinging a tennis racket, and this showed up in their muscle activation—even though they weren't actually moving those muscles.

The moral of the story: the more you practice mental practice, the better you'll get at it.

Common questions about mental practice

When I started to practice mentally, I had a hard time clearly imagining certain aspects of playing—particularly hearing the specific quality of sound I wanted—but with practice this has become much easier. As I discussed in the previous chapter, you don't have to hear and feel all the different layers and aspects of playing all at once. It's still extremely valuable to practice mentally even if it's only one or two aspects of playing. Because mental practice is often a new idea to people, I often get many questions about exactly how to do it. Let's look at some of the most common.

Can you move during mental practice or is it better to stay still?

In most of the studies on mental practice, the mental practicers were required to stay completely still while practicing mentally (and often their bodies were monitored to make sure they were staying still). But what if you did move? Would that be better? Only a few studies have looked at this so far, but they've found that when people moved slightly, doing a very small version of the motion they were practicing, it was better than practicing mentally while staying stationary.[13] For us as musicians, this would be like moving your fingers very slightly when imagining fingering a passage, or doing tiny bow movements in the air. For wind and brass players, it might mean making tiny embouchure adjustments. Or it might mean showing the direction or shape of the phrase with your hands or body. So feel free to move if you want to. But if you're in public and moving would seem strange, it's still going to be beneficial if you stay still.

Should you devote a block of time solely to mental practice? And for how long?

You definitely could devote a block of time solely to mental practice, and that works very well. At various points in my life, I have done mental practice for blocks of 30 minutes to an hour at a time. A big meta-analysis—comparing the results of many different studies—done in 1994 found that the optimal amount of time to practice mentally without a break is 20 minutes, presumably because it's taxing on the brain and it's hard to focus for longer than that.[14] Most of the time, though, I intersperse mental practice with physical practice. Often, before I play something on my instrument, I will practice it mentally first. I work out the flaws, phrasing, etc. inside my head, and then try it on my instrument. I assess what I heard come out of my viola, and then I practice it mentally again before trying it once more on my instrument. I go back and forth in this way, alternating mental and physical practice. It's no secret that playing an instrument can be hard on the body, and many professional musicians advocate spending as little time as possible actually playing to protect yourself from unnecessary wear and tear. You're not going to hurt yourself by practicing mentally, so you can get much more done without fear of injury or physical fatigue.

Should you close your eyes or look at the music?

This completely depends on the purpose of your practicing. Mental practice can be a very powerful method for working on memorization (as we've seen and as we'll discuss more in Chapters 12 and 13), but you don't have to have your music memorized to practice mentally. I often learn orchestra music for an upcoming gig while on airplanes, for instance. Whatever practicing you would do with your instrument, you can do that same thing inside your head—and yes, doing interleaved mental practice works great![15] Some

130   THE POWER OF THE MIND

people find that at first, they need to close their eyes to really hear and feel everything clearly in their mind. If that's the case for you, then pick a very small section that you can remember and just work on that inside your head with your eyes closed. Then pick something else small and work on that, and so on. But it's not *necessary* to memorize it or close your eyes. It's just as effective with your eyes open, looking at the music, as long as you can still imagine it clearly.

Can mental practice improve things like intonation or quality of sound?

Yes. Absolutely. Believe it or not, you can hear and feel when you play something out of tune inside your head. Try it right now with something you *always* miss while playing. You missed it inside your head, too, right? You can also feel and hear when you play something with a bad sound. At the very least, you can tell that the sound or the intonation isn't completely clear in your mind. The more experience you gain with mental practice, the more you will discover this. Once you can hear and feel yourself play a given note in tune, chances are it will be in tune on your instrument (something we'll discuss more in Chapter 15). If you can really, truly hear the exact quality of sound you want, chances are you'll be able to achieve that sound more easily on your instrument. Without these internal representations of pitch and sound, we have very little information to help guide us while actually playing. We need to be able to hear these things inside our heads accurately so we know what we are aiming for. After all, if we don't have a clear mental image of how something should sound, how can we tell if our playing matches what we want? We don't have anything to compare it to. If your answer is, "I'll compare it to a tuner or a piano," my question is, "Will you be able to do that in a concert?" If you don't have a strong internal representation of how something should sound, you are flying blind. We always need to be comparing what we hear coming out of our instruments to what we *want* to hear, but if that internal representation is weak, the comparison can't be made, and our playing suffers because of it. Mental practice helps strengthen this skill.

But *how* do you get better at this if you can't already do it? To ensure you can hear whether something is in tune, first test to see if you can sing it in tune out loud. There's a reason why sight-singing classes are such a staple of formal music education! Then try to hear the exact same pitch inside your

MENTAL PRACTICE AND THE BRAIN   131

head. If you can't hear it, go back and forth between singing and audiating—hearing inside your head—and you'll find that the perception of the pitch clarifies itself in your imagination. Then try putting it into the context of your piece, again by singing first and then audiating. Start with just a few notes and then gradually expand.

For quality of sound, find an example of the sound you are going for, either on a recording or by playing it yourself. Go back and forth between listening to that sound and audiating it, just as you did for pitch. You may find that descriptive analogies of the sound—bright, dark, smooth, round, etc.—help you imagine it more clearly. Once you can hear it on a single pitch, see if you can hold on to that sense of the sound for one bar or one phrase. At first you may lose it, but the more times you are able to get it back, the more easily you'll be able to hold onto the sound and imagine it clearly.

Does mental practice work for kids?

To my knowledge, there has not been any research on mental practice in children. However, I've introduced the concept of mental practice to children as young as elementary school age with excellent results. When I ask children to practice mentally, however, I make a slight modification in my instructions. Rather than asking them to feel or hear the music in their heads, I ask them to imagine that the wall in front of us is a giant TV and they are going to imagine watching themselves play on the TV. I focus their attention on the specific skill I'm trying to improve, and I ask if they can see themselves doing it perfectly on the TV. For instance, if a student is forgetting to slur two notes together, I will ask them to watch themselves play those two notes on the TV and see their bow do the slur. After we've done this a few times, then we try it on the instrument. Almost always, the problem is solved.

Does listening to recordings count as mental practice?

Listening to recordings is very important for musicians, but it's not mental practice. Mental practice is an active process of *creating* the music inside your head, just like when you actually play. Listening is passive. If you could learn to play a piece just by listening, you could just listen to your favorite recording over and over again and then one day you'd magically be able to play

132   THE POWER OF THE MIND

just like the performer. Obviously that's not how it works. You could practice mentally *while* listening (kind of like AOMI, discussed in the previous
chapter) and that would work much better. But passive listening alone is not
going to have the same effect as practicing mentally.

Hopefully these chapters have convinced you to try mental practice. And
hopefully the discussion in this chapter on the effect of training will help you
stick with it if you feel like you aren't able to imagine things very clearly. Just
start with one aspect of playing. Don't try to hear and feel everything all at
once. Eventually, your auditory and kinesthetic imagery will become more
vivid and detailed. But just like anything else, you have to practice to get
there. Mental practice takes practice, too.

11

How to Focus to Play Your Best

In the mid-1990s, researcher Gabriele Wulf had a realization while learning to windsurf. She had read detailed instructions about what to do with her body and had looked at many pictures with step-by-step directions, but no matter how hard she tried, it wasn't working. Out of frustration, she decided to focus instead on the board and how *it* should move. Suddenly everything became much easier. She wondered if something as simple as a change in focus—on the board versus her body—was unique to just her, or whether it was a useful strategy for others.[1] Being a research psychologist, she decided to test this idea in her lab. From her first published study on this idea in 1998, she has completely overturned decades—and probably centuries—of tradition in how athletic and musical skills should be taught in order to promote optimal performance for the learner.

Internal versus external focus

Her very first experiment to test this idea was a simple one.[2] She used a ski simulator, shown in Figure 11.1, which consists of a small platform on wheels.

The participants stood on the platform, propelling it back and forth over a curved track, making movements like someone skiing a slalom course. The goal was to move the platform from side to side as much as possible. Some of the participants were told to "exert force on the outer foot" while the platform was moving in the direction of that foot (so, exert force on the right foot when the platform is moving to the right). Others were told to "exert force on the outer wheels" while the platform was moving in the direction of those wheels (so, exert force on the right wheels when the platform is moving to the right).[3] The wheels lie directly under the feet, so this is a very small difference in instructions. Despite this tiny difference, the group focusing on the *wheels* did much better, both during the two days of practice and in the final test on the third day. In fact, compare the feet-focus group to the wheel-focus group

Learn Faster, Perform Better. Molly Gebrian, Oxford University Press. © Oxford University Press 2024.
DOI: 10.1093/oso/9780197680063.003.0012

Figure 11.1 A ski simulator.
Reproduced with permission from Wulf, G., et al. (1998). Instructions for motor learning: Differential effects of internal versus external focus of attention. *Journal of Motor Behavior.* 30(2): 169–179. © Taylor & Francis Ltd, http://www.tandfonline.com

in Figure 11.2: at the end of Day 2, the feet-focus group hadn't even caught up to where the wheel-focus group was by the end of Day 1!

This seems hard to believe. How can focusing on the wheels—which are right under the feet—result in significantly better performance? Why should it matter at all?

Dr. Wulf and her colleagues then did a follow-up experiment, and the results were even stranger.[4] In this experiment, they used something called a stabilometer, basically a small seesaw that you stand on and have to keep level. On the seesaw platform were two small pieces of tape to show the participants where to position their feet, with the tip of each foot touching these tapes. Some of the participants were told to keep their feet as level as possible. Other participants were told to keep the tapes as level as possible—again, a tiny difference that common sense would say shouldn't matter. But once more, the group focusing on the tapes were able to stay much steadier than the group focusing on their feet.

There was a lot of skepticism when this study was first published. Understandably! Why would focusing on little tapes—that the tip of your shoe is touching—be significantly better than focusing on your feet?

This is now a very well-established finding. Focusing on what your body is doing (having an *internal focus*) is not as effective as focusing on

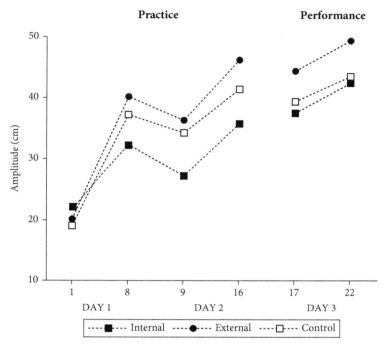

Figure 11.2 Performance of the three groups on the ski stimulator.
Reproduced with permission from Wulf, G., et al. (1998). Instructions for motor learning: Differential effects of internal versus external focus of attention. *Journal of Motor Behavior.* 30(2): 169–179. © Taylor & Francis Ltd, http://www.tandfonline.com

something outside your body (having an *external focus*). This is known as the "constrained action hypothesis," which says that when we exert conscious control over the motor system—when we try to control our actions by paying attention to what our *body* is doing—we get in the way of automatic processes that would normally regulate and coordinate the motion on their own. We constrain the motor system and end up doing the motion less efficiently. When we focus on something *outside* of our body, however, we allow the motor system to coordinate the action in an automatic way.

Said another way: when you allow your muscle memory to just do its thing, the result is much better than if you try to micromanage it through overly intrusive conscious control. This seems to hold true whether the skill is new or already well-learned.

If the constrained action hypothesis is true, you would expect to see a few things. First, you would predict that paying attention to controlling the body would use more attentional resources. If paying attention to something outside the body allows unconscious processes to take over, that should be less taxing for the (conscious) brain. To test this, participants did the stabilometer test with either an external or internal focus—focus on the tapes versus the feet—but they also had to press a button every time they heard a beeping sound.[5] The external-focus participants had a faster reaction time to the beep, meaning they were indeed using fewer cognitive resources to balance.

The second thing you would expect to see is more efficient muscle activity. If an internal focus of attention constrains the motor system and forces it to be used in an inefficient way, that should cause more muscle activity than necessary. To test this, researchers put electrodes on people's muscles to monitor the amount of muscle activity while they were shooting basketball free-throws.[6] The internal-focus group was told to focus on the snapping motion of their wrist during the follow-through of the shot. The external-focus group was told to focus on the center of the basketball hoop. Not only did they find that the external-focus group was more accurate with their shooting, but there was a lot less muscle activation as well, particularly in the biceps and triceps. In Figure 11.3, you can see that the biceps and the triceps show increased muscle activation in the internal focus group (black bars), meaning they are being used inefficiently. A similar study with throwing

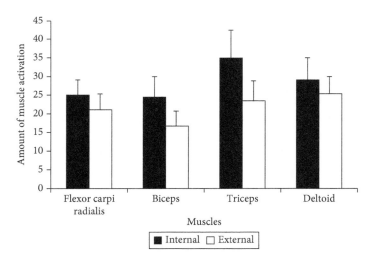

Figure 11.3 Muscle activation in the internal versus external focus groups.
Modified from Zachry, T., et al. (2005). Increased movement accuracy and reduced EMG activity as the result of adopting an external focus of attention. *Brain Research Bulletin.* 67(4): 304–309. © Elsevier 2021.

darts found the same thing,[7] as did an experiment looking at how high people could jump from a standing position.[8]

Since Dr. Wulf's initial shocking study in 1998, this idea of an external versus internal focus has been tested in many different sports, including golf, discus throwing, soccer, volleyball, long jump, running, and swimming. All show an advantage for adopting an external focus. In sports that use some sort of equipment (e.g., golf club, soccer ball, etc.), focusing on the equipment or the goal of the motion results in better performance than paying attention to what the body has to do to execute that motion.[9] Focusing on the golf club head or where the ball is going, for instance, is better than focusing on what the arms are doing. Focusing on throwing a discus as far as possible results in longer throws than focusing on what the arm has to do in order to throw well.[10]

These sports studies make a strong case for the importance of adopting an external focus, at least for athletes. What about musicians?

External focus in musicians

In a study from 2018, 23 musicians were asked to perform a piece of their choice in a concert hall environment.[11] Both instrumentalists and singers were included, and all were graduate or undergraduate music majors. First, they performed their piece without any specific instructions. Then, they were asked to play with different points of focus. In the external-focus performance, the musicians were told to "focus on playing for the audience and the expressive sound of the music." In the internal-focus performance, they were told to "focus on the precision of [your] finger movements (or lip movements for the singers) and correct notes."[12] The order was randomized, so some musicians did the external-focus version first, whereas others started with the internal-focus version. All the performances were then rated by professional musicians on a variety of technical and expressive criteria.

You might guess that the internal-focus performance was dry but more technically accurate, whereas the external-focus performance was more musically compelling but not as clean. But that's not what the researchers found. The students received the highest scores for both musicality *and* technical precision when they adopted an external focus, putting their attention on giving an expressive performance. You can see this clearly in Figure 11.4; the technique and musicality scores are both higher in the

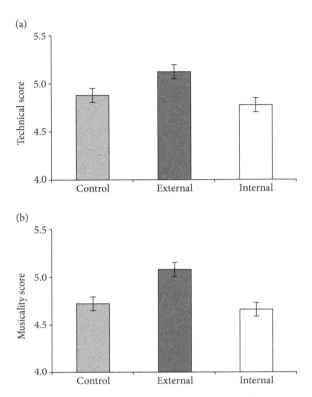

Figure 11.4 The scores on technical precision and musicality for the three conditions.

Adapted from Mornell, A., et al. (2019). Adopting an external focus of attention enhances musical performance. *Journal of Research in Music Education.* 66(4): 375–391. © 2019 by SAGE Publications. Reprinted by permission of SAGE Publications, Ltd.

external focus condition. Said another way, not only does focusing on musicality and phrasing result in a more expressive performance, but it also results in a cleaner performance from a technical perspective. Paradoxically, the more you focus on technical precision in performance, the less clean your playing will be.

Two different studies on singers also back this up. In both studies, one done with untrained singers and one done with trained singers, an external focus resulted in a better sound.[13] There was an interesting difference between the singers in these two studies, however. In both studies, they were asked to sing with a variety of different focus instructions. In the untrained singers, the various points of focus were: "(a) sing while feeling the vibrations on the throat with the palm of one hand, (b) sing with the index and middle fingers placed on either side of the nose, directing the sound to the fingertips, (c) direct the sound to a microphone; (d) direct the sound to a point on the wall across the room," or without any specific instructions.[14] In the study with trained singers, they were asked to sing while focusing on "keeping the vibrato steady," "the position of their soft palate," "directing their sound to points in the room at three different distances from the singer," or imagining "filling the room" with sound.[15]

The untrained singers performed the best when they were directing their attention to something closer to their body—either their fingertips on the side of their nose, or to the microphone. For the trained singers it was the opposite: their sound was best when they had to imagine filling the room with their sound, the point of focus farthest from their body. The external focus conditions were the best for both groups, but the *proximity* of their focus to their own body was different based on their level.

This last finding is an important detail to be aware of, especially for teachers. Where exactly you put your external focus seems to matter, and that differs based on level of expertise. For instance, researchers have found that beginning golfers do best when they are told to focus on the movement of the club rather than the trajectory of the ball through the air.[16] That's a focus closer to the body. But the opposite is true for expert golfers: they do better when focused on the flight trajectory of the ball, rather than focusing on the position of the clubface in the swing.[17] The same thing was found in volleyball players: those with more skill did better when their external focus was further from the body, whereas those with less skill did best with an external focus closer to the body.[18]

Just as we discussed in Chapter 8 on variable practice, skill level matters. When you are starting to learn a new skill, focus on something closer to your body. As you get better at the skill, move the focus farther and farther away. For us as musicians, the focus that is the farthest from our bodies is either filling the space with our sound, or conveying what we are trying to express to the audience.

A few other notes on this research may be of particular interest to wind and brass players and singers. Researchers have found that runners who adopt an external focus show the lowest levels of oxygen consumption, which is a measure of physiological efficiency and is correlated with better running performance.[19] Swimmers who adopt an external focus swim faster and more efficiently as well.[20] In the case of the runners, the external focus was to their

140   THE POWER OF THE MIND

surroundings. For swimmers, the external focus was on pushing the water back or down. Particularly in passages where breathing and stamina are a concern, an external focus will help you there. No studies have been done as of this writing on how an internal versus external focus affects the ability to sustain a sound, but based on all the prior research in this area, one would predict that an external focus would allow someone to sustain longer before needing to take a breath. As many choir directors know from experience, focusing on the shape or arrival point of the phrase or the specific quality of sound is more beneficial than focusing on the mechanics of breathing.[21]

External focus and teaching

If you're a teacher reading this, I'm sure you're wondering about technique and form. If someone is learning a new physical skill and they aren't thinking about what their body has to do to perform that skill correctly, won't they be learning bad form? It's a great question. After all, sloppy technique is going to lead to worse performance in the long run.

A study on volleyball players used both beginners and skilled players to find an answer to this question.[22] In this experiment, the participants were working on what's known as the tennis serve, and they were assessed on their ability to hit a target with the volleyball using this serve. Everyone was given the same instructions on how to do the tennis serve, which explained what they were supposed to do with their bodies (i.e., very internal focus instructions). Where the two groups differed was on the kind of *feedback* they were given about their actual performance once they started practicing. The internal-focus group was given feedback like "shortly before hitting the ball, shift your weight from the back leg to the front leg." The external-focus group was told "shortly before hitting the ball, shift your weight towards the target."[23] The researchers made sure the external- and internal-focus feedback was as similar as possible.

For both the beginners and the more advanced players, the researchers found that the external-focus feedback group not only performed at a higher level, but their form was also better than the internal-focus feedback group. Interestingly, among the beginners, the internal focus group did the *worst* during the practice sessions, but in the test on the final day—when they weren't given any feedback—they caught up to the external focus group. The researchers hypothesized that the internal-focus feedback was holding them back from performing as well as they could. When that feedback was gone, they were released from focusing overly much on their bodies and therefore performed better.

This experiment should give teachers some peace of mind: giving specific instructions that focus on the body are fine to explain how to do something initially. However, once student starts to work on the skill, we should give feedback that encourages them to focus on the instrument itself or on the effect we want their movements to have. Drawing attention to the specific motions of their bodies will be detrimental.*

What about doing something complex, though? Most of the athletic skills we discussed so far aren't as complicated as what many musicians must do to play well. Maybe for a complex coordination pattern, like those often required of musicians, it's necessary to focus on what the body is doing. A study on golfers looked at exactly this question.[24] This experiment was specifically looking at something called the X-factor stretch, which describes the rotation of the shoulders relative to the pelvis during a golf swing. How much a golfer rotates is of critical importance for generating enough speed to hit the ball far enough, and so a larger X-factor (more rotation) results in hitting the ball farther. I know nothing about golf, but apparently this is a difficult skill to execute well.

There are a number of elements involved in executing this rotation optimally, but in this particular experiment, the golfers were given very simple instructions. The internal focus group was told, "Transfer your weight to your left foot as you hit the ball." The external focus group was instructed, "Push against the left side of the ground as you hit the ball."[25] Once again, the researchers found that an external focus resulted in much better form for the X-factor stretch, and participants also hit the balls farther as a result. You can see the higher form scores for the external-focus group clearly in Figure 11.5.

From these two experiments, the golf study and the volleyball study, it seems that even for developing proper form, an external focus is better.

For teachers, this is all essential information that should hopefully change how we teach. One particularly concerning study found that giving feedback encouraging an internal focus was most detrimental *early* in learning, exactly when we might be most likely to focus a student's attention on what

---

* You may notice that this is in direct contrast to old way/new way, discussed in Chapter 3. In that method of rapid error correction, you *do* want to have conscious control over what the body is doing to correct a deeply ingrained, unconscious bad habit. Once the new habit has been established, however, returning to an external focus will be the most beneficial.

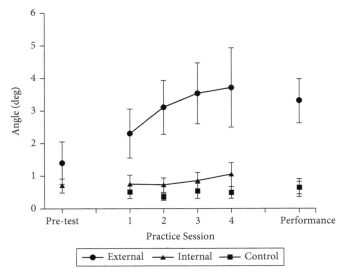

Figure 11.5 The X-factor stretch score for each group.
Adapted with permission from An, J., et al. (2013). Increased carry distance and X-factor stretch in golf through an external focus of attention. *Journal of Motor Learning and Development.* 1(1): 2–11. ©Human Kinetics, Inc.

their body should be doing.[26] Interestingly, making analogies for how a student should use their body mitigates the detrimental effect of internal-focus instructions. Telling a basketball player to release the ball as if they are waving goodbye works much better than telling them to release the ball by flipping the hand down. When we make analogies in our teaching, the student is still focusing on the effect of the action, and the motor system is left free to coordinate the movement without interference from our conscious minds. It's not that we must avoid talking about the body at all costs. But as teachers, we need to be mindful of our language and try as much as possible to either phrase our instructions in terms of analogies, or to focus our students' attention on the *effect* of their movements, rather than the movements themselves.

Some concrete examples might make this easier to understand, so I'll use a few from my own teaching. For background, some common bow-hold issues for violists are:

- The first finger (index finger) presses into the stick too much
- The second and third fingers ride up so they are on top of the stick rather than hanging over

- The pinky is straight rather than bent
- The thumb is straight rather than bent and/or is pressing into the stick

For each of these issues, Figure 11.6 shows an example of an internal focus instruction and an external focus instruction.

You can see that although many of these descriptions are quite similar— and the external focus instructions mention parts of the hand and fingers—they are subtly different. The external focus instructions include analogies and put the focus on feeling the *bow* rather than feeling the fingers. Teachers have long observed that using analogies helps students, and many of us have always used them as an integral part of our teaching. This research explains why they work so well and is hopefully encouragement to continue developing our analogy toolbox. As teachers, we of course need to be aware of the precise physical mechanics, but we must be mindful of how we communicate that information to our students. As players, especially advanced players with training in pedagogy, we are often aware of the physical mechanics necessary to play well, but while playing, we should translate that information into an external-focus objective to perform our best.

Technical issue	Internal Focus	External Focus
First finger pressing into the stick	Bend the first finger and touch the middle joint of the finger to the stick of the bow. Allow it to be heavy, but don't press.	Bend the first finger and feel the stick under the middle joint. Imagine your finger is a heavy backpack hanging off the stick of the bow, rather than pressing down from above.
Second and third fingers riding up	Touch the first knuckle line to the stick. Don't let the fingertips contact the top of the stick.	Feel the stick in contact with the first knuckle line. Feel the frog in close contact with the fingerprint part of your finger, as if there were suction cups there.
Pinky straight	Bend your pinky more.	Bring the back part of the frog more into the palm of your hand (impossible to do without bending the pinky).
Thumb straight and/or pressing	Bend the first joint of the thumb and keep the thumb in light contact with the bow without pressing.	Pretend you are picking up a water bottle sideways with your hand (nobody would do that with a straight thumb). Then think of the thumb like a shelf on which the bow can rest.

Figure 11.6 Examples of internal and external focus instructions for various bow hold issues.

144   THE POWER OF THE MIND

My students know that I teach using lots of wacky analogies, but since learning about this research, I am even more intentional with the language I use. Whenever I'm tempted to give feedback that will focus a student's attention on body mechanics, I quickly rethink what I'm about to say and express the feedback in terms of their instrument or bow. I've also found that this is extremely helpful in my own practicing. When I am trying to solve a technical problem in my playing, envisioning the solution in terms of an analogy or something outside my body always works much better than focusing on the minutiae of what my fingers or arms must do.

Another bonus is that an external focus helps us play better under pressure. This is especially evident when performing from memory, a topic we'll discuss in the next two chapters.

12

The Most Effective Ways
to Memorize Music

I was a Suzuki kid growing up. For the first three years of lessons, I learned to play exclusively by ear. Even once I learned to read music, listening to the Suzuki recordings was the main way I learned my music. And every time I would perform in a solo recital, I played from memory. This was never a big deal for me—it's part of the Suzuki culture and playing a solo piece with music in a concert would've been like performing in my pajamas. It just wasn't done.

I never really had memory slips in performance growing up, but I did have one extremely unusual experience that has always stuck with me. I was playing a simple sonata movement in a solo recital. Halfway through, I noticed for the first time that the piano was playing the melody I had just played. Why I had never noticed this before is beyond me, but I was probably about 12 at the time, so I'll chalk it up to being a typical kid. Despite the fact that I was on stage, performing in a solo recital, I was curious how much of the melody the piano got to play, so my entire attention was focused on listening to the piano, even though I was still playing. Unfortunately, once the piano melody finished, I realized I had no clue where I was in the piece. But somehow, I was still playing, from memory. Amazingly, instead of stopping or getting anxious, I just listened to myself for a while. Eventually I figured out where I was and my brain rejoined my body. But how could my body just continue to play "without me" and not make mistakes?

Types of memory

Especially for string players and pianists, performing from memory is a frequent part of our lives, but is something that also creates a lot of anxiety for many people. Understanding the science of memory can help us memorize

Learn Faster, Perform Better. Molly Gebrian, Oxford University Press. © Oxford University Press 2024.
DOI: 10.1093/oso/9780197680063.003.0013

more effectively and consistently so we can trust that our minds won't go blank when we get on stage.

Most musicians blame Liszt for the modern-day expectations around memorized performance, but it was actually Clara Schumann who first changed the conversation around performing from memory. She performed Beethoven's *Appassionata* Sonata from memory in 1837 (when she was only 17), and that was the turning point in the culture of performing from memory.[1] Musicians had performed from memory before this, of course, but it was seen as arrogant and was actively discouraged. These days, solo pianists almost always play from memory. String players are expected to play from memory as well, unless they are playing chamber music or a more contemporary work. The conventions around memorized performance are slowly relaxing, but the expectation to perform from memory is still a major part of many of our lives.

We tend to think of memory as one unitary cognitive skill, but in reality, there are many different types of memory that all work together, shown in Figure 12.1. This cooperation is so seamless, we don't usually notice they are separate from each other. But we know they are separate because of research on individuals who have brain damage; one type of memory can be gravely damaged, while others are completely intact.

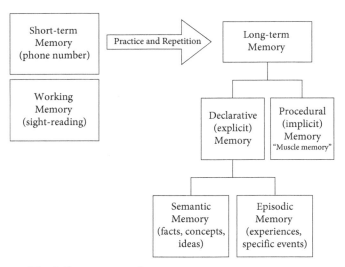

Figure 12.1 The different types of memory.

The most famous story demonstrating this is that of patient H.M. He underwent brain surgery for intractable epilepsy in 1953, with his surgeon removing both the right and left temporal lobes because that was where the seizures were originating from. He seemed completely fine when he woke up, until it became clear that something was seriously wrong with his memory. When he met a new doctor or nurse he would interact normally, but when he met them a second time, he would have no idea who they were. Even if they had just left for a few minutes, they would have to be reintroduced. It turned out that H.M. could not form any new memories—called anterograde amnesia—because something called the hippocampus had been removed as part of the surgery. Because of that catastrophic result, neuroscientists learned that the hippocampus (we have two, one on each side) is necessary for forming new memories.

Despite this severe deficit, H.M. could still remember things from his presurgery past just fine—events that had happened, facts, etc. He could also learn new motor skills—which rely on what we musicians call "muscle memory"—but had no memory of having done the activity before. He was trained to do a challenging reverse tracing task in a mirror, for instance, and although he had no memory of his previous training sessions, he mastered it easily, demonstrating that his muscle memory was fine.[2] Incidentally, this is also why musicians with Alzheimer's can still play their instruments quite well, even though their memories of past events and loved ones' faces may be nonexistent.[3]

It was H.M.'s hodgepodge of memory abilities and deficits which first demonstrated that different types of memory exist and are separate from each other. When we perform music from memory, we are using these various types simultaneously. Once we understand these different kinds of memory, we can prepare better for memorized performance by strengthening the types that will help us most.

One of the biggest distinctions between memory types is declarative memory (also called explicit memory) versus procedural memory (also called implicit memory). Declarative memory comes in two flavors: semantic and episodic (also called autobiographical memory). Semantic memory is our memory for facts, whereas episodic memory is our memory for events that we have experienced in our lives. Usually when people say they have a bad memory, this is what they are referring to—it's hard for them to remember facts or events in their lives, so they feel like they have a bad memory.

148   THE POWER OF THE MIND

The opposite is procedural memory. This is the scientific term for muscle memory. Muscle memory doesn't reside in our muscles—it resides in the pattern of neuronal activity in our brains, just like declarative memory. But unlike declarative memory, procedural memories can't be described in words. Procedural memory is also very strong and durable, which is why they say you never forget how to ride a bike: even if you haven't ridden a bike in years, the minute you ride one again, your body will remember how to do it.

H.M. had intact motor memory, but damaged declarative memory. That's why he could remember how to do the reverse tracing task (procedural memory) but couldn't remember his previous practice sessions on the task (declarative memory). Motor memory is also why I was able to continue playing without mistakes in that recital even though I didn't know where I was. My muscle memory knew; it was my declarative memory that was temporarily lost.

As can be seen from the story of H.M., there is also a distinction between long-term memory and short-term memory. We have declarative long-term memories (intact in H.M) and declarative short-term memories (disrupted in H.M.). We also have long- and short-term procedural memories (both intact in H.M.). Long-term memory is extremely durable and stable and has essentially unlimited capacity. Short-term memory, on the other hand, has a very limited capacity and is prone to breaking down, especially under pressure. If someone were to tell you their phone number but you had nothing to write on, you would probably repeat it over and over in your head until you were able to write it down. That would be using your short-term memory. But if something surprising and unexpected happened before you could write it down, that would disrupt your ability to continue repeating the number in your head, and you would probably forget it.

There is also something called working memory, which is like short-term memory, but has a slightly different function. Working memory enables you to remember something that you are also manipulating and using at the same time. For example, if you were holding my phone number in short-term memory, but I also asked you to calculate the sum of the individual numbers, that would be using your working memory. Remember the numbers, but also add them up. You can imagine how taxing this would be on your brain!

When we are sightreading, we are using working memory to keep track of the key signature and any accidentals we encounter along the way. We must hold this information in memory but also use it to play the right notes. That's why it can be much more difficult to sightread something in a key with many flats or sharps, especially if it also has many accidentals. That's a lot of information to hold in your mind, taxing working memory.

Like short-term memory, working memory has a limited capacity and breaks down easily, especially under pressure. Because of that, we definitely do not want to rely on it when performing from memory. We want to rely on long-term memory. To understand how to strengthen our long-term memories for the music we are trying to learn, it's important to understand how long-term memories are made, so that will be the main focus of these next two chapters.

There are three stages when it comes to long-term memory formation: encoding, consolidation, and retrieval. We need to make sure we are doing a good job with each step of the process; if any one of these stages is neglected, that will make it seem like we can't remember whatever we are trying to memorize. Let's look at each step to understand what they are and how we can get better at each one in learning our music.

Encoding

Encoding describes how the information gets into your brain in the first place. There are many ways to encode new information, but researchers have found that something called deep encoding works best. To illustrate what deep encoding means, let's look at a famous study that was done on memory for words.[4] In this experiment, two groups of college students were shown a series of words, one at a time. Some of the students had to supply a definition for each word, while others just had to say the last letter of each word. After they finished, they were given a pop quiz to see how many words they could remember. They had not been told ahead of time that they would be given a quiz, so nobody was actively trying to memorize the words they were shown. As you might expect, the students who had to define the words remembered more of them. This is an example of deep encoding: they had to interact with each word, connect it to information already stored in their memory, and describe what it meant. The other students engaged in shallow encoding: they didn't even have to read the word at all, much less think about what it meant. As a result, they could only remember a few.

One strategy that works quite well to ensure deep encoding is something called chunking. Chunking is taking individual pieces of information and grouping them together into a meaningful whole. This enhances encoding

150 THE POWER OF THE MIND

for a couple of reasons. First, there are fewer things to remember: a few large chunks, rather than many individual pieces. Second, to create the chunk in the first place, you must understand how the individual pieces of information are related, connecting the new knowledge to information you already have stored in long-term memory, which is deeper encoding.

As an example, start a timer for five seconds and try to commit the following letters to memory:

I   B   F   A   S   U   A   I   C

Now restart your timer and try to commit these letters to memory:

C   I   A   U   S   A   F   B   I

The second list was probably much easier—if English is your native language—because the second list is three acronyms: CIA USA FBI. You can chunk the letters into three groups, and you can connect these groups to information you already have stored in memory about what each entity is. Incidentally, the first group is just the second group backward, so not only is it the same number of letters, it's also exactly the same letters. They are only more difficult to memorize because they are not as easily combined into meaningful groups.[*]

Experts in a given field often look like they have incredible memories compared to the rest of us, but it's actually because they are able to chunk information in a way that makes it easier to remember. People who perform amazing feats of memory—like memorizing a whole deck of cards or the digits of pi—are using chunking to help do this. They aren't memorizing 52 separate cards; they are chunking the cards into larger patterns.

This is also partly why every teacher assigns scales and etudes, and why every collegiate music program requires theory, history, and ear training of its students. These areas of study help you build meaningful chunks, which makes it easier to learn and memorize music. When you practice scales and arpeggios, you are building and reinforcing your muscle memory chunks, your aural memory chunks, and your declarative memory chunks for which notes belong in which keys. If you can remember back to your very first scale, it was probably pretty hard for you. But now, that scale is simple. When you

---

[*] If the first list was easier because you made it into a word, or it contains acronyms you recognize, the point still stands. When you can chunk the letters into larger, more meaningful units, the list is easier to remember.

THE MOST EFFECTIVE WAYS TO MEMORIZE MUSIC   151

play a one-octave D major scale, you don't have to think "Hmmm . . . I know it goes D then E, but is the next note F-sharp or F-natural?" That's because "D major" is a chunk. You know that it has F-sharp and C-sharp, and you don't have to think twice about it. You also don't have to think twice about where to put your fingers to play those notes, because that's a chunk as well.

In theory class, we learn about common chord progressions. For example, I ii V I is a very basic chord progression in many styles of Western music. If you know this, it's much easier to learn a series of chords. You don't have to think of each individual note or even each individual chord because it's part of a larger pattern, a larger chunk. You can also recognize the underlying chord progression more easily if it's hidden by decorative notes, making the passage much easier to learn and remember. In history class, we learn about the common musical forms used in different eras. A piece by Bach is not going to be in sonata form, but the first movement of a sonata by Mozart likely will be. You can use this knowledge of both form and history to help you chunk the music into larger sections, which will help you remember it better. So take your technique practice and your theory, ear training, and history classes seriously. They will make it significantly easier for you to learn music and memorize it.

When artists like Hilary Hahn or Lang Lang perform giant concertos from memory effortlessly, it's not because they have far superior memories compared to everyone else. A large part of that ability is due to chunking. How easily we can play from memory in a performance situation is also related to how *big* our chunks are. When you look at novices in any field, they obviously don't have any chunks yet because they are just learning. In their brains, researchers find a lot of activity in working memory areas and hardly any in long-term memory areas, which isn't surprising.[5] Because of this, novices usually don't perform very well, especially under pressure. As people practice and get better at a given activity, they start to create more chunks. As a result, activity in working memory areas goes down while activity in long-term memory areas goes up. This is exactly what we want when we perform. As we discussed previously, working memory is taxing, fragile, and prone to breaking down under pressure, so we want to rely on long-term memory as much as possible. As we continue to practice, we group our chunks into even bigger chunks, something I call super chunks (the actual term is *knowledge structures*). When this happens, activity in long-term memory areas is very high, with minimal activity in working memory areas.

For Hilary Hahn and Lang Lang, big swaths of a piece are one big super chunk, so there is less to remember. For a student just learning a major

152   THE POWER OF THE MIND

concerto for the first time, they have many smaller chunks, which will make it more difficult for them to perform it from memory compared to Hilary Hahn or Lang Lang. But if they continue working, eventually these chunks will start to get grouped together, making memorized performance easier and easier.

Encoding strategies for musicians

To dig deeper into this question of how professional musicians perform from memory and what their preparation looks like, psychologist Roger Chaffin teamed up with a variety of musicians to probe their processes.[6] The musicians who worked with him recorded every single practice session on a piece they were preparing to perform from memory. They would also keep a detailed practice log, as well as comment on their process and what they were doing—or trying to do—in each practice session. Once they had performed the piece in public from memory, Dr. Chaffin then analyzed the hundreds of hours of practice footage to see if there were any commonalities in people's processes. He found that the musicians all used what he called "performance cues"—information from the music itself to help them chunk the individual notes and rhythms, keep track of where they were, and to help cue recall for a specific section.

Based on his observations, he divided the performance cues into four different categories: structural cues, expressive cues, interpretive cues, and what he called basic cues. Structural cues are information from the formal structure of the piece, such as the beginning of the development section, or right after the final repeat. Knowing where you are in the structure of the piece is very helpful in staying oriented and supplies a framework on which to "hang" the notes and rhythms. Making sure you understand the structure and knowing where you are within that structure is therefore a critical step in the memorization process.

Expressive cues are concerned with the emotional content of a given passage or section: the joyful part, the wistful part, etc. Therefore, making sure you have clear emotions and characters for everything you are playing is also extremely helpful when trying to memorize something. There always needs to be a *reason* for what you are playing, beyond the fact that it's what the composer wrote. It will help you play more expressively of course, but it will also help you memorize more easily as well.

THE MOST EFFECTIVE WAYS TO MEMORIZE MUSIC 153

Interpretive cues are markings provided by the composer, like changes in tempo or character. These are slightly different from expressive cues in that they are written in by the composer, rather than generated by the player.

And finally, basic cues are matters of technique, like fingerings, bowings, or breath marks.

In addition to collecting and analyzing all the recordings and written records of the musicians, Dr. Chaffin also contacted them 18 months to two years later and asked them to write down from memory as much of the piece as they could remember. The musicians did the best they could, and then sent him whatever they were able to write down. He then analyzed what they wrote to see which performance cues were the most durable over time, meaning they still cued recall for the actual notes and rhythms on the page.

After doing his analysis, Dr. Chaffin found that structural cues and expressive cues—knowing where you are in the structure and what you are trying to express—were the most durable. Interestingly, he found that the least durable cues were basic cues (matters of technique). In fact, he found that these sometimes had a negative effect: they promoted forgetting over time. We want our performance cues to have a deeper meaning and significance than just "second finger on this note" or "take a breath here." This takes us back to the idea of deep encoding: you must really engage with the music in order to understand the structure and what you want to express at each moment. Basic cues are much more superficial, so it's no wonder this more shallow form of encoding doesn't hold up well over time.

As an encoding strategy, it can be very helpful to have multiple copies of your music, each with different aspects of the piece marked. Having one copy with all the structural landmarks clearly indicated, another with expressive words written in for each phrase or section, a third showing the shape and direction of each phrase, etc. will aid in the memorization process enormously. We tend to think this kind of pencil-and-paper work isn't "real practicing" but it's essential for providing us with a framework within which to memorize.

It is also important that we solidify and encode information using the various kinds of memory we use in memorized performance, namely muscle memory, auditory memory, and declarative memory. What does it feel like to play this piece? What does this piece sound like? What are the actual notes, rhythms, articulations, etc., that make up this piece?

Most of us have one type that is stronger than the others, and usually we try to rely on that one exclusively. But if that one fails in a performance, we are left without a backup, and then we have a memory slip. If we strengthen

154 THE POWER OF THE MIND

all three, however, it's very unlikely that all three will fail at exactly the same moment. If our strong suit fails, we still have two backups. Also, when we strengthen all three equally, they reinforce each other, which encodes them in our memories more strongly.

Because they all work together, it can be difficult to isolate and strengthen only one at a time without the other kinds jumping in to help—especially when you are strengthening the one that is weakest. Let's look at some strategies to strengthen each one individually.

Strengthening muscle memory

Try playing your piece on your instrument with no sound. For string players, this means fingering without the bow, or doing the bowing above the string (or with your bow upside down in your elbow for violin and viola players). Because tapping the fingers on the strings produces a pitch, I also advocate that string players put on headphones with white noise playing so they don't get any auditory feedback. You can also slip a cloth between the strings and the fingerboard to dampen the pitch. Wind and brass players should play without any air. For pianists, either play on an electric keyboard with the sound off or put a blanket over the strings of the piano and wear noise-canceling headphones. People who have weak muscle memories almost always rely on the auditory information coming from their instrument to help keep track of where they are, so you want to get rid of any pitched sound completely. Another great strategy for string players is to detune the instrument so the strings are random pitches.[7] Then try playing from memory. You want your fingers to be in the right places, which means it will sound completely absurd since the strings are tuned incorrectly. Within a string, it will sound okay (unless you have perfect pitch), but the minute you cross strings or play double stops, it will sound ridiculous. It's a great test of your muscle memory—and also quite fun because of how horrible it sounds.

Strengthening auditory memory

Try singing from memory without your instrument to help. Ideally, you should be able to sing from memory on a neutral syllable (la la la), on note names, and solfège. For string or keyboard players, singing on finger numbers can also be helpful. This is a great challenge and will strongly reinforce how it sounds and what the notes are.

If you have a strong muscle memory, but a weak auditory memory, you also need to work on joining the two. One way to practice this is to sing the note out loud first and then put the finger down. If your muscle memory is the stronger one, your finger will want to go down before you've sung the note, but be disciplined and make sure the singing always precedes the fingers. This exercise should also be done on a neutral syllable, on note names, finger numbers, and solfège.

Strengthening declarative memory

Try drawing a formal diagram of your piece from memory. It can be a formal diagram like you might create for theory class, or it can just be a visual depiction of the structure in any format that makes sense to you. Also try what Roger Chaffin asked his musicians to do: get a blank piece of staff paper and write out as much as you can from memory. Write notes, rhythms, articulations, dynamics, tempo markings, text, etc. Don't forget about the key signature and time signature as well. This can be extremely beneficial in helping you figure out where the holes are in your memory for a piece.

Auditory-motor coactivation

I mentioned joining the different types of memory, particularly muscle memory with auditory memory. There is fascinating research that suggests that this joint auditory-muscle memory is one aspect of performing that separates professionals from amateurs. In one experiment on violinists, researchers had the musicians finger their piece silently.[8] In the professional violinists, the auditory cortex was active when they did this. The auditory cortex is usually only active when we are hearing something, but these violinists were fingering silently. There was no sound, and yet their auditory cortex was behaving as if there were. It was the fingering itself that was cueing recall for the sound and the brain behaved as if there were actual sound happening. But this was not seen in the amateurs: only their motor cortex was active.

On the flip side, when pianists were played a recording of a piece they knew how to play and had to listen without moving, their motor cortex was

156   THE POWER OF THE MIND

active in a very specific way.[9] Normally, the motor cortex is active only when you move. As we discussed in Chapter 9 on mental practice, the motor cortex is divided into different regions, with a specific part of the motor cortex controlling each part of the body. In the study on pianists, researchers found that when the thumb would play a specific note, the thumb area was active. When the pinky would play a note, the pinky area was active. And again, the pianists weren't moving, but their motor cortex was behaving with the same precision as if they were.

Taken together, these two studies suggest a coactivation of the auditory and motor cortices, at least in professional musicians. Many teachers, including myself, have noticed that Suzuki-trained students—and other students who were trained in a tradition that emphasizes learning by ear, like bluegrass or jazz—memorize music very easily. This is definitely true for me: I don't have to work at memorization. Music just gets memorized. Students whose first experience playing music was by reading notes from the page, however, seem to have a much more difficult time memorizing. This distinction is so common that many teachers could probably predict with a high level of accuracy which of their students were trained by ear versus taught to read notes from the beginning, just based on their ease with memorization.

I have a theory—which has not been backed up directly by research yet, so this is one of the only speculative parts of this book—that students who learn by ear from the beginning foster this auditory–motor connection in the brain from a very young age. Traditionally trained students, on the other hand, form a connection between the motor cortex and the visual cortex. Take away the visual and you are left with muscle memory, which is a form of implicit memory. By definition, we don't have good conscious access to our implicit memories, and so traditionally trained students feel at a complete loss if they aren't looking at their music, even if they have played the piece many times.

To help remedy this situation, I ask students to do two things: play something from memory every single day—even if it's just a little bit of music—and figure out something by ear every single day. When figuring out music by ear, start with easy songs—children's songs, folk songs, etc. Then tackle slightly harder tunes; movie and TV themes are great for this. For an advanced student who has not learned out of the Suzuki books, learning books 1 through 3 completely by ear is a great exercise. In playing something from memory every day, I advise students to try a bit of the music they are currently working on. I find that these activities, when incorporated into daily practice, vastly improve a student's ability to play from memory. My guess is they work so well because they are promoting the development of the auditory–motor coactivation in the brain. We will have to wait for science to catch up with what many teachers have already observed, but the two studies discussed above already provide fascinating clues as to what may be happening in the brain.

The most important information to remember about encoding is this: the more you can elaborate and connect new material to information you already know, the more easily you'll remember it. If you come up with a story that fits the music, cover a copy of your music with specific character words/colors/emotions, etc., or do a detailed harmonic or structural analysis, these activities will help you understand the music on a deeper level, which will help you remember it more successfully.

So far, we have just been discussing encoding, the first step in the memorization process. Deep encoding is critical to get the information into your brain—without that, the next two steps will be at a profound disadvantage. But deep encoding is not enough—all three steps are critical. In the next chapter, we'll discuss steps two and three in the process: consolidation and retrieval.

13

Boost Confidence
in Memorized Performance

In the previous chapter, we discussed encoding, the process of getting information into your brain in the first place. In this chapter, we'll discuss steps two and three: consolidation and retrieval. Step two in the memorization process, consolidation, is how information gets moved from short-term storage to long-term stable storage. Sleep is absolutely critical for this step. We discussed sleep at length in Chapter 5, but it's worth revisiting some of that information here.

Consolidation

We touched briefly on the role that the hippocampus plays in memory when we discussed H.M., the patient who had his hippocampi removed. He could no longer form new memories, but memories formed long before his surgery were still intact. This is because when we learn new information, it gets stored temporarily in the hippocampus. Since H.M. had no hippocampi, he had nowhere to store new information and so it was forgotten. For the rest of us, after information is stored in the hippocampi, it then gets transferred out to the neocortex for more long-term storage while we sleep. This is why H.M.'s memories from before the surgery were fine: that information had been transferred out of the hippocampi and was being stored in the neocortex, which was largely unaffected by the surgery.

This transfer process is called consolidation. If we don't get enough sleep, the process is disrupted, and we'll lose what we learned during the day (either completely or partially). You can do a great job at encoding, but if you don't get enough sleep, you will have difficulty remembering what you worked so hard on. So don't neglect sleep in favor of more practice—you'll learn and memorize faster if you prioritize sleep.

Learn Faster, Perform Better. Molly Gebrian, Oxford University Press. © Oxford University Press 2024.
DOI: 10.1093/oso/9780197680063.003.0014

160   THE POWER OF THE MIND

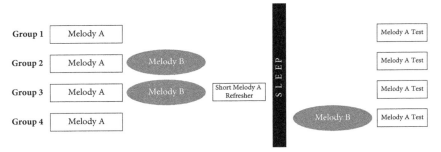

Figure 13.1 The practice schedule for the four groups.

In Chapter 5, we also discussed the research that shows you get a boost in your ability to perform something after a night of sleep. But that research didn't specifically test memory. Does a full night of sleep after trying to *memorize* something also result in improvement the next day? A study on pianists aimed to answer this question.[1] In this experiment, there were four different groups, all trying to memorize short melodies. The schedules for the various groups are shown in Figure 13.1 to help you keep them straight.

Group 1 worked on a short melody (Melody A) and tried to memorize it. The next day, after a full night of sleep, they were tested on their memory for the melody. Group 2 worked on Melody A, after which they worked on memorizing a second melody, Melody B. The next day, they were tested just on their memory for Melody A. Group 3 worked on Melody A and Melody B, just like Group 2, but after they were done with Melody B, they were given a quick refresher on Melody A. Then the next day, they were tested on their memory for Melody A. Group 4 worked on Melody A and went home. The next day, they worked on Melody B. After they were done, they too were tested on their memory for Melody A.

The findings are very interesting, shown in Figure 13.2. In this graph, higher scores are better. You can see that Group 1 did indeed get a boost in their memory performance. They were better at performing Melody A from memory on Day 2, compared to their memorized performance at the end of Day 1. Groups 2 and 4, who worked on Melody B in between practicing and performing Melody A did *not* get a boost in performance. They didn't get worse, but their performance on Day 2 was the same as their performance on Day 1. The most interesting group is Group 3. They are the ones who learned Melodies A and B, but then got a little refresher on Melody A before going

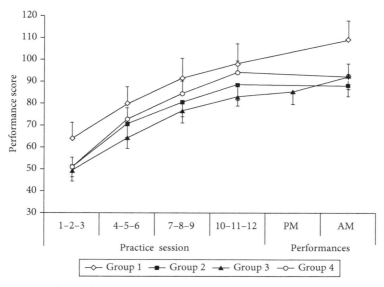

Figure 13.2 The performance of the four practice groups in playing the short piano melody from memory.

Adapted from Allen, S. (2013). Memory stabilization and enhancement following music practice. *Psychology of Music.* 41(6): 794–803. © 2013 by SAGE Publications. Reprinted by permission of SAGE Publications, Ltd.

home (that's the PM performance data point). Like Group 1, Group 3 also got a boost in their memorization performance on Day 2.

How does this translate into real-world practice? Obviously, we are always working on more than just two short melodies in our practicing. This research suggests that you will get a boost in performance if you practice something last in the day, get a full night's sleep, and then practice that same thing first the next day before you practice anything else. As musicians, we can use this strategically. For that one passage that you just can't memorize no matter how hard you work on it, practice it last in the day and then first thing the next morning—with a full night's sleep in between—and you will have more success on the second day.

Retrieval

The final step in the memorization process after encoding and consolidation is retrieval: getting the information back out of your brain again when you

162 THE POWER OF THE MIND

need it. The best way to get better at retrieval is to . . . practice retrieval. This may sound obvious, but in both music and other pursuits we don't practice this step of the process enough. Students often think that they can perform in studio class using the music and then play from memory on their recital the following week. One week is not nearly enough time to practice retrieval. The retrieval process needs to be as automatic, easy, and well-rehearsed as everything else.

To take an example from academic pursuits, students frequently study for tests by rereading the passages they highlighted in their textbook. Research has shown this is the worst possible way to study because it is not practicing retrieval, it is practicing reading.[2] If you find it's hard to remember the material when you're taking an exam, this is why: you have likely never practiced retrieval. You have not tested whether you can produce the information from scratch. The best way to study for a test is to take a test—without your notes or books—because it forces you to practice retrieval. You can then see where your memory breaks down, so you know where to focus your studying going forward.

You can do a great job at encoding and consolidation, but if you don't practice retrieval, it can look like you don't remember the information. Each step of the process needs dedicated practice if you want it to hold up under pressure.

For musicians, this means practicing playing from memory often. All the musicians Roger Chaffin worked with emphasized the need to practice their retrieval strategies. This means going through your performance cues, making sure you always know exactly where you are in the music and what the exact notes and rhythms are, until this process is automatic. If the retrieval process isn't automatic, it will break down under pressure. The musicians Dr. Chaffin worked with also stressed the need for many performance cues so that they could start anywhere. If you do have a memory slip, you want to be able to restart close to where you stopped. Your audience is not going to be very happy if you're 10 minutes into the Bach Chaconne and you have a memory slip and have to start all over again from the beginning. If you can only play it from the beginning, you don't actually have it memorized. As an example, most of us don't truly have the alphabet memorized. What comes after J? Or right before V? Probably you have to start from the beginning of the alphabet to figure it out (or at least from LMNOP for the question about V). When we perform, we need to be much more flexible than this.

To give an example of the sort of timeframe you should be aiming for: in my own work, my goal is to have the piece memorized at least six weeks before I'll have to perform it from memory. Two months is even better. As I mentioned earlier, I memorize easily, but even so, I want to have it memorized at least six weeks out from the concert. I require this of my students as well. For those last two months, ideally I'm practicing it completely from memory, even when I'm breaking it down to work on small details. If I can break it down in that way without looking at the music, it further solidifies the actual notes and rhythms in my memory.

If the goal is to be completely without music a minimum of six weeks before the performance, when should we start memorizing? Should we wait until we can play the whole thing well, or should we start memorizing while we're still learning the piece? A study on singers aimed to answer this question.[3] The singers in this experiment were students, professionals, and amateurs, and the goal was for them to learn and memorize a new song in six 15-minute practice sessions. In the sixth session, they had to perform the song from memory as best they could. Based on how they did in that final session, the singers fell into two groups: fast accurate memorizers, or slow inaccurate memorizers. Interestingly, there were students, professionals, and amateurs in each group, so it wasn't that the students were all inaccurate memorizers while all the professionals were accurate memorizers.

The main difference in approach between the groups was *when* they started to work on singing from memory. The accurate memorizers started attempting a bit of music from memory in the very first practice session, whereas the inaccurate memorizers didn't start really testing their memory until the third session. You can see this in the left-hand graph in Figure 13.3, which shows number of measures attempted from memory by both groups during each practice session. The accurate memorizers were attempting a lot from memory even in the first two practice sessions, whereas the inaccurate memorizers were hardly attempting anything at all.

The right-hand graph of Figure 13.3 shows the average number of mistakes each group made in every practice session. You can see that the accurate memorizers were making many memory mistakes in the first and second practice sessions, but that's because they were practicing retrieval. They would try some from memory, get it wrong, and then update their memory so they could do better the next time. The inaccurate memorizers, on the other hand, weren't attempting anything from memory, so they weren't making as many mistakes, but that also meant they weren't testing their

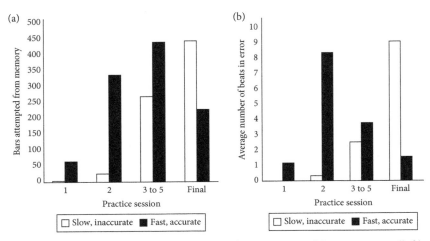

Figure 13.3 Graphs showing the number of bars attempted from memory (left) and number of word errors made from memory (right).

Adapted from Ginsborg, J. (2002). Classical singers learning and memorising a new song: An observational study. *Psychology of Music*. 30(1): 58–101. © 2002 by SAGE Publications. Reprinted by permission of SAGE Publications, Ltd

memory or learning from their mistakes. In the final session, when everyone had to sing the entire song from memory, the accurate memorizers did great. The inaccurate memorizers on the other hand, made many mistakes and had to keep trying it over and over to get it right.

This study makes a convincing case to start testing your memory from the very beginning of working on something new if you know you're going to be performing it from memory eventually. On that very first day of practice, attempt *something* from memory, even if it's just one bar. With anything you work on that day, try to do at least a portion of it from memory. It doesn't matter if it's significantly under tempo, or if you still have choreography to work out. If you're a pianist, maybe you can only play part of the right hand from memory. That's okay—it's better than nothing. It doesn't have to be perfect (or even good) to start testing your memory. You could also just test your aural memory by singing how it goes without actually playing anything. The more you can practice retrieval, the better off you'll be. Even if you get it wrong, it will help solidify the right answer in your memory. As we discussed in Chapter 2, making mistakes is a necessary part of learning. Whenever there is a mismatch between what you intend and what you produce, that causes your brain to pay attention and update itself so you can get it right—or at least get closer—the next time.

BOOST CONFIDENCE IN MEMORIZED PERFORMANCE   165

In fact, researchers have found that just the act of *trying* to answer—even if it's wrong—helps solidify the correct answer in your memory once you look it up. You will remember the correct answer much better in the future than if you hadn't tried to answer at all or just looked it up immediately.[4] So when you're trying to play something from memory and you can't remember what comes next, try to figure it out. It's okay if you're wrong. The mere act of trying to remember how it goes—rather than just looking at your music right away—will help cement it in your memory. Even better than looking at the music: try to figure out how it goes by listening to a recording and reconstructing how to play it.

Other strategies for practicing retrieval

Mental practice can also be a very powerful tool for working on memorization and retrieval. As we discussed in detail in Chapter 10, the combination of mental and physical practice together is much more successful in preparing for memorized performance than just physical practice alone. When you don't have the aid of your body moving or the sounds coming from your instrument, it tests whether you truly have it memorized. Start with just one phrase. Can you hear it in your head from memory? Can you feel exactly what your body has to do to play each note? Do you know what every note is, and can you feel yourself playing each one? String players, for instance, often find that they cannot remember the bottom notes of chords. Pianists tend to forget what the left hand is doing more often than they forget the right hand. Make sure you truly feel your fingers playing those left-hand notes or the bottom notes of chords, and that you know exactly what the notes are. Eventually, you want to be able to play the entire piece through in your head in this way with no holes in your kinesthetic, auditory, or declarative memory awareness.

Often, students will try to memorize by playing a section using the music and then immediately try to play that section without the music (as I mentioned in Chapter 6 when we discussed the forgetting curve). This strategy just uses your short-term memory and won't help ensure it's in long-term memory. And in a concert, this definitely won't help you. You won't be able to play each section with the music right before you play without the music. If you can play it from memory right after you've looked at the music, but you can't play it from memory 10 minutes later or after practicing

166 THE POWER OF THE MIND

something else, you don't have it memorized. Instead, test your memory multiple times a day *without* looking at the music first. The spaced practicing schedule I use, taking days and weeks off from a given passage (as described in Chapter 6) also works very well for memorizing music.

Interleaved practice is also extremely effective for working on memorization. Here are a few suggestions to use this principle to work on retrieval and test your memory.

Serial practice (described in more detail in Chapter 7)

Make a list of the spots you want to test for memory and then play each one on the list, one after another. Don't look at the music before you play each one. If the memory is flawless, you get a tick mark next to that spot. If there are hesitations or stops and starts, it doesn't count, even if you don't play any wrong notes. If there are hesitations, it means your retrieval process needs more work. If it's not error-free and fluent, you don't get a tick mark (and you must erase any you've already accumulated for that spot). The goal is five tick marks on each spot.

Play in a random order

Assign each section of your piece a number. Make sure these sections start and end where it makes musical sense. Don't just divide it up by line because chances are, the end of the line is not the end of the phrase. Then, write each number on a separate slip of paper and put these into a box. Draw the slips one by one. Whatever number you draw is the section you have to play from memory. Again, don't look at the music before you try to play each section. This tests whether you can start anywhere or have fallen into the trap of only being able to play from the beginning. You can also use a set of dice or a random number generator for this instead of slips of paper.

Interval timer practice

Choose a passage you want to test and set your interval timer to go off every three to ten minutes. Start practicing a completely different piece. When the timer goes off, stop what you're practicing and perform the chosen passage from memory. Again, don't look at the music first. You can also combine this with the previous suggestion: when the timer goes off, draw a number and perform that section from memory.

Combine with mental practice

Combine any of the strategies above with mental practicing for an added retrieval test and performance benefit.

I always recommend to my students that they do a minimum of 10 practice performances before the actual concert. If they will be performing from memory, all ten of those need to be from memory as well. All ten do not have to be in front of an audience, however. The first few should just be alone with your recording device. If you can play your music fluently from memory on three separate occasions while you video yourself, then you are ready to try it out in front of someone. If you can't do it successfully from memory in front of your recording device, you definitely won't be able to do it in front of an audience. Give yourself plenty of time to have enough practice performances so you trust that your memory is solid. This is why I aim to have my music memorized at least six weeks before the performance: I need the remaining time to practice performing from memory.

Choking

Even armed with all this new information and these practice techniques, every musician's worst nightmare is still having a memory slip. Nothing is scarier than the prospect of standing on stage and going completely blank, having absolutely no idea what comes next and no way to get back on because your music is in your case backstage. When we mess up despite excellent preparation and adequate skill level for the music, it's called choking. Choking isn't specific to just memorization, but it's probably what scares people the most about playing from memory. Most musicians have had the experience of getting up on stage and having everything go completely wrong. We wish the floor would open up and swallow us, or our instrument would explode, or some catastrophe would happen in the concert hall so we

168   THE POWER OF THE MIND

don't have to keep playing. We get off stage in tears, furious with ourselves, baffled as to why things went so wrong.

If we didn't prepare well for the concert, that's one thing. You can't expect to play well without good preparation. And if we attempted to perform something that is beyond our current skill level, that's not going to work out very well either. But if we were well prepared and the music is well within our ability level, it can be maddening to have things go so wrong on stage. This is what is meant by choking. It's something that every musician, athlete, actor, and dancer will experience at some point in their lives, even those at the very highest levels of their field. But we can still try to protect ourselves from having it happen to us.

There are two main hypotheses as to what causes choking: distraction and something called *explicit monitoring*. The distraction hypothesis suggests that choking is due to either external or internal distractions—that we are not focused the way we need to be—and so we mess up. Explicit monitoring (also called skill-focus) is essentially micromanaging every single aspect of what you are doing, rather than just trusting your muscle memory to do it correctly.[5] It's like if you are taking a test and the teacher comes and stands right next to your desk and stares down at your paper—you start to massively second guess yourself in that situation. Explicit monitoring is essentially doing that to yourself: standing watch over every little thing and saying, "Are you sure that's right? Are you sure that's a B-flat and not a B-natural coming up?" By the time we get to a performance, all our movements should be automatic. Thinking about each and every one will cause us to revert to an earlier level of ability and we won't play well.

To test these two theories—distraction versus explicit monitoring—researchers put athletes in high-pressure situations to see if they could increase the likelihood of choking. To test whether external distractions cause of choking, researchers put athletes in a high-pressure situation and made them do something distracting while performing, like count out loud backward from one hundred by sevens.[6] It turns out, this *doesn't* increase the rate of choking (in fact, some people perform *better*), so external distractions can't be the cause.

To test the explicit monitoring hypothesis, researchers put athletes in a high-pressure situation and videotaped them, explaining that the video would be sent to an expert to assess their form.[7] This dramatically increased the likelihood of choking, so explicit monitoring seems to be a big cause of this phenomenon.

What about internal distractions? In a study on tennis serves, when researchers put people in a high-pressure situation and didn't increase the pressure by videotaping them or give them a distracting task, the people who choked all reported distracting thoughts and difficulty concentrating.[8] So from this research, it seems like choking is caused both by internal distractions as well as explicit monitoring.

How can we protect ourselves against choking? Just saying "Don't explicitly monitor!" or "Don't think distracting thoughts!" isn't going to work very well. The minute I tell you *not* to think about a white elephant, you start thinking about a white elephant. And if you could just tell yourself to focus on the task at hand and get rid of distracting thoughts, you wouldn't have distracting thoughts in the first place. We all know it's not as easy as that. Fortunately, researchers have found a few things that will help protect us against choking.

The first is to think about big-picture things, rather than the little details of how to play correctly. For us as musicians, this means to focus on the phrasing, the quality of sound, and what we are trying to express to the audience. This, as you'll hopefully recognize, is an example of external focus, as we discussed in Chapter 11. Not only does an external focus make learning easier, but it also helps us perform better too. When we're focused on the effect we are trying to achieve, we perform better and we are much less likely to choke.[9]

The second strategy is to videotape yourself in practice to get used to being watched.[10] This helps us learn to cope with the tendency to explicitly monitor everything so we can develop more helpful ways of thinking. When we video-record ourselves in practice, we need to make sure we are thinking about big-picture things (sound, phrasing, expression) so that we trust that this kind of focus will work when we get to the performance. This is especially critical when playing from memory. If we haven't practiced performing from memory while adopting an external focus in front of a video camera, we won't trust that it will work once we get to the performance. We'll revert back to our tendency to explicitly monitor what we're doing, making it more likely we'll choke.

The field of performance psychology is dedicated to helping musicians, athletes, and other performers do their best under pressure. It's beyond the scope of this book to delve too deeply into performance psychology—because this book is about practicing and I'm not a performance psychologist—but an excellent resource for musicians when it comes to performance psychology

170 THE POWER OF THE MIND

is Dr. Noa Kageyama's website BulletproofMusician.com. He has countless articles, interviews, and courses you can take to learn more about the tools performance psychology has to offer and to help refine your ability to perform well under pressure.

Hopefully these two chapters on memorization have given you some ideas to boost your confidence when it comes to memorized performance. If you try even one of the memorization strategies in these chapters, you will be able to play more reliably from memory. If you do all of them, you will feel much more confident and consistent on stage without music. It can be overwhelming to use many new practice strategies all at once, so incorporate them one at a time. Start with the strategy that seems the most interesting or enjoyable to you. Once that becomes a regular part of your practice, then add another. Keep going in this way and eventually, you will have incorporated all of them and performing from memory will feel enjoyable and effortless.

SECTION IV
CHALLENGES SPECIFIC TO MUSIC

Most of the research discussed in this book is broadly applicable to any skill you wish to learn, not just music. In this final section of the book, we'll look at some music-specific challenges and what research has to say about how to improve in the areas of rhythm, tempo, pitch, intonation, and playing faster.

14

Improving Rhythm and Tempo

I used to be a notorious rusher. Rarely would I get yelled at by my chamber music partners for dragging—it was almost always for rushing. This really started to become an issue when I was preparing orchestral excerpts for auditions. Tempo precision is paramount, and even though I thought I was steady as a rock, I would listen back to recordings of my run-throughs and I was always rushing. And it's not like I wasn't practicing with a metronome. I used the metronome so much it felt like I had to change the batteries every week! Then my teacher told me to practice with the metronome clicking on the offbeats or just on the downbeats to fix my rushing problems. Lo and behold, it worked! But why?

The metronome and brain activation

Playing with good rhythm and a solid sense of pulse are fundamental to successful performance. Some musicians would even argue that rhythm is the number one most important ingredient for good playing, even ahead of pitch, tone, or expression. Rhythm is the framework on which everything else sits. Music also creates a sense of movement when we hear it, in a way that language and ambient noise don't. We talk about a phrase feeling "stuck," or having a nice sense of flow. Some music has a great groove and makes us want to dance, while other pieces may give us a sense of peace and repose. The reason music is so tightly linked with a sense of movement is because the motor systems in our brains respond to hearing music, even if you aren't moving; the motor areas in your brain are being activated, telling you to move. You must actively suppress moving if you're in a situation where it's more appropriate to stay still.

Understanding this connection with the motor areas of the brain is the key to improving your rhythm and sense of pulse. Ask a musician how they work on rhythm and tempo and most will say: use a metronome. However, because of how the brain works when it comes to the pacing of movements, the

Learn Faster, Perform Better. Molly Gebrian, Oxford University Press. © Oxford University Press 2024.
DOI: 10.1093/oso/9780197680063.003.0015

174   CHALLENGES SPECIFIC TO MUSIC

standard way of using a metronome will not improve your sense of pulse or rhythm beyond a certain point. A metronome—as typically used—will show where you are rushing or dragging, and will help clarify where rhythmic figures lie in relation to the beat. But paradoxically, it will not actually help you develop a steady sense of pulse.

In this chapter, we'll look at how we can develop a better sense of pulse, as well as better precision and accuracy in both hearing and performing rhythms. Let's start by explaining why my teacher's suggestion to have the metronome click on the offbeats or just on the downbeats solved my rushing problems.

In an experiment looking at brain activation in response to a metronome, researchers put nonmusicians in an fMRI machine—which shows the brain areas that are active when someone performs a given task—and asked them to do two simple things: tap along with a metronome, and then continue to tap at the same tempo without the metronome.[1]

The brain activity while doing these two tasks—tapping with the metronome on versus off—was very interesting. Although the activation for the two tasks was similar, it was not identical. There were several areas of the brain that were only active when the metronome was off. This means that when the metronome is off, our brains are doing something fundamentally different than when the metronome is on. This is why I could play just fine with the metronome, but I rushed without it. It's also why some people have difficulty playing rhythms accurately when the metronome is off, but not when it's on. The areas of the brain that are active when the metronome is off are collectively known as the sensorimotor loop. These areas are in charge of the internal self-timing of movements, among other things. The minute there is something external helping us pace things (like a metronome), these areas no longer get involved.

The brain needs a chance to practice the skills it will need in a performance situation. Because musicians never perform with a metronome clicking—except for session players recording movie soundtracks and the like—the sensorimotor loop doesn't get to practice if we always practice with a metronome. I sometimes hear students practicing with the metronome always on, no matter what they are practicing. I think when students do this, they believe it will make them rock-solid steady. Not only will this way of practicing *not* lead to the desired result, but it also leads to a wooden sense of timing and phrasing that lacks flexibility and nuance. Of course it's important to practice with a metronome, but like any other tool, it should be used strategically.

Now that you understand this, how can we practice to ensure we are steady while also letting the brain practice the skills it needs in a performance situation? The answer is to have the metronome click progressively less often. To do this, first confirm that you can play exactly with the metronome by having it click on each beat, as usual. Then, have it click every other beat (so, only on 1 and 3 in 4/4). Once that's easy, have the metronome click on the downbeat only, just like my teacher advised me to do. Then every other downbeat only, then every third downbeat only, and so on.* When the clicks come further and further apart like this, the sensorimotor loop will get involved to help you stay steady, but the objective metronome is still there to make sure you are *actually* steady.

My teacher's suggestion to have the metronome click on offbeats only—on the "and" of each beat, rather than on the beat itself—will also help develop a strong sense of inner pulse. In this case, your ability to feel the beat must be stronger than the clicks you are hearing from the metronome. To make the metronome sound like it's clicking off the beat, turn on the metronome and tap offbeats. Then count out loud with your tapping. This should make the taps feel like the beat and the metronome clicks feel like offbeats.

Some metronome apps, like TimeGuru or TonalEnergy, have a random mute function, which allows you to determine how large a percentage of the beats you want the metronome to randomly mute. With it set on 80%, for example, 80% of the beats will be muted. The metronome still flashes on every beat, so you can look at it to get yourself started; just don't look while you're playing since the sensorimotor loop is also sensitive to visual pacing cues, not just auditory ones. TimeGuru also has a gradual mute function that is useful. With this function turned on, it will start with all the beats audible and then randomly mute more and more beats over time.

These exercises are challenging, but very rewarding. If you are exactly with the metronome when it clicks after a long silence, you know you are absolutely steady and you feel a real sense of accomplishment.

---

* To get your metronome to click only on every third downbeat, for instance, it's not necessary to put it on an extremely slow tempo that is fraction of your goal tempo. Most metronome apps will allow you to selectively mute certain beats. If you want it to click every third downbeat in 4/4, for example, set the metronome to 12/4 and silence all the beats except for the first one.

Improving sense of pulse

What if you try these ideas with the metronome and you just can't do them? What if no matter how hard you try, you always rush when the metronome isn't clicking every beat? Or what if you just can't hold onto the beat when the metronome is clicking on offbeats? How can you practice to get better at this and improve your internal sense of pulse?

It seems like actual physical movement is key and the more it involves the whole body, the better.

There have been several studies using rhythms with an ambiguous meter to figure out how people create a sense of pulse. In most of these experiments, the meter can either be heard in 2 or 3. The researchers then manipulate people's experience in various ways to see what influences their sense of meter. Figure 14.1 shows an example of a rhythm with an ambiguous meter and how it can be heard in two different meters, depending on where the stress is placed.

In the first study looking at this, researchers had the participants listen to the ambiguous version, bouncing up and down along with the experimenter, bending their knees in time with the rhythm. Group A bounced in 2, bending their knees every other beat. Group B bounced in 3, bending their knees every third beat.[2] Afterward, participants listened without moving to rhythmic clips that had accents added to make it clear whether it was in 2 or 3. They had to say which one—the one in 2, or the one in 3—matched the rhythm they had heard when they were bouncing with the experimenter. Not surprisingly, if they had bounced in 2, they said the rhythmic clip that sounded in 2 matched (and vice versa if they had bounced in 3).

This isn't all that surprising. To probe this further, the researchers then had another group of people just *watch* the experimenter bounce to the ambiguous rhythm without actually moving themselves. Afterward, when participants were played the rhythms with the accents added, it didn't matter which meter the experimenter had bounced in. People were just as likely to say the 2/4 meter matched as the 3/4 meter, regardless of which one *actually* matched. From this experiment, it seems that moving themselves—and

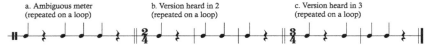

Figure 14.1 a. Ambiguous rhythm. b. Same rhythm in 2/4. c. Same rhythm in 3/4.

not just watching someone else move—was critical for influencing the participants' perception of the meter.

Then the researchers asked: do people have to *actively* move themselves? If someone else moves them—like a parent bouncing a baby on their lap—is that enough to influence the perception of the meter?[3] Obviously, you can't bounce a full-grown adult on your lap to see what happens, so in order to test this, the researchers built a kind of seesaw bed so they could rock participants up and down in time with the rhythm. The bed was constructed such that the researchers could either rock the participants' whole body, just their head, or just their legs. The researchers found that when they rocked people's whole bodies or just their heads, that strongly influenced their sense of meter. But when the researchers just rocked people's legs, that didn't do anything: just like the people who only watched the experimenter bounce, people who only had their legs moved were just as likely to say 2/4 matched as 3/4.

Passive movement will therefore influence a sense of meter, but only if your whole body or at least your head is moving. Why would that be? The researchers wondered if it had something to do with the vestibular system, our sense of balance. The vestibular system is housed in our inner ears and the movement of fluid inside the vestibular structures is what helps us maintain our balance. You can stimulate the vestibular nerve with an electrode attached right behind the ears. This makes people feel like their head has moved even when it's completely still—which must be a very strange sensation! The researchers designed an experiment to stimulate the vestibular nerve or the elbow (as a control condition) in either a 2/4 pattern or a 3/4 pattern.[4] After the stimulation, they found that people were significantly more likely to say the version in 2/4 matched when their vestibular nerve had been stimulated in 2 (and vice versa for the 3/4 meter). The elbow stimulation didn't do anything. It seems from this finding that the vestibular system *is* involved in creating a sense of meter.

What does this all mean for musicians?

It means that you are going to create a much stronger sense of pulse if your whole body, or at least your vestibular system, is involved. One of the best ways I've found to improve sense of pulse is to have students walk in place to the beat while they are playing. This is significantly better than tapping your foot (or even conducting) and the research we just discussed explains why: when you walk in place, your vestibular system is engaged, which seems to be critical for developing a strong sense of pulse. Proponents of Dalcroze have known this for a long time: engaging the whole body in music-making

178 CHALLENGES SPECIFIC TO MUSIC

helps students understand musical concepts on a very deep level, especially rhythm and sense of pulse.

The method I use to introduce and develop the ability to walk in place depends on the age and level of the student. If the student is advanced, I simply ask them to walk in place at the tempo of the beat and play at the same time. Some students try to cheat by just raising their heels up and down, but again, this isn't going to have the same effect because they are not engaging the vestibular system by doing this. Some students suddenly start walking like penguins, forgetting they have joints at their knees and hips, and try to walk while keeping their legs completely straight. You want to walk in as normal and natural a way as possible. It's often helpful to start walking first and then join in with your playing. This can be very challenging when you're new to it, so stick with it if you can't get it right away. If you sit when you play (like cellists or keyboardists), swaying back and forth in time is a decent replacement for walking because you still get the vestibular involvement.

With younger and/or less advanced students, I usually use the following steps to help them learn to walk and play on their own:

1. I walk and play for them first as a demonstration so they can understand what I want them to do.
2. We walk together while I play so they can feel how their walking lines up with my playing.
3. We walk together and they sing along with me as I play.
4. We both walk and play together.
5. We walk together while they play alone.
6. They walk and play on their own without me doing anything.

Everyone is helped in their sense of pulse when someone else is also moving alongside them, but especially younger children.[5] We are a social species, and so having another human being moving with us can help develop sense of pulse enormously.*

Once a student can confidently walk and play at the same time, I encourage them to walk musically: deeper steps on strong beats, more shallow steps on weak beats. I tell them I should be able to tell the meter and character of the music just by watching how they step. I find this to be an incredibly useful

---

* This is especially true for children and explains why they often have such a hard time playing with a metronome. It's much more fruitful for the teacher to play or move with the student than to try to get them to play with a metronome on their own.

practice method that helps even when I'm performing, even though I'm obviously not walking when I'm on stage. The practice of walking in place, especially walking musically, engrains a deep sense of pulse and propulsion in my body, and I often feel as though I'm still walking when I'm performing even though I'm not.

In addition to developing a strong sense of pulse, a sense of metrical hierarchy (weak versus strong beats) also seems to be especially important for rhythmic accuracy (as well as playing expressively). This is true for both rhythmic execution and accurate perception, a critical skill when playing with other people. To demonstrate this, a pair of researchers tested musicians and nonmusicians on the accuracy of both their rhythmic perception and performance.[6] In the perception test, participants heard a repeated rhythmic pattern followed by a bar of rest, as shown in Figure 14.2. After the bar of rest, there was one final note that was almost on the next downbeat, but was a little off—sometimes by a tiny bit, sometimes by a lot. The participants had to say whether it sounded early or late. In the performance test, they heard a rhythmic pattern repeated three times (like that in Figure 14.2), which they then had to perform by tapping. The researchers measured their rhythmic accuracy, but also the force of their tapping to see whether it differed between strong and weak beats.

Not surprisingly, the researchers found that the musicians performed better on both tests than the nonmusicians. The most interesting finding was that the *metricality* of the tapping—the difference in tapping force between strong, medium, and weak beats—was significantly correlated with how accurate participants were on both the performance and the perception tests. The people who tapped the rhythms with a better sense of metrical hierarchy were more accurate in both tapping those rhythms *and* in perceiving whether notes were early or late in the perceptual test. And to be clear, nobody was tapping more strongly on weak beats than strong beats; some people just weren't making much difference between weak and strong (or medium) beats. Going back to our discussion of chunking from the chapter on memorization: when we can embed knowledge into a larger structure and context, we do better. In this case, having a clear sense of metrical hierarchy

Figure 14.2 An example of a rhythmic pattern the participants heard.

makes us better at performing and listening when it comes to rhythmic accuracy. Walking musically helps develop this as well: the more we can embed a sense of metrical hierarchy in our bodies, the stronger and more reliable our sense of pulse will be.

The most important takeaways from the research on rhythm, tempo and meter are these: if staying steady on your own is difficult for you, move as much as you can. Walk and play simultaneously all the time, walking as musically as you can. But make sure it's in time—just walking randomly around the room isn't going to do anything. Move when you listen to music, involving your whole body, in a way that matches with the rhythmic structure. Again, moving randomly isn't going to help in this case. Be sure you understand the rhythmic hierarchy in your music and that you are making it clear to a listener. Finally, test how steady you are with the ideas for metronome practice presented in this chapter. Developing a strong internal sense of pulse is the framework on which everything else rests.

15

Improving Pitch and Intonation

As a string player, I have always wanted a magic bullet to just make my intonation perfect. Unfortunately, there is no getting around the fact that continually improving our ability to play in tune is a lifelong process for almost all musicians. Given how important pitch and intonation are in Western music, there is surprisingly limited good research on developing skills in these areas. Even more surprisingly, there seems to be little relationship between the ability to perceive pitch, the ability to match pitch by singing or playing, the ability to sing in tune versus play in tune, and the ability to play or sing with good intonation in a musical context.[1] It seems that these skills, although all important for playing with good intonation, are somewhat independent from each other. They each need to be honed individually; improving at one won't automatically improve the others.[2]

In this chapter, we'll look at what the (scant) research has to say about improving pitch perception, the role of singing in improving intonation, whether using a tuner is a good method to improve your ability to play in tune, and the role of audiation. If you are a keyboardist, it may seem like this chapter is less relevant to you, but audiation is a fundamental skill we all need to develop, so I hope you'll stick around.

Pitch discrimination

Being able to tell whether two pitches are different from each other is a foundational skill for any musician. For those of us who have to worry about intonation while playing, our ability to perceive very fine distinctions between two pitches is paramount. If we can't hear the difference between an in-tune F and an ever-so-slightly flat F, we won't be able to identify mistakes and fix them.

Research on pitch discrimination in musicians versus nonmusicians routinely finds that musicians have more highly developed abilities in this area, which isn't a surprise. Researchers usually measure this by determining

Learn Faster, Perform Better. Molly Gebrian, Oxford University Press. © Oxford University Press 2024.
DOI: 10.1093/oso/9780197680063.003.0016

182   CHALLENGES SPECIFIC TO MUSIC

the smallest difference between two notes that can still be heard as two distinct pitches, known as the pitch discrimination threshold. The smaller the pitch discrimination threshold, the better. One experiment found that musicians had a pitch discrimination threshold that was six times smaller than nonmusicians.[3] Perhaps not surprisingly, string and wind players had a smaller pitch discrimination threshold than pianists in this study, probably because we must actively monitor our intonation while playing in a way that pianists don't.

The researchers in this study wanted to see if they could train the nonmusicians to discriminate pitches as well as the musicians could. The training method involved playing two pitches, and the nonmusicians had to say which one was higher in pitch. The distance between the pitches kept shrinking until the nonmusicians couldn't hear a difference anymore. They were given feedback to help them improve, and after only four to eight hours of training, the nonmusicians were able to hear differences in pitch that were as small as the ones the musicians could hear.

From this, it seems like better pitch discrimination is a skill that can be learned relatively quickly. For musicians wanting to improve their pitch discrimination ability, there is an app called InTune that essentially works the same way as the experiment. The app plays two notes and if the second note is higher, you swipe up. If it's lower, you swipe down. The notes get closer and closer together until you can't tell the difference anymore, and the app gives you feedback to help you improve. Over time, you'll be able to hear smaller and smaller distinctions between the notes, just like the nonmusicians in the study. If you have difficulty hearing the difference between an in-tune C and one that's a little out, this app would be a good first step in developing a more refined sense of pitch.

Fine-tuning your perception can also help you hear dissonance more accurately, probably one of the hardest things to hear when it comes to pitch and intonation. When I was younger, I used to think that you didn't have to worry about intonation for dissonant intervals because it was literally impossible to tell if they were in tune or not. Imagine my surprise when my teacher pointed out that I was playing a tritone out of tune. That was truly shocking to me, to realize that dissonant intervals could be in tune, just like consonant ones.

But just like anything else, you can practice and get better at hearing dissonant intervals more accurately. A study on nonmusicians suggests an effective way to do this.[4] In the experiment, participants heard various dissonant

IMPROVING PITCH AND INTONATION 183

intervals and had to try to match the pitch of one of the two notes, receiving feedback on how they did. Over time, not only did their pitch-matching ability improve, but they heard the dissonant intervals as less dissonant. So to hear dissonance more accurately, practice playing a dissonant interval or chord and then try to sing one of the notes out loud. The top note is usually the easiest to hear, so start there. Then try to sing the bottom and middle notes. Over time, it will get easier and easier to pick out the individual notes and your ability to judge the intonation of dissonance will improve as well.

Singing to improve intonation

Once you can hear extremely fine-grained differences between pitches, the next step is to improve intonation while playing or singing. One common strategy to improve this ability among instrumentalists is to have us sing out loud. Often in band, for instance, students are encouraged to sing the tuning pitch before playing it on their instruments. "If you can sing it, you can play it" is a common refrain. But what does the research show?

Band directors will be disappointed to know that there doesn't seem to be any support for the idea that singing the tuning pitch will improve overall intonation ability.[5] In fact, when students are given an intonation intervention that involves singing in a general way, it doesn't seem to do anything to improve intonation while playing.[6] Does that mean singing is useless?

Fortunately, no. In a few studies where the singing intervention was directly related to what the students were playing, it *did* make a difference. One study found that when students played what they were working on, then sang it, and finally played it again, they made significant improvement on intonation-related skills by the end of the experiment.[7] Another study found that when students were learning to hear and play intervals more accurately, singing and then playing them was more beneficial than just singing or just playing them.[8] From this, it seems like singing *in general* doesn't necessarily have much benefit when it comes to improving intonation, but singing what you are working on is very beneficial.

So when your teacher asks you to sing in your lesson, they aren't trying to make you uncomfortable. It *will* help to improve your intonation. When I am having difficulty getting a particular note in tune, I will stop right before the note in question and sing it out loud before I try to play it. Sometimes, I find that I can't sing the right pitch. No wonder I can't play it in tune—I don't

184   CHALLENGES SPECIFIC TO MUSIC

know what it's supposed to sound like! If I can sing it accurately, that doesn't automatically mean I can play it in tune, but being able to sing it is a necessary first step. For us instrumentalists, we shouldn't neglect singing: it's a valuable tool to help us with intonation.

Tuners versus drones

The next step in the process would be actually playing in tune. Again, just because you can hear it or sing it does not automatically mean you can *play* it in tune. Does playing with a tuner help? There is surprisingly little research on this, given how common it is as a practice method, particularly for wind and brass players. Most of the research on using tuners to improve intonation was done with beginning players, and as a result, it's not clear how relevant it is for more advanced players. One study with high school and college trombonists, however, provides some clues.

This experiment was rather devious. The trombonists heard a recording of a professional trombonist playing A440, and they were told to match the pitch on their instruments.[9] There was a tuner on the stand that was there for them to refer to if they wanted, and they had three different tries to match the A. Unbeknownst to the trombonists, the researchers sometimes tampered with the tuner on the stand. On the first try, the tuner display was accurate: if they played A440 perfectly in tune, the tuner showed they were in tune. On the other tries, however, it was either set to A437 or A443, so playing A440 would show up as out of tune on the tuner. The question was: would the trombonists adjust their intonation based on what they were *hearing* or what they were *seeing*?

Before I tell you the outcome, I want to emphasize that nobody was forced to use the tuner. They were just told "Please perform in tune with the trombone stimulus sounding in the headphones. A tuner is provided for your reference and as an aid to your performance."[10] That's it.

What did they find?

There wasn't much difference in their intonation when the tuner was set flat versus in tune, but when the tuner was set sharp, the trombonists played *much* sharper. They essentially ignored what they were hearing and went with the tuner. This was true for both the high school and college trombonists, although the high school trombonists were more influenced by the tuner than the college players were.

IMPROVING PITCH AND INTONATION 185

This study illustrates the danger of the tuner: to play in tune, we need to rely on our ears, not our eyes. You won't have a tuner in the concert to help you tune every note you're playing. If you haven't developed the ability to adjust intonation based on what you're hearing, it's going to be hard to play in tune. This echoes the research on simultaneous feedback that we discussed in Chapter 2: when we get simultaneous feedback, we can't develop a good internal sense of how something should feel or sound.

My position has always been that it's much better to practice intonation with a drone instead of a tuner. To play in tune with a drone, you must listen carefully and adjust based on what you are *hearing*, not what you are seeing. Unfortunately, nobody has tested the use of drones versus tuners in advanced players to see which one works better long-term, so I don't have any specific data to back this up. But over and over again in this book, we have seen the importance of letting the brain practice what it will have to do in a performance situation. When it comes to intonation, all you will be able to rely on in a performance are your ears, so you should be practicing in a way that uses your ears, not your eyes. That means drones, not tuners.

Audiation

But is practicing with a drone enough? After all, you won't have a drone in a performance situation either. The short answer is probably not. What we really should be relying on in a performance situation is our inner ear, something scientists call auditory imagery and musicians call audiation. Audiation, hearing something inside our heads, seems to be a critical skill for accurate intonation, both in terms of perception and performance. Being able to hold a drone in your head or hear pitches accurately before you play them is of critical importance when performing. An external drone is a good first step, but it shouldn't be the last step.

To test whether people's perception of intonation and ability to audiate are related, researchers gave people two different tests.[11] In one test, the participants heard an ascending major scale and when the final tonic was played at the top, they had to say whether it was in tune or not. The top note was either in tune or mistuned by -60, -40, -20, +20, +40, or +60 cents. In the second test, participants heard either the first three or the first five notes of an ascending major scale and then they had to imagine the rest. When the final tonic was played at the top, they again had to say whether it was in tune or

186 CHALLENGES SPECIFIC TO MUSIC

not. Researchers found that it didn't matter whether people heard the whole scale or had to imagine part of it: their accuracy in determining whether the final tonic was in tune or not was the same in both cases. If someone wasn't very good at imagining the missing notes, they also weren't very good at determining whether the tonic was in tune when they heard the whole scale.

The researchers repeated this experiment with the leading tone instead of the tonic because it's harder to imagine the leading tone accurately. This time there was a big difference between listening to the whole scale and having to imagine part of it, with everyone doing worse when they had to imagine. However, the people who had musical training—and therefore had practiced audiation—were much more accurate at both tasks, showing again that the ability to audiate clearly is closely related to how accurately you can perceive the intonation of a note.

In most studies on audiation, researchers ask people how vividly they can hear something in their heads. Usually, people's self-reports match their performance on the audiation tasks. But maybe some people just *think* they aren't good at audiation, but they actually are. After all, you can't directly measure how vividly someone imagines something in their head. All you can rely on is what people *say* about their experience audiating. There is some evidence, however, that people's self-reports are accurate because of how their brains behave.

Neurons communicate using electrical signals (as we discussed in Chapter 1) and these electrical signals can be detected by putting electrodes on people's heads. Researchers record what are called *event-related potentials* (ERPs), which are specific brain-wave patterns that correspond to discrete events, like hearing a wrong note or having an expectation fulfilled. When scientists look at a given ERP, they are usually measuring its amplitude: the size of the brain wave. And typically, they are looking to see whether a given ERP behaves differently in different scenarios.

One specific brain-wave pattern, called the N1, is known to get smaller and smaller when people hear a succession of notes. If the notes stop and then start up once more, the N1 will be bigger again in response to the first note after the break.[12] This is a way to test audiation: if people are still hearing notes in their heads during the break, the N1 should stay small when the actual notes start playing again. If not, the N1 should be big again after the break.

The researchers repeated the experiment where people either heard a full scale or imagined part of the scale and then had to report whether the leading tone or the tonic was in tune or not. This time, however, the researchers were also measuring their brainwaves.[13] When people heard the full scale, the N1 got smaller just like it's supposed to. The interesting finding was the difference between people who were good at audiation versus those who weren't when they had to imagine part of the scale. The people who were good at imagining the rest of the scale *still* showed a small N1 when the final note was played after the break. This means they were still hearing the notes in their heads, just as they reported. The people who weren't as good at audiation showed a big N1 again because they weren't hearing anything in their heads. This is evidence that when people say they can hear notes accurately in their heads, they're telling the truth. In good audiators, the brain behaves as if it is still hearing the notes, which translates into better ability to judge intonation.

But does this have any bearing on the ability to play or sing in tune? It seems to, at least for singing. When people were asked to sing a short melody in their heads and then sing it out loud, those who reported more vivid audiation also sang more in tune.[14] Interestingly, people who have difficulty both singing in tune and audiating clearly also show more activity in their vocal apparatus while audiating.[15] To measure this, researchers attached electrodes to people's necks to measure the laryngeal activity while they imagined a short tune. In the people who reported difficulty with audiation, researchers found more laryngeal activity. Even though the participants weren't actually singing, their vocal apparatus was more active while they imagined the tune as compared to people who audiate more clearly. It may be that the body is trying to help supplement the deficient auditory imagery in people who aren't yet proficient at this skill.

For those of us who spend large chunks of our time working on intonation, this research gives us a good framework for how to go about the process. Make sure your pitch perception is as finely tuned as possible. For us instrumentalists, sing what you are playing to make sure you can vocalize it accurately. A tuner may help in the beginning stages, but a drone will likely help more in the long run because we need to develop the ability to adjust intonation with our ears, not our eyes. And finally, work on audiation. As we discussed in the chapters on mental practicing, being able to hear and feel things in your head is a skill you can improve on.

If audiation is hard for you, all is not lost. Devote time every day to improving the vividness of your aural imagery. Sing scales, intervals, and simple songs in your head to get better at hearing them. Practice singing a drone in your head while you play or sing out loud. At first, you may not be

188 CHALLENGES SPECIFIC TO MUSIC

able to hold the drone in your head very well, but this will get better with practice. And at all times when you are playing or singing, you should hear what you are about to play in your head before you play it. If this is hard for you, that's fine and completely normal. I advocate that my students start to develop this skill first in their scales. Play the first note of the scale and don't play the second until you can hear it clearly in your head. Then play the second note. Sing the third in your head before playing the third. Continue in this way, singing each note in your head and not playing the next note until you've audiated it clearly first. Over time, your auditory imagery will get clearer and clearer, and your ability to judge intonation and play in tune will improve as a result.

16

How to Play Faster

In 2018, I was working on a piece that I was scheduled to premiere in a few months. It was challenging but not unplayable, except for the final fast section. I used every practice technique in the book, and I just couldn't get it even close to the required tempo. Even worse, each day when I returned to that section, it was like I had never seen it before. I had already asked the composer to change certain notes three times—something I almost never do unless it's literally unplayable—so now I felt like I had to find a way. But *nothing* was working.

I think we've all been there. Besides playing from memory, one of our biggest challenges is playing fast. Many times, students feel they can play it just fine slowly, but not up to tempo, and they're not sure how to practice to get it there. There is also conflicting advice about how to practice fast music. Some students are told they should practice slowly and work it up. But how? Others are told *not* to practice slowly, that you must practice it at tempo. In reality, both of these things are true. It is necessary to play slowly to make sure it is free from mistakes and sloppiness. But just because you can play it slowly does not mean you can play it fast. Many students think that once they get it clean at a slow tempo, they'll automatically be able to play it at the faster tempo. Then they're disappointed when they can't. Bridging the gap between a slow tempo and a fast tempo often takes many steps and a lot of time. This process can be significantly shortened, however, by using good practice methods.

Basic methods

I'm going to start by briefly describing some standard practice methods for working on speed. These will likely be familiar to many readers, but I include them for those who haven't encountered them before, and to explain why they work. When we know the purpose of a specific practice method and how it works, we can use it in a more targeted and precise manner. After

Learn Faster, Perform Better. Molly Gebrian, Oxford University Press. © Oxford University Press 2024.
DOI: 10.1093/oso/9780197680063.003.0017

190 CHALLENGES SPECIFIC TO MUSIC

I detail these common practice methods, we will look at some less conventional ones, including the solution I finally found for that stubborn passage in the piece I was premiering.

Rhythms

One of the most common methods for working on fast passages is to play them in a variety of rhythms, like dotted-eighth sixteenth and the opposite rhythm (sixteenth dotted-eighth). The purpose of this practice method is to make only some of the notes fast, rather than all of them. For this practice method to have the maximum benefit, it's necessary to make the rhythm as snappy as possible. Think a double dotted-eighth followed by a 32nd note. The double dotted-eighth can be as long as you want, but the 32nd to the following note should be as fast as you can play cleanly.

But two rhythms are not enough—you need more rhythms to practice with. Figure 16.1 shows the various rhythms you should do, at a minimum. In Appendix D, I've also included what I call "bonus" rhythms. These are rhythms for practicing scales that violinist Joseph Gingold gave his students. They are great for scales, but they also work wonderfully for fast passages. Again, the point is that only some of the notes are fast, not all of them. That way, your brain and body get a little break on the longer notes. If the passage itself is slurred, you should practice in all these rhythms first without slurs and then with the marked slurs.

Slurring patterns

Another common method for fast passages is to play using different slurring and articulation patterns (different bowings for string players). Included in Figure 16.2 are a variety of these for you to try. The purpose of these is to create a more flexible version of the skill by making it harder to play the passage, as we discussed in Chapter 8. It can be difficult to coordinate these various slurring patterns to play them cleanly, highlighting areas where the coordination is not yet well organized. Once you are able to play these various patterns cleanly at or near tempo, playing as-written will then be much easier.

HOW TO PLAY FASTER   191

Figure 16.1 Rhythmic patterns to practice with (the original passage is shown at the top).

Metronome clicking up

The final common method to work on fast passages is to click up the passage with a metronome. To use this technique, start the metronome at a slow, comfortable tempo—I always say to start at a tempo that is so slow you couldn't possibly make a mistake—and gradually make it faster by five or ten clicks until you reach your goal tempo. This is much more effective than trying to get gradually faster without the metronome. Each increase in speed should only feel ever so slightly faster. When we make it faster on our own without a metronome, the jumps between tempos will be too big.

Figure 16.2 Slurring patterns to practice with (the original passage is shown at the top).

There are two common mistakes people make when clicking up with the metronome: starting too fast and/or clicking up by too much at once. You should always start at a tempo that feels easy. If you are making any mistakes at all, even little ones, you are starting too fast. Playing fast is taxing on working memory (discussed in Chapter 12) and if you start at a tempo that is already putting a heavy load on working memory, you will run into a wall very quickly. My rule of thumb is to start at half tempo (or slower). If that feels at all too fast, slow it down by at least 10 to 20 clicks. It's much better to start too slow than too fast. It should feel almost boring and trivial at your start tempo—but make sure you are still demanding absolute precision and cleanliness.

When you start clicking up, each new tempo should feel slightly faster than the last one. If it feels significantly faster, you've gone up by too much at once. If it doesn't feel any faster at all, you're going up by too little at a time. Usually,

HOW TO PLAY FASTER   193

I click up by fives, but it depends on the tempo, the note values, the meter, and the difficulty of the passage. Sometimes I click up by threes, other times by 10s. But clicking it up by one at a time (60, 61, 62, etc.) is going to be a waste of time because the difference between tempos is too small to be noticeable. This gets back to the idea of desirable difficulties from Chapter 8: each increase in speed should feel slightly harder than the last tempo you played.

Those three methods—rhythms, slurring patterns, clicking up—are the three most common strategies for working on fast passages. I had done all of these (many times) on that passage in the piece I was scheduled to premiere. But it wasn't enough. One day, out of desperation, an idea came into my head based on the concept of interleaved practice, discussed in Chapter 7. It worked so well it felt like magic. I call it interleaved clicking up and I now use it instead of the three practice methods I described above. It works that well.

Advanced methods

Interleaved clicking up can seem confusing and complicated when it's first described, but it's not actually that hard or confusing to do. I will describe the method here, but I also have a video on my website that demonstrates this method—which you can play along with—to help you understand it better. Everyone who has tried this method swears by it now, so I promise it's worth it. I've included both a written description and a visual depiction of the method here (Figure 16.3) because I think you need both to understand it.

Interleaved clicking up #1 instructions

- Each box below represents a single beat or a single measure. I will describe the process with each box representing one beat. The numbers inside the boxes are metronome markings.
- Step 1: Start by clicking up only the first beat of the passage by 5s, starting at a slow tempo (60 in this example) and working up to your tempo goal tempo. Usually I do a beat plus a note so I end on the beat (1e&a 2).
- Step 2: Go back to the start tempo (60) and play the first two beats at that tempo. Then do the *new beat only* at 65. Then both beats at 70. Then the new beat only at 75. Then both beats at 80. Continue this pattern until you reach the goal tempo.

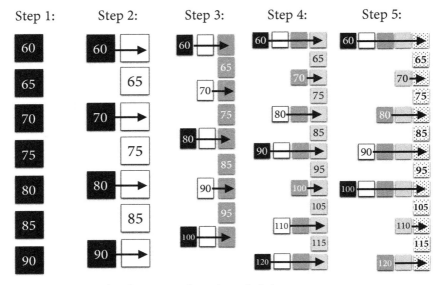

Figure 16.3 Graphic depiction of interleaved clicking up.

- Step 3: Go back to the start tempo and play the first three beats at that tempo. Then do the *new beat only* at 65. Then the second and third beats at 70. Then the new beat at 75. Then all three at 80. Continue this pattern until you reach your goal tempo.
- Continue this pattern, adding a new beat each time as illustrated in Figure 16.3, until you've done the whole passage.
- This works equally well working forward or backward (so starting with the first beat/bar and working forward or starting with the last beat/bar and working backward).

This method of practicing works as well as it does for a few reasons. First, every beat is getting isolated and focused on, since whenever a given beat is the "new beat," it gets clicked up by fives. Second, you are both isolating and putting in context at the same time. Third, the "older" the beat gets, the less often you do it. When you get to step four, for instance, you are only doing the first beat at 60, 90, and 120. That gives your brain a little bit of time to forget about the first beat, so it is more strongly reinforced when you do play it again (as we discussed in Chapter 6 on spaced practice). Eventually, the only time you will play the beats at the beginning of the passage are at the start tempo and the goal tempo. Again, this method is best understood by doing it, so go check out the video if you feel overwhelmed and confused by this explanation. I promise it's worth it.

I often use this method to learn a fast passage from scratch. I usually do interleaved clicking up going both forward and backward. If the passage is harder at the end, I will usually start by doing it backward. For extremely hard fast passages, I do this method by the beat first. After a few days of that, I do it by the bar. Then by every two bars. Then by the line. I only do each tempo once. If you are starting slowly enough, it should be perfect on the first try at each tempo. If it's not, that either means you're starting too fast or your chunk is too big (or you aren't focused). Sometimes a whole beat is too much (especially if there are six to eight notes in the beat). If that's the case, try starting with half or a quarter of the beat instead.

One of the hardest aspects of working on fast music is getting to the point where you can play it cleanly at tempo on the first try. All the methods mentioned thus far will help you get it up to tempo, but that's just the first step. Working it up to tempo is one thing, being able to just play it at tempo is another story. We need different practice methods that simulate playing it at tempo, while also allowing us to work up to it. The first practice method I use for this I call interleaved clicking up #2. For this method, you need three to five fast passages. If they are very short (just a few measures), you probably want seven to ten instead.

Interleaved clicking up #2 instructions

- Click up passage A by 5s, then passage B by 5s, then passage C by 5s.
- Click up passage A by 10s, then passage B by 10s, then passage C by 10s.
- Click up passage A by 20s, then passage B by 20s, then passage C by 20s.
- Click up passage A by 30s, then passage B by 30s, then passage C by 30s.
- Play passage A at the start tempo, a tempo exactly halfway between the start and the goal, and then the goal tempo (e.g., 60, 90, 120). Do passage B the same way. Then do passage C the same way.
- Play passage A at the start tempo and then the goal tempo. Play passage B the same way. Then play passage C the same way.
- Play passage A at tempo, followed by passage B at tempo, followed by passage C at tempo.

You need multiple passages for this method to work so you can forget a little about each passage while you are doing the others. If the passages are short, you need more of them so there is enough time to forget about each passage before you come back to it. In addition to allowing your brain time to forget, you also

196 CHALLENGES SPECIFIC TO MUSIC

increase the difficulty level whenever you return to a passage because you are clicking up by bigger intervals each time. Desirable difficulties again. By the time you get to the last step, it feels like playing it at tempo on the first try.

At-tempo chunking

Another effective practice method for being able play at-tempo is chunking, an idea we first talked about in relation to memorization. To review, chunking is taking separate pieces of information and putting them together into one larger chunk. Part of the issue with working up a fast passage from a slow tempo is that at slow tempos, we tend to think of each note individually. But to play fast with fluency, we can't be thinking of each individual note—we need to think in terms of much larger groups. Even the fastest brain can't think individual notes fast enough to direct the muscles to play them smoothly and effortlessly. This is where chunking comes in. I call this type of practice *at-tempo chunking* (but others may have different names for the same idea). You should do this method at your goal tempo or slightly faster. I always try to practice fast passages five to ten percent faster than my goal tempo because if the goal tempo is the fastest I can play it, it will never feel comfortable under pressure. I want to be able to play it faster than the goal so the goal tempo feels easy and manageable.

For at-tempo chunking, start by playing one beat plus a note (1e+a 2) as fast as possible (or at tempo) *cleanly*. Ideally, you will feel this one beat plus a note as a unit. If you find that there are a pair of notes within the beat that aren't clean, just do those two notes as fast as possible until they are clean and then reintegrate them into the chunk. Once you can do this beat plus a note cleanly, move onto the next beat and play that beat plus a note cleanly. Keep working in this way, doing one beat plus a note cleanly, until you have gotten through the entire passage.

Once you can play the entire passage this way, go back and now do two beats plus a note (1e+a 2e+a 3) as fast as you can cleanly. Do the entire passage that way. One note of caution: if you're in 4/4 (for instance), it's easy to do beats 1 and 2 and then beats 3 and 4, but you also need to make sure you do beats 2 and 3 together as a chunk (and then 4 and 1 of the next bar). Once you've done the whole passage two beats plus a note as fast as you can cleanly, go back and do three beats plus a note as fast as you can cleanly. Keep working in this way until you can play the entire passage.

When I start learning a fast passage from scratch, usually I start with interleaved clicking up #1. Then I move on to interleaved clicking up #2 and at-tempo chunking. Often after I've done at-tempo chunking, I find it helpful to follow that with clicking the passage up from the start tempo to the goal tempo by 10s. The at-tempo chunking helps me think in bigger groups and the clicking up by 10s enables me to check in at slower tempos and reinforce the cleanliness I've been working on.

Irregular groupings

Irregular groupings in a fast passage (like septuplets or 11-tuplets) can be difficult to practice since they don't divide nicely into equal groups and are therefore awkward to click up with a metronome. A modified version of at-tempo chunking works extremely well with passages like this. The first step is to identify the smaller groups within the tuplet; you might group it as 4+3+4, for instance. It doesn't matter how you group it, just make sure the groupings feel easy and intuitive to you.

Let's use a notorious passage from the end of the first movement of the Bartók Viola Concerto as an example (Figure 16.4a). These runs are very fast, are not any kind of recognizable scale, and are in groups of 11. You can see from the dotted vertical lines in Figure 16.4a that I've grouped them into chunks of three and four notes. To learn this, I practiced each individual chunk as fast as I could cleanly, shown in Figure 16.4b. Then I did pairs, shown in Figure 16.4c (the number of each chunk is provided above the notes for clarity). Next, I did three groups in a row (Figure 16.4d). I continued this until I could play all the runs together as one big chunk.

Techniques that only work at fast tempos

Techniques that simply don't work at slow tempos, like double-tonguing (for wind and brass players) or sautillé (for string players), can also be difficult to know how to practice. The issue is that the technique only works when it's fast, but coordinating everything is a challenge at tempo and it needs to be slowed down somehow—but then the technique changes or doesn't work at all. An effective solution for this conundrum is to practice with each note repeated several times—often called practicing in multiples. That way, the fast

198 CHALLENGES SPECIFIC TO MUSIC

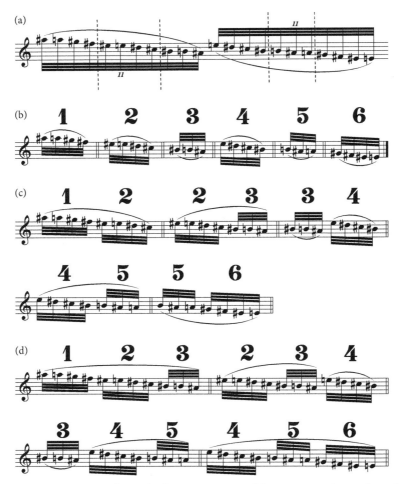

Figure 16.4 a. Passage from the first movement of the Concerto for Viola and Orchestra by Bartók with my chunks marked. b. Step 1 for practicing: individual chunks. c. Step 2 for practicing: pairs of chunks (with original bowing). d. Step 3 for practicing: groups of three chunks (with original bowing).

Viola Concerto, Sz. 120 by Béla Bartók© 1950 By Boosey & Hawkes, Inc. Boosey & Hawkes, Agent for Rental. Copyright Secured. Reprinted by Permission.

technique—say sautillé or double-tonguing—can be used for the multiples, but the fingers don't have to move so quickly.

To use this method, start with eight repetitions on each note. Make sure these repetitions are at a tempo where the technique in question works. After working to get eight repetitions per note clean, then do four repetitions,

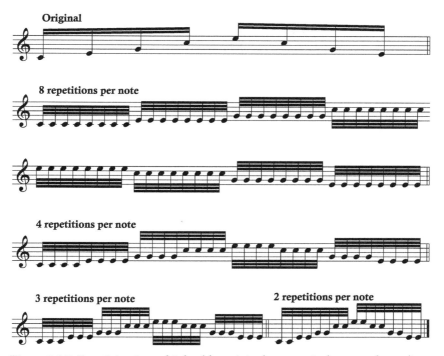

Figure 16.5 Practicing in multiples (the original passage is shown at the top).

three, and finally two (as shown in Figure 16.5). Once you've done two repetitions per note, then use at-tempo chunking, playing as-written, to become comfortable with the entire passage at tempo.

Mix and match the practice techniques described in this chapter and find what works best for you. Playing fast often requires a variety of practice strategies to make the passage feel comfortable and reliable. Often, I will do a different practice method each day. As mentioned earlier, this also falls under the category of variable practice, something discussed in Chapter 8. Whenever we do variable practice, the skill becomes more flexible, which makes it feel more solid and reliable.

Finally, be patient. Playing fast is difficult and if you try to rush the process, it will end up taking more time in the long run. Make sure you start practicing your music early enough before the performance so you have plenty of time to make the fast passages clean, fluid, and comfortable.

Conclusion

Bringing It All Together

Phew! That was a lot of information! Now that you've read this whole book, hopefully you have come to understand that deliberate practice is about training your *brain* more than anything else, as well as how to go about this training in the most effective way. It's understandable if you feel overwhelmed by all the new information. In this final chapter, we're going to explore some ideas to help with putting it all together. Specifically, we're going to talk about time management, focus, motivation, and strategies to cope with feeling overwhelmed by how much you have to practice.

The power of a practice journal

In Chapter 1, we talked about how good practicing is problem solving. One of the most powerful problem-solving tools is a practice journal. Your practice journal should be a place where you write down problems and their solutions, both the ones you come up with on your own and the ones your teacher helps you find. You should also write down everything your teacher points out in your lesson that you didn't notice before, plus any advice they give you on how to improve in these areas. While practicing, your practice journal serves a few purposes:

- It helps you organize your priorities and goals for each practice session.
- It helps you remember the solution you found the next time you go to practice. Just the act of writing it down will help you remember, but if you forget, it's right there for you.
- It's likely you will have a similar problem in the future, so you can go back and see how you solved the problem in the past.

Learn Faster, Perform Better. Molly Gebrian, Oxford University Press. © Oxford University Press 2024.
DOI: 10.1093/oso/9780197680063.003.0018

202 CONCLUSION

- It helps you track your progress. It can be very hard to see your progress in the moment, but if you look back at old entries in your practice journal, it's easy to see how far you've come.

You should have a clear goal or goals for every practice session, as we discussed in Chapter 2. For every practice session, you should go in knowing exactly what you hope to accomplish and how you plan to accomplish it. Your goals may be extremely specific: fix the intonation on beat 2 of measure 5, make the rhythm in bars 61–67 steady, and clean up the articulation in bars 100–101; or they may be more open-ended: figure out why the timing at the beginning of the development section isn't working, or figure out the right tone color for the opening theme. Whatever your goals are, it's imperative that they are specific, clear, and articulable. Without a clear set of goals, it would be like getting in the car, driving around randomly, and then coming home upset that you didn't go to the grocery store to get more milk. Without a clear intention to go to the grocery store, it's unlikely you will arrive there by chance. Practicing is the same.

Use your practice journal to help set and keep track of your goals. At the end of each practice session, write down the problems you solved along with their solution(s), as well as anything that still needs work. From this list of things that still need work, mark the top three priorities. These are your goals for your next practice session. If you do this at the *end* of each practice session, then you know exactly where to start when you come back to practicing. You don't have to waste time the next time you practice trying to remember where you left off or what still needs to be fixed. And this process of writing down what needs work and your goals for the next time shouldn't take a lot of time—two to three minutes, maximum. It also doesn't have to be pristinely neat—the only person who has to be able to read it is you! Use bullet points and abbreviations. No need to write out full sentences or paragraphs or even full words. A typical entry in my practice journal reads:

- m. 14 int b. 3
- m. 26 DS b. 2
- C-D art.
- pg. 2 top BS? CP?

Translation:

- Fix the intonation on beat 3 of measure 14.
- Address the double stop (usually it's an intonation issue) on beat 2 of measure 26.
- Address the articulation between rehearsals C to D.
- Experiment with bow speed and contact point at the top of the second page.

You will come up with your own abbreviations and shorthand, but the most important thing is keeping track of what needs work so your goals are clear for your next practice session.

Scheduling

As we discussed in Chapters 4–6 on taking breaks, there is a very strong culture in classical music (especially at music school) of practicing for long blocks of time, as many hours per day as you possibly can. Hopefully you understand from reading those chapters why this sort of schedule doesn't work very well. There also seems to be a biological limit for the amount of time we as humans can spend doing intensively focused work each day. Surprisingly, there isn't much (if any) empirical data to back this up, but musicians, scientists, writers, and scholars throughout history have found that they can only focus intensively for four to five hours per day. Beyond that, they just aren't productive and they are better off doing something else that takes less brain power.[1] If you are practicing six, seven, or eight hours a day (or more!) you aren't being as productive as you think you are. All those hours past five aren't very focused and therefore not a good use of your time.

In terms of the amount of time we can focus without taking a break, 60 to 90 minutes seems to be the sweet spot. Most people have heard of circadian rhythms—the 24-hour sleep/wake cycle—but we also have something called ultradian rhythms. These are smaller cycles of about 90 to 120 minutes that we move through both when we are asleep and when we are awake. When we're awake, we have about 90 minutes of alertness followed by about 20 minutes of rest (when we feel less alert). Even if you don't know anything about ultradian cycles, I'm sure you've noticed that there are certain times of day when you feel alert and awake, and then other times that you feel sleepy and just want to take a nap. We often think during these sleepy times when it's hard to stay focused that we're just lazy or unmotivated, but actually we're completely normal! It's just our ultradian cycle at work. You can push through the downward swing of the ultradian cycle, but then your brain won't get the rest it needs, so you won't be as alert and focused during the next upswing. But, if you take a 20-minute break every 90 minutes or so, you'll be much more focused than if you push through without a break.[2]

We also need to give our *bodies* a chance to rest and recover. Playing an instrument is taxing, and the small muscles we use to play need downtime as well. When I was a teenager, I got tendonitis from playing and Dr. Michael Charness, an expert on musicians' injuries and the Director of the Performing Arts Division at Brigham and Women's Hospital in Boston, was the doctor who treated me. After taking significant time off, I had to stick to a very strict schedule of practice once I came back to playing so I didn't reinjure myself. His recommendation was that musicians never practice for more than 25 to 30 minutes without at least a five-minute break.[3] After 60 to 90 minutes, you should take a longer break. To this day, I use a variant of the schedule I adopted as a teenager because it works incredibly well, both to protect my body and for optimal focus. On an ideal day, I practice four hours. A light day is three hours, a heavy day is four and a half. I break it up as follows:

Ideal day

Total practice time: 4 hours
Morning practice: 30 min. (5 min. break) 30 min. (5 min. break) 30 min. = 90 min. total
Afternoon practice: 30 min. (5 min. break) 30 min. (5 min. break) 30 min. = 90 min. total
Evening practice: 30 min. (5 min. break) 30 min. = 60 min. total.

Light day

Total practice time: 3 hours
Morning practice: 30 min. (5 min. break) 30 min. (5 min. break) 30 min. = 90 min. total

Afternoon practice: 30 min. (5 min. break) 30 min. (5 min. break) 30 min. = 90 min. total

Heavy day

Total practice time: 4.5 hours
Morning practice: 30 min. (5 min. break) 30 min. (5 min. break) 30 min. = 90 min. total
Afternoon practice: 30 min. (5 min. break) 30 min. (5 min. break) 30 min. = 90 min. total
Evening practice: 30 min. (5 min. break) 30 min. (5 min. break) 30 min. = 90 min. total

Between each practice session, there is at least a 90-minute break, if not longer. Often the break between practice sessions is more like two to three hours. For me, a 30-minute block of time is the longest I can practice before I feel my focus start to wander. During my five-minute break, I do something restful to give my brain a break. Usually I read a bit of a novel—never anything dense or difficult to read. Sometimes I take a quick walk. I try to avoid checking email or social media because we all tend to get sucked into that, pulling us away from what we actually want to spend our time doing.

Focus

But what if you can't focus for 30 minutes straight? Learning to focus is a skill and something you can work to improve. If it's hard for you to maintain focus, set an alarm for a very short amount of time—two minutes or five minutes—and practice while staying focused for just that long. Then take a short break. Then do the same amount of time again. Once that short amount of time feels easy, set your alarm for longer and repeat the process. If you keep doing this, working up slowly, you'll eventually find that focusing for 30 minutes is something you are able to do.

You can also give yourself an uncomfortably short amount of time in which to accomplish something. If you normally spend 20 minutes working on scales, give yourself five minutes only. With such a restricted time limit, you will have to be incredibly efficient in how you work. This will help you learn where you are wasting time in your practice and how you can work more effectively. You also won't have time to space out and lose focus. People who tend to lose focus in the middle of a practice session often like the idea (presented in Chapter 7 on interleaved practicing) of setting an interval timer to go off every three to five minutes, telling them it is time to switch to something else. These incredibly short slices of time force you to zero in on precisely what needs fixing and to use the most effective method possible to address the issue.

If you tend to practice mindlessly without clear goals, set a timer to go off every five to ten minutes. Every time the timer goes off, say out loud the precise goal you're working toward in that moment, the strategy you are using, and why that strategy works. Pretend you are explaining to a nonmusician friend exactly what you are doing and why. This will help you become more aware of your tendency to practice mindlessly, without a clear goal or method. This awareness will then help you reduce the amount of time you practice in this way.

Motivation

One of the most common questions I get from my students is, "What do I do when I can't find the motivation to practice?" I like to think of big-M Motivation and small-m motivation. Big-M Motivation is your overriding *why*. Why do you play your instrument? Why are you trying to get better? What are you trying to achieve long-term? Without Motivation, we can't do anything. If there isn't a big-picture reason for you to be playing your instrument and trying to improve, practicing is going to feel pretty pointless. Maybe you want to have a career as an orchestral musician in a top orchestra. Maybe you want to share music with people around the world who don't have easy access to it. Maybe you want to get into your dream school. Maybe you just absolutely love to play and it's the thing that makes you happiest in the world, so you want to become the best player you can. Whatever your reason, the only thing that matters is you have one.

But small-m motivation: that's a different story. Small-m motivation is the day-to-day motivation that waxes and wanes. Some days you're really going to want to practice, and you just can't wait for class to be over so you can get back into the practice room. Other days, practicing is going to be the last thing you feel like doing. It would be so much nicer just to sleep all day, or

CONCLUSION 207

play video games, or party with your friends. When people ask about motivation, they are always talking about small-m motivation.

Here's my answer: motivation is irrelevant.

I know that sounds harsh, but bear with me.

When people ask, "How do I find the motivation to practice?" what they are really asking is, "How do I make it easier to start practicing when I don't feel like it?" And when that's the question, there are many strategies you can use to make it easier to open the case and get started.*

Research on habit formation has found that it has nothing to do with willpower or motivation and everything to do with setting up systems and structures in your life that make it easy to do the right thing (practice) and hard to do the wrong thing (slack off). People who practice regularly without any seeming struggle have set up their lives so they don't have to make the choice in the moment whether to practice or when to practice. If you constantly have to make the choice, moment to moment, of whether you feel like practicing or not, it's not going to happen. You'll just keep putting it off. But if you can decide ahead of time when you'll practice, you make things much easier for your future self.

There have been dozens of books written on this (my favorite is *Atomic Habits* by James Clear), so I'll just describe a few strategies here.

Make a schedule

This one may seem obvious, but I can't tell you how many times I've asked students about their daily schedule of practicing, homework, etc. and they don't really have one. They have their daily class and work schedule, but they haven't blocked out how they are going to use their free time. They just sort of wing it, using their free time in whatever way they feel like in the moment. This is a recipe for disaster (or at least, a recipe for inefficient time use). Again, if you are deciding in the moment how you are going to use your free time, you will be wasting time making the decision. If, however, you've decided ahead of time how to use that time, you'll be more efficient and get more done. At the end of every day before I go to bed, I plan out exactly how

---

* I realize that a lot of this advice may not work for those with ADHD (or those struggling with their mental health). As I said in the introduction, specific strategies for neurodivergent individuals are outside my area of expertise and, unfortunately, I am not able to address these issues in this book, as much as I would like to.

208　CONCLUSION

I'm going to use my free time the next day. Sometimes, if I have a busy day coming up and a lot that needs to get done, the schedule has to be pretty strict. If I have more flexibility, I make looser plans. But I always make a plan so I have fewer decisions to make in the moment. This helps me stick to my practicing goals.

Be flexible

An all-or-nothing mindset can be very destructive to regular practicing. Setting aside specific times to practice each day—and deciding that the night before—is extremely effective in helping you use your time well. But unexpected things do happen, and your plans can get disrupted. Sometimes people feel if they don't get their morning practice in because of an unexpected issue cropping up, then the whole day is shot and it's not worth practicing at all. Hopefully you can see that this is illogical. If you planned to practice for three hours and you lost an hour in the morning, doing two hours is better than doing zero hours. Add this up over the course of a week and it's a huge difference. If the plan was three hours a day—21 hours a week, assuming you practiced every day—and you lost an hour every day, you still got 14 hours of practicing in. That's a lot more than zero hours. Sometimes, if you miss an entire day of practicing, it can be hard to get back on the practicing train. You feel like, "Well, I already missed a day. What's one more day?" and before you know it, you've missed a whole week. I have a rule for myself with habits I'm trying to form: I'm never allowed more than one day off in a row. It's okay to take today off, but then tomorrow I *have* to practice (or exercise, or whatever). If you know tomorrow is going to be hard to practice, better to practice at least a little bit today so you can take tomorrow off. That way you keep the habit and you feel good for having practiced.

Start small

Sometimes we don't feel like practicing because we're so tired and overworked. We see a whole hour looming in front of us and it just seems like too much. If that's the case, figure out one small thing that you *need* to practice and give yourself permission just to practice that one small thing, even if it only takes literally two minutes. Often once you get started, it's easier to keep going. But if you don't want to keep practicing and the two-minute spot is all you got done that day, at least you did *something*!

Use the Red-Yellow-Green method to combat overwhelm

Often when people feel unmotivated to practice, they are actually overwhelmed. They don't know where to start, so they feel paralyzed. In Chapter 2, we discussed the method of dividing your music into Red, Yellow, and Green sections. As a review, Red sections are emergencies and need the most work. Yellow sections need work, but aren't an emergency. And Green sections are in pretty good shape. I often find that when students have their music mapped out in terms of priority like this, it's much easier to get started with practicing. They don't feel overwhelmed by the amount they have to do, so they know exactly where to start and why. Some of my students use this method as a matter of course: their first step when they get any new piece of music is to map out the Red, Yellow, and Green sections based on difficulty. Once they've worked through everything, they reassess and reassign the colors. It helps them get started initially and enables them to keep going without getting paralyzed by indecision.

Habit bundling

When you use habit bundling, you link something you do anyway (or enjoy doing) with a new habit you are trying to form. Much of the research on habit bundling was done with people trying to exercise more.[4] When people were only allowed to listen to their favorite podcast or watch their favorite show while at the gym, they were much more likely to exercise, and to exercise more. With practicing, you could decide you are only allowed to play through your favorite piece *after* you've practiced for a certain amount of time, for instance. If bribing yourself in this way doesn't seem like it will work for you, you can also link practicing to something you already do regularly, taking away the decision of exactly *when* to practice. For me, I always practice after I eat a meal: my morning practice block happens after breakfast, the afternoon block is right after lunch, and the evening block is after dinner. That way, I never have to decide when I'm going to practice. Eat-practice has become a routine, so the decision is already made.

210   CONCLUSION

Make it social

Humans are social creatures. It's much easier to do something you may not feel like doing if there are other people involved. Find a practice buddy and agree to coordinate your schedules so you can practice at the same time each day. Or find a friend and hold each other accountable—agree to play for each other once a week a few days before your next lesson. Use the habit bundling idea with friends: first you practice, then you go out to coffee or dinner or something together. It's not a cop-out to rely on your friends to help you stick with the practicing habit—it's taking advantage of a strength humans have (our social connections with each other). And your friends will thank you—they are probably struggling to practice consistently, too!

Prioritize rest

As we discussed in chapters 4–6, taking breaks and resting is necessary for learning. Sometimes when we lack motivation, we're just tired and burnt out. If you prioritize rest and rejuvenation, you'll find that it's easier to stick to your schedule and your goals. We are human beings. We cannot practice four to five hours a day, every single day without ever taking any time off, nor should we. Treating yourself with kindness and compassion is always a better option than beating yourself up.

These are just a few of the ideas that have proven successful in helping people establish new habits. But the idea that we should always feel motivated to practice and be able to practice hours and hours every day effortlessly is a fantasy. I think part of where this mistaken idea of day-to-day motivation comes from is the myth of inspiration—musicians are artists, and we "just can't work when we aren't inspired." If you talk to professional artists in any field—musicians, writers, painters, sculptors, dancers, architects, photographers—they will all tell you that inspiration is irrelevant. The American artist Chuck Close has a famous quote: "Inspiration is for amateurs. The rest of us just show up and get to work. If you wait around for the clouds to part and a bolt of lightning to strike you in the brain, you are not going to make an awful lot of work. All the best ideas come out of the process; they come out of the work itself."[5] If you put in the work, motivation and inspiration will follow. If you don't, they won't.

Hopefully you have found some new ideas in this book you are excited to try out. Don't feel like you have to do everything all at once. My aim with this book is to provide a comprehensive overview of the research on learning and memory and how it applies to practicing and performing, in the hopes that many people will find solutions to the problems and frustrations they face while practicing. I know the amount of information can be overwhelming. To get started, just pick one idea that seems intriguing to you and try it out. Over time, you can add more and more ideas that you've learned about in here. You don't have to do it all at once. And you don't even have to do all of it ever. I never take naps, for instance, even though I am well aware of the research showing how beneficial they are. It just doesn't fit into how I have to schedule my days most often.

I believe that when we understand better how our brains work, we can learn music more effectively, which will make practicing much more enjoyable. And as a result, we will give more convincing, joyful, engaging performances that we feel good about. I hope this book has inspired you to experiment and change your routine in a way that will allow you to get more out of your practicing. Making music is one of the most amazing and complex activities human beings engage in. When we take advantage of how our brains learn most effectively, we can accomplish incredible things.

Let's go practice.

APPENDIX A

Complete List of Practice Strategies

Section I

Chapter 1: Good Practicing and How It Changes the Brain

- Start with your hard spots:
  - Figure out *why* you are having trouble as precisely as you can.
  - Break the problem down into smaller, manageable parts.
  - Solidify the solution using one of the methods below:
    - Play it correctly at least five times in a row.
    - Overlearning: If it took you 10 tries to get it right, do at least 5 correct repetitions (50% overlearning); 10 is even better (100% overlearning).
- Ask: "Which pathway am I reinforcing by how I'm practicing?"
- Intonation:
  - Stop on the note in question.
  - *Don't* adjust.
  - Figure out whether it's flat or sharp.
  - Stop on the note in question until it's perfectly in tune without adjusting to achieve at least 50% overlearning.

Chapter 2: Practice Like a Pro

- Keep going when you feel frustrated.
- Use the Three Step Model:
  - Step 1: Set specific goals.
  - Step 2: Monitor your progress toward those goals closely.
    - Record yourself and listen back to help with this step.
  - Step 3: Evaluate how you did and precisely why things did or didn't go well.
- Divide your music into Red, Yellow, and Green sections. Start with the Red sections.
  - Red = emergencies.
  - Yellow = not great, but not emergencies.
  - Green = acceptable for now.
- Work backward.

Chapter 3: Use Errors to Your Advantage

- Amplification of error:
  - Exaggerate the main cause of the bad habit.

214 APPENDIX A

- Old way/new way:
  - Step 1: Watch a video of the old way and the new way.
  - Step 2: Perform and describe the old way.
  - Step 3: Perform and describe the new way.
  - Step 4: Alternate between the old way and the new way (perform and describe).
  - Step 5: Do the new way several times.
- Instead of practicing in front of a mirror, video-record yourself and watch back.

Section II

Chapter 4: The Fastest Way to Learn Music: Take More Breaks

- Practice for shorter amounts of time with breaks in between.
- Microbreaks:
  - Do three correct repetitions.
  - Take a 10-second break.
  - Do three more correct repetitions.
  - If any of the repetitions had errors, start over and repeat the process.
- During longer breaks, practice contrasting music.
- Avoid retroactive interference:
  - Take a 6-hour break between practicing two very similar passages when they are new.

Chapter 5: Can You Learn Music in Your Sleep?

- Get a full night of sleep to enhance performance the next day.
- Take a short nap or just rest quietly after practicing to boost learning.
- Take a nap between practicing similar passages to mitigate retroactive interference.

Chapter 6: What's the Perfect Schedule of Breaks?

- Err on the side of longer breaks.
- Breaks should be shorter when music is new, longer when you know it better:
  - Microbreaks.
  - Revisit the same passage two to three times within a day when new.
  - Once something is comfortable, take a day or two off from practicing it.
- My practice schedule for new music:
  - Three days in a row then take a day off.
  - Every other day three times (Monday, Wednesday, Friday), then take a week off.
  - Three days in a row, then take two weeks off.
  - Three days in a row.
  - Three is the average: sometimes it's two days, sometimes four.

APPENDIX A 215

Chapter 7: Be More Consistent in Performance

- Use interleaved practice to help prepare for performance.
- Serial practice:
  - Make a list of hard spots and perform each spot, one after the other.
  - A good performance gets a tick mark for that spot.
  - A poor performance means you must erase any tick marks you've already gotten for that spot.
  - The goal is to get five tick marks per spot.
- Interval timer practice:
  - Every time the timer goes off, perform your chosen spot.
- Time-constrained practice:
  - Switch what you're working on every two to five minutes.
- Perform in a random order:
  - Divide your music into sections, number them, and then draw numbers at random.
- Interleaved practice for new music:
  - Return to spots practiced previously after working on other music in the interim.
- Late night/early morning mock performance.

Chapter 8: Why Exact Repetitions May Not Be the Best Goal

- See Appendix C for instrument-specific ideas.
- Practice at a variety of tempos.
- Practice with different expressive parameters (separately or combined):
  - Articulations.
  - Tone colors.
  - Dynamics.
  - Vibratos.
- Play with opposite articulations and/or dynamics.
- Create a skeleton version of the piece.
- Fill in longer note values with subdivided repeated notes.
- Play a passage with a variety of different emotional intentions.
- Play a passage as if you were different famous musicians.
- Alternate between physical and mental practice, one bar at a time.
- Introduce small physical challenges:
  - Eyes closed.
  - Walking in a circle.
  - Walking backward.
  - Standing on one leg.
  - Bend knees/going up on tip-toes.

Section III

Chapter 9: The Power of Mental Practice

- Try to feel and hear everything you need to be aware of while playing, but inside your head.

216   APPENDIX A

- Try dynamic mental practice: move slightly while you hear/feel the music inside your head.
- Try AOMI: watch someone (or yourself) perform what you're working on while practicing mentally at the same time.

Chapter 10: Mental Practice and the Brain

- 20 minutes of mental practice seems to be the optimal amount of time before taking a break.
- Try alternating between mental and physical practice.
- Try to hear the exact quality of sound and intonation you want.
- For kids: imagine watching yourself playing on a big TV on the wall.

Chapter 11: How to Focus to Play Your Best

- Focus on quality of sound and expressive intent rather than the details of what your body must do.
- Focus on what the instrument has to do rather than what the body has to do.
- A focus closer to the body is better at lower skill levels; a focus farther from the body is better at higher skill levels.
- Give feedback that focuses on the effect of the action rather than the physical mechanics of the action.
- Use analogies instead of language that focuses on body mechanics.

Chapter 12: The Most Effective Ways to Memorize Music

- Chunk your music for deeper encoding.
- Use performance cues to help with encoding:
  - Structural cues (best).
  - Expressive cues (best).
  - Interpretive cues.
  - Basic cues.
- Have multiple copies of your music marked differently:
  - Structural landmarks.
  - Harmonic analysis.
  - Expressive words for each phrase/section.
- Solidify muscle memory, auditory memory, and declarative memory separately:
  - Muscle memory
    - Play without sound (from memory).
    - De-tune your instrument and play from memory.
  - Auditory memory
    - Sing from memory (neutral syllable, solfège, note names, finger numbers).
    - Sing then play one note at a time.

APPENDIX A   217

- Declarative memory
  - Draw a formal diagram from memory.
  - Write out your music from memory on a blank piece of staff paper.
- Work on developing the auditory/motor coactivation:
  - Figure out something by ear every day on your instrument.
  - Play something from memory every day on your instrument.

Chapter 13: Boost Confidence in Memorized Performance

- Get enough sleep for optimal consolidation.
- Practice the hardest section to memorize last before sleep and first thing the next day.
- Practice retrieval until it is automatic.
- Aim to have all your music memorized at least six weeks before the performance.
- Start testing your memory from the very beginning of learning something new.
- If you can't remember what comes next, try to figure it out by listening to a recording rather than looking at the music right away.
- Mental practice from memory.
- Use the serial practice list technique to test memory (Chapter 7).
- Play from memory in a random order.
- Use an interval timer to test memory.
- Video-record yourself playing from memory in the practice room.
- Play from memory while thinking about big picture things:
  - Sound.
  - Expression.
  - Phrasing.
  - Character.
  - Musical intentions.
- Play from memory for others often leading up to the performance.

Section IV

Chapter 14: Improving Rhythm and Tempo

- To improve sense of pulse, have the metronome click:
  - On off-beats only.
  - Every other beat.
  - Every downbeat only.
  - Every other downbeat only.
  - Every third downbeat only.
  - Use TimeGuru or TonalEnergy with the random mute function.
- Walk in place to develop an internal sense of pulse.
- Walk in place musically, so step depth shows metrical/musical hierarchy.

218 APPENDIX A

Chapter 15: Improving Pitch and Intonation

- Use a pitch discrimination app like InTune to improve your ear.
- Practice singing the individual notes of dissonant intervals out loud while playing both.
- Sing what you are playing out loud.
- Use a drone instead of a tuner.
- Work to develop your audiation abilities:
  - Sing scales, intervals, and simple songs in your head.
  - Sing a drone in your head while playing.
  - Play a scale and don't go to the next note until you can hear it in your head first.

Chapter 16: How to Play Faster

- Play in different rhythms.
- Play in different slurring patterns.
- Click up the passage with the metronome.
- Use interleaved clicking up #1 to learn fast passages.
- Use interleaved clicking up #2 to simulate playing at tempo.
- Use at-tempo chunking to simulate playing at tempo.
- Use at-tempo chunking for runs in asymmetrical tuplets.
- Practice in multiples (8, 4, 3, 2) for techniques that don't work at slower tempos.

Conclusion: Bringing It All Together

- Use a practice journal to write:
  - Goals.
  - Problems and their solutions.
  - A list of what your teacher said in your lesson.
  - A list of what to work on in your next practice session.
- Scheduling:
  - Don't practice more than five hours a day.
  - Take at least a 5-minute break every 25–30 minutes.
  - Take at least a 90-minute break every 60–90 minutes.
- Focus:
  - Put on a timer for a short amount of time and gradually increase to work on the ability to focus.
  - Give yourself an uncomfortably short amount of time to work on something.
  - Set a timer to go off every 5–10 minutes and when it does, explain out loud your goal in that moment, what strategy you are using, and why.
- Motivation
  - Figure out ahead of time when you are going to practice. Put it in your planner.
  - Be flexible: if your schedule gets disrupted, don't throw it all out the window.
  - Start small: do one tiny thing that feels manageable.

APPENDIX A   219

- Use the Red-Yellow-Green method (Chapter 2) to combat overwhelm.
- Use habit-bundling to link something you like to do/are already in the habit of doing with practicing.
- Find a practice buddy and hold each other accountable.
- Prioritize rest: if you're exhausted and burnt out, you won't feel like practicing.

APPENDIX B

Sample Spaced Practice Calendars

Piece: Bach Suite 6 Prelude

Section 1: mm. 70–74
Section 2: mm. 83–89
Section 3: mm. 1–22

Section 1 schedule

Monday	Tuesday	Wednesday	Thursday	Friday	Saturday	Sunday
Practice 1	Practice 2	Practice 3		Practice 4		Practice 5
	Practice 6		Practice 7			
			Practice 8	Practice 9	Practice 10	
					Practice 11	Practice 12

Section 2 schedule

Monday	Tuesday	Wednesday	Thursday	Friday	Saturday	Sunday
	Practice 1	Practice 2	Practice 3		Practice 4	
Practice 5		Practice 6				
		Practice 7	Practice 8	Practice 9		
				Practice 10	Practice 11	Practice 12

Section 3 schedule

Monday	Tuesday	Wednesday	Thursday	Friday	Saturday	Sunday
		Practice 1	Practice 2	Practice 3		Practice 4
	Practice 5					
	Practice 6	Practice 7				
		Practice 8				

222 APPENDIX B

Combined schedule

Monday	Tuesday	Wednesday	Thursday	Friday	Saturday	Sunday
Section 1 #1	Section 1 #2 Section 2 #1	Section 1 #3 Section 2 #2 *Section 3 #1*	Section 2 #3 *Section 3 #2*	Section 1 #4 *Section 3 #3*	Section 2 #4	Section 1 #5 *Section 3 #4*
Section 2 #5	Section 1 #6 *Section 3 #5*	Section 2 #6	Section 1 #7			
		Section 2 #7 *Section 3 #7*	Section 1 #8 Section 2 #8	Section 1 #9 Section 2 #9	Section 1 #10	
	Section 3 #6			Section 2 #10	Section 1 #11 Section 2 #11	Section 1 #12 Section 2 #12
		Section 3 #8				

APPENDIX C

Variable Practice Strategies

This is, of course, not an exhaustive list. There are an infinite number of variable practice methods, but hopefully those listed here and in Chapter 8 will get you started. A huge thanks to Fred Sienkiewicz (a trumpet player) for the brass and woodwind ideas, Jeffrey Sykes (a pianist) for the piano and voice ideas, and Michelle Gott for the harp ideas. Although the suggestions in this appendix are specific to each instrument family, I encourage you to read them all. I think you'll find that there are intriguing suggestions that could be creatively modified for use on any instrument.

Brass and woodwinds

- Play with the opposite hand (left hand for trumpet, euphonium, trombone, tuba; right hand for horn).
- Sing on brass articulations like "da" or "ta" to model the motor actions of the wind production/air support needed to play.
- Buzz on the mouthpiece alone. A variation on this is to use the Jo-Ral *Short-Cut* or any of the home-made variants (3" length of 3/8" hose with a funnel) to similar effect.
- Isolate and rehearse only the respiratory and tongue functions by blowing air through the instrument in the rhythm of the music, without vibrating the lips. Can be combined with fingers for further integration.
- Buzz a single pitch by removing the leadpipe of the instrument, and blow and tongue using the mouthpiece and the leadpipe only. This setup usually has 3–4 partials available to the player; try to find a partial near the register of the music. Can be combined with fingering for further coordination benefits.
- Practice a passage first with the mute that offers the most resistance or back-pressure possible (usually a practice mute), and gradually work through less-resistant mutes until you reach open (i.e., practice, Harmon, cup, straight, open).
- Practice on a bigger instrument. For instance, horn players have the option of playing most notes either on the "F side" or the "B-flat side" of the horn. For trumpets, practice solos or excerpts meant to be performed on C, E-flat, or Piccolo trumpet on the larger B-flat trumpet. This also works for any of the woodwinds if you have access to other instruments (bass clarinet, alto flute, etc.).
- Practice on a "natural" instrument: For both trumpet and horn, practice Baroque or Classical music written for natural trumpet or natural horn on either a period instrument (if available) or a home-made hose-a-phone to vary the conditions of the embouchure coordination. Playing without valves highlights and intensifies the aural precision and the coordination of the lips and air.
- Play a very low or very high passage in a more comfortable octave to isolate the music from the difficulties associated with register.
- Practice sitting on a chair with both feet held in the air by extending them straight out. This engages the intercostal muscles and the diaphragm in a pedagogically helpful way. A similar effect is observed playing standing on one foot.

224 APPENDIX C

- Practice lying down flat on the floor, facing the ceiling. This helps with relaxing the neck and shoulders while playing, and models good posture.
- Practice the music with every note articulated only by the air (no tongue). For cross-improvement of rhythm and subdivision, breath attack on every (smallest appropriate) subdivision.
- Practice a passage entirely while flutter tonguing. This causes the breath support and embouchure to work harder to accurately get and sustain the pitches.
- Change your tonguing. Whereas normal articulations are done with a "ta" articulation, double tonguing with a "ta-ka" articulation, and triple tonguing with "ta-ta-ka" or "ta-ka-ta," the following possibilities vary the experience: "ka" for single tonguing, "ka-ta" for double tonguing, and "ka-ta-ta" for triple tonguing, in each case putting the ka syllable on the strong beat.

Harp

- Use an egg shaker in one hand to generate the beat while playing a passage with the other hand. This will test rhythmic consistency and coordination. Be sure to then switch hands to test both sides.
- Sing one line while playing the other.
- Play without doing the pedal changes. It will sound completely wrong, but will help solidify muscle memory for the hands.
- Say the pedals out loud while playing with the hands alone.
- Only do the pedals (in time) with no hands.
- Only play every other note in fast passages while making sure the fingering is still consistent.
- Practice playing detached (lifting off the strings) in passages where you would otherwise connect note to note.

Keyboard

- Play hands separately. This is worth doing even in later stages of working on a piece.
- Alternate hands separately: play one measure right hand only, then the next left hand only, etc., but play continuously.
- Play the left-hand part with right hand and vice versa, either separately or simultaneously. This helps with understanding articulation, balance, and voicing.
- Play with hands crossed.
- In textures that require the hands to be crossed, play with uncrossed hands. This can usually be done by separating the hands by an octave or two.
- Play the two hands with greater distance separating them, at least an extra octave, but sometimes two is possible (or desirable). If possible, also do the opposite (less space between the two hands).
- Change which hand is "leading." Let the left hand dictate where the right hand plays or vice versa. This helps strengthen the less dominant hand, strengthens rhythmic execution, and creates more nuanced voicing.
- Play the passage in a completely different register than normal. Particularly when playing very low, you must listen in a different way, especially to articulation.

APPENDIX C   225

- If one hand (or staff) has two voices, play the two voices with separate hands.
- In fugues or other highly contrapuntal music, play the voices separately and in all possible combinations of two voices using separate hands. You can also sing one voice while playing another one or two voices.
- Play the melody using only a single finger and the weight of the arm and/or play the melody alternating single fingers of both hands, i.e., the two thumbs in alternation. This helps connect the arm to the fingers and gives a sense of how weight is transferred across the keyboard. It can also help find a deeper, more resonant sound at the piano.
- Play as if the melody is the accompaniment and the accompaniment the melody. This can help refine expression and phrasing, particularly in the accompaniment.
- Play only the thumbs, but in time. Since hand positions are often defined by where the thumb plays, this can help clarify that.
- Play the melody and accompany yourself with a variety of stereotypical patterns: waltz, march, Alberti bass, bossa nova, tango, siciliano, stride bass, etc.
- Syncopate the melody against the accompaniment.
- Improvise a new melody over the accompaniment. This can help you clarify the harmonic/melodic push/pull of the original melody.
- Impose limitations on your pedal usage:
  - Play without pedal.
  - Play a passage and allow yourself to use the pedal for only one second, or two seconds.
  - Only the three most important spots in a passage and no more.
  - Play with the lightest film of pedal throughout and use articulation to still make your ideas clear.
  - Change the timing and placement of your pedal usage.
- Practice on every different piano you can find. Don't avoid the bad ones; do what you can to make them sound good (without hurting yourself).
- If you have access to a prepared piano, practice your "regular" music on it. This is a great memory test as well.
- Vary where you are looking as you play:
  - Right hand; left hand; between the two hands.
  - Look at the departure point of a leap; look at the arrival point of a leap.
  - Look at the more stable hand in a leap; look at the hand that moves more.
  - Close your eyes or turn out the lights.
  - Have the light on half the keyboard, the other half in the dark.
  - If you're reading music, look at your hands. If you're playing from memory, don't look at your hands.

Strings

- Play with backward bowing. If it starts down bow, start up bow and vice versa.
- Confine yourself to one part of the bow, especially focusing on extremes (e.g., doing everything at the extreme tip or extreme frog).
- Use a different or opposite bow stroke. For instance, if it's marked spiccato, play it legato; if it's legato or slurred, play it spiccato.
- Play all down bows or all up bows, but preserve your phrasing and dynamics.

226 APPENDIX C

- Play in a variety of different bowings (like those listed in Chapter 16).
- Confine yourself to very little bow (one to three inches) and see if you can still bring out your phrasing.
- Use twice as much bow speed as you think you should, while still trying to get a good sound and clear phrasing.
- Isolate bow speed, contact point, bow weight, and vibrato individually and try to bring your phrasing and shapes across just using the one parameter you're focusing on (e.g., try to achieve all your musical ideas through contact point alone).
- Play completely without vibrato and try to convey your phrasing just with the bow.
- Play everything with the opposite bow speed, contact point, bow weight, and vibrato you intend.
- Play the melody in a different octave than marked.
- Play the correct notes, but in a different position than usual. You could either improvise new fingerings/shifts or try to play the entire passage confining yourself to one position only.
- Play the melody only on one string.
- Play the melody only on one finger while trying to preserve good intonation.
- For double-stops:
  - Play both notes with your left hand, but only bow on one string. Do this for both the top notes and the bottom notes. This will help isolate them and will improve intonation.
  - Sing along out loud with just the top line and then just the bottom line while playing both notes.
  - Sing one line out loud while playing the other.
  - Record yourself playing one line (with a fingering you would use if it were just a single line and didn't have double stops) and then play along with your recording as-written to test intonation.
- Play open strings only. This is especially useful for cleaning up passages with many/difficult string crossings.
- Play left hand only. This is especially useful for passages that require a lot of left-hand articulation. It will illuminate where the left hand is unclear.
- Before each string crossing or shift, stop and say out loud, "Shift" or "Cross." This will help clarify the coordination demands.
- Use the "spotlight" method to work on intonation. Pick one note in the passage that returns often. Whenever you come to that note in the passage, hold it as if it had a fermata on it. This will help draw attention to these notes and also ensure that different instances of the same note match.

Voice

Text only

Once you've mastered the basic pronunciation of the words, try speaking them in a variety of ways:

- Speak the words slowly and evenly.
- Speak the words both in a conversational rhythm and in the rhythm of the music. This is quite basic and can be combined with any of the ideas that follow.

APPENDIX C   227

- Speak the words as if you were Dr. Martin Luther King Jr., or President Obama, or your favorite actor/actress.
- Speak at different pitch levels, with different articulation, and most especially with different speeds. When you speak slowly, make sure to sustain words rather than leaving space between them. Speak with changing pitch levels, changing articulation, and changing speeds.
- Imagine you are speaking to 10,000 people in a colosseum and the sound system is broken, but you can't yell.
- Whisper the words like an intimate secret.
- Imagine you are telling a ghost story to a class of 5-year-olds.
- Use the words for baby-speak with your dog or cat.
- Use the words in an improvised rap style.
- Paraphrase the words in different styles/characters (e.g., in Shakespearean English, like a political stump speech, or like the characters in your favorite TV show). This is a helpful exercise for internalizing the gist of texts that are often abstract.

Combining text with singing

- With good technique, sing the words on a single pitch in an even rhythm. You can combine this with any of the suggestions above. Warning: some voices get tight when they stay on a single pitch. If that's you, then try the third suggestion down instead.
- Sing the vowels of the words in their proper order (no consonants) on easy vocalise patterns (e.g., 1-2-3-2-1, 5-4-3-2-1, or 1-3-5-8-5-3-1). Vary the placement of the vowels within this pattern and feel free to create single-vowel melismas. Vary the speed and dynamics of this.
- Pick an easy vocalise pattern and sing the words using that pattern. Vary the placement of the words within this pattern. Stressed syllables can have multiple notes (i.e., melismatic) or not. Unstressed syllables can be melismatic, too, but keep them unstressed. Vary the speed and dynamics of this.
- Pretend all the notes of your song are of equal length, i.e., all quarter notes. Sing the vowels of your words using the now-equal-length notes of the song. Then do the same using the full words.
- Sing only the vowels using the notes and rhythms of the song.
- Sing short passages at different pitch levels than written.
- Vary the focus of your singing. Imagine singing to one person. A small group. A large group. One person moving toward you. One person moving away from you, etc. Imagine singing to a camera: a very narrow, close focus. Imagine singing for a camera that's a mile away.
- At every breath, take the time you need to get a full, relaxed breath. It will create gaps in the music, which is fine. Try to retain the quality and experience of your breath as you make the gap smaller and smaller.
- Sing each word separately, stopping after every complete word no matter where it may be in a phrase. This helps especially with songs in foreign languages; it helps you understand the beginnings and endings of words and the natural stress patterns of words, and it shows you how the syllables of words need to be bound together with unbreakable legato.

228   APPENDIX C

- Sing standing, sitting, squatting, leaning against the wall, lying on the floor on your back and on your stomach, lying on your side, with one foot level and the other on a step up or down, hanging from a pullup bar, while dragging something across the floor, while lifting something above your head, etc. Varying the position you're in while singing varies the demands of the supporting musculature—and it's a great prelude to the physical flexibility demanded by opera staging. Obviously, pay attention to your technique here—don't do anything that will hurt you vocally; always optimize technique.
- Make a word-for-word translation into your native language and sing using this translation, as awkward as this can be. The closer you are to perfect word-for-word in this, the better. Do not try to normalize your translation. This is incredibly effective for helping you understand music in foreign languages.

APPENDIX D

Bonus Rhythms

Glossary

Amplification of error—A practice method to fix bad habits by exaggerating the error, making it more obvious and therefore easier to correct.

Anterior—Toward the front.

AOMI—Stands for *action observation and mental imagery*. A form of enhanced mental practice where the student watches someone perform the skill while also imagining themselves performing the skill at the same time.

At-tempo chunking—A practice method for working on fast passages that involves playing very small amounts of music at tempo (starting with just one beat or less), with the goal of playing that small chunk cleanly.

Audiation—Hearing music inside your head. A synonym for auditory imagery.

Auditory cortex—The area of the brain responsible for processing sound. Located in the temporal lobes.

Auditory imagery—Hearing music (or other auditory information) inside your head. A synonym for audiation.

Auditory memory—Memory for sound (music, speech, etc.).

Auditory-motor coactivation—When the auditory cortex and the motor cortex are activated together. Seen in professional musicians in response to hearing music and/or playing music silently.

Basic cues—Information in a piece of music that pertains to matters of technique, like fingerings, bowings, or breath marks. From Roger Chaffin's list of the four types of performance cues musicians use to orient themselves while playing from memory.

Blocked practice—A practice method where the musician spends a large chunk of time focusing on one task before moving on to something different.

Cerebellum—Part of the brain, located at the back of the head below the cerebral cortex. Involved in motor coordination (among other things).

Chaffin, Roger—A psychologist who studied musicians, specifically the preparation necessary to perform music from memory.

Challenge point—A concept of structuring practice that asserts that the most learning will occur when the task is neither too easy nor too hard, but rather is right at the edge of the learner's current capabilities. The challenge point changes depending on the experience and skill of the learner.

Choking—A failure in performance despite adequate preparation and skill level for the task at hand.

232 GLOSSARY

Chunking—Grouping together separate pieces of information into one unified concept, making them easier to remember.

Consolidation—The second stage of memory formation, where the information to be remembered is transferred from short-term to long-term storage. Happens primarily during sleep.

Constrained action hypothesis—Describes why a focus outside the body (an external focus) is superior to focusing on bodily movements (an internal focus) by positing that when we exert conscious control over our movements, we get in the way of automatic processes, constrain our actions, and therefore perform at a lower level.

Contextual interference—Describes the phenomenon of switching between different tasks (sections of a piece, technical skills), which causes cognitive friction (interference) and is more difficult than sticking with just one task. This friction causes the brain to work harder, resulting in better learning.

Contracting schedule (spaced practice)—A schedule of breaks where the breaks get shorter and shorter over time.

Declarative (explicit) memory—Memory for facts and other information that you can verbalize.

Deep encoding—Deep encoding occurs when new information is connected to other information already stored in long-term memory, resulting in better memory for the new information.

Deliberate practice—A form of practice where the learner focuses on improving their weaknesses and is ideally guided by an expert teacher. First described by psychologist Anders Ericsson.

Desirable difficulties—Practice methods that require greater effort to play a given section well (variable practice or interleaved practice, for example) result in better retention and performance long-term. The difficulties created by the practice methods are therefore desirable.

Ebbinghaus, Hermann—A psychologist from the late 19th century who first discovered the importance of taking breaks and who originally plotted the forgetting curve.

Encoding—The first stage of memory formation, when the new information enters the brain.

Episodic (autobiographical) memory—Memory for events that we have experienced personally.

Ericsson, Anders—The psychologist who first described deliberate practice and did seminal research in this area.

Event-related potentials (ERPs)—Electrical responses in the brain to specific events, used to determine how the brain reacts to and processes information.

Expanding schedule (spaced practice)—A schedule of breaks where the breaks get longer and longer over time.

GLOSSARY 233

Expressive cues—Information on the emotional content of a section of music. From Roger Chaffin's list of the four types of performance cues musicians use to orient themselves while playing from memory.

Explicit monitoring—Paying close attention to and controlling every detail of one's actions, micromanaging every aspect of an action or performance.

External focus—Focusing on the effect of one's actions or on something outside the body (e.g., the movement of the bow on the strings), as opposed to the body itself.

Fixed schedule (spaced practice)—A schedule of breaks where the breaks are always the same length.

fMRI machine—Stands for *functional magnetic resonance imaging*. A machine that measures blood flow in the brain as a proxy for brain activity.

Forgetting curve—A decline in memory retention over time, first described by Hermann Ebbinghaus in the late 19th century.

Frontal lobe—One of the four lobes of the brain, located in the front right behind the forehead.

H.M.—A patient who underwent surgery for epilepsy and had both hippocampi removed, resulting in him being unable to form any new memories.

Habit-bundling—Pairing an enjoyable or habitual activity with a less enjoyable activity for the purpose of sticking to the habit of the less enjoyable activity (e.g., listening to a favorite podcast only when at the gym to get into the habit of exercising regularly).

Hippocampus—Part of the brain involved in memory and necessary for making new memories. Removed in patient H.M.

Homunculus—A model or rendering of what humans would look like if our body parts were proportional to how much brain real estate is devoted to each body part, resulting in enormous hands and lips and tiny legs and arms.

Illusion of mastery—The mistaken belief that performance gains *during* a practice session are an accurate reflection of how much improvement and learning has taken place.

Interleaved (random) practice—A practice method where the learner alternates frequently between different sections or items to be learned rather than spending a large chunk of time focusing on one thing.

Interleaved clicking up—A method of working fast music up to tempo using a metronome that uses the principles of interleaved practice.

Internal focus—Focusing on the specifics of what the body must do to perform a given action (in contrast to an external focus).

Interpretive cues—Markings in a piece of music provided by the composer that indicate a change in tempo or character. From Roger Chaffin's list of the four types of performance cues musicians use to orient themselves while playing from memory.

234 GLOSSARY

Knowledge structures ("super chunks")—An interrelated collection of information about a given topic or idea, integrated into a larger framework for understanding and/or remembering that information.

Long-term memory—Memory for facts, events, and skills that were learned and retained in the past (not recently).

Long-term potentiation (LTP)—The first step in strengthening synapses so neurons can communicate more effectively. This is a structural change in the neurons on either side of the synapse.

Lyndon, Harry—An Australian educator who invented the old way/new way method of correcting bad habits.

Mental practice—A practice method done entirely inside one's head by imagining how the music sounds and feels to play.

Mirror neurons—Specialized neurons that are active when we watch someone else perform an action.

Motor cortex—Part of the brain, located in the frontal lobes, and active whenever we move.

Motor cortex excitability—A measure of motor cortex activity in the brain, related to reaction time. More motor cortex excitability means a faster reaction time.

Motor evoked potential (MEP)—Electrical signals recorded from muscles when we move or imagine moving.

Motor imagery—Imagining what it would feel like to move, but without actually moving.

Muscle memory—Also known as procedural memory or motor memory, this is our memory of how to do something (ride a bike, play an instrument).

Myelin—A layer of fat that wraps around the axon of neurons and allows electrical signals to move more quickly and efficiently down the axon.

Myelination—The process of wrapping myelin around an axon.

Neural pathway—A series of interconnected neurons that sends information from one area of the brain to another.

Neuron—The name for the cells in the brain.

Neuronal ensemble—A group of neurons that works together to perform a given action.

Neurotransmitter—An umbrella term for the chemicals our brains use to communicate (dopamine, serotonin, etc.).

NREM sleep—Stands for *non-rapid eye movement* sleep, a specific type of sleep.

Old way/new way—A method for fixing bad habits that involves consciously and repeatedly comparing and contrasting the bad habit (old way) with the new habit to be formed (new way).

Overlearning—Overlearning happens when a learner continues to reinforce a skill after they have figured out how to do it. Overlearning is necessary to make it stick long-term.

Parietal lobe—One of the four lobes in the brain, located on the top toward the back.

GLOSSARY   235

Performance cues—Information in a piece of music that helps performers know where they are in the piece when playing from memory. Described by Dr. Roger Chaffin in his studies on preparing for memorized performance.

Pitch discrimination threshold—The smallest distance between two notes that can still be distinguished as different (higher or lower). This is different for each person depending on their training.

Posterior—Toward the back.

Premotor cortex (PMC)—Part of the brain, located in the frontal lobes and involved with motor skills.

Proactive interference (or inhibition)—When old information inhibits the ability to learn new information that conflicts with the old information.

Procedural (implicit) memory—Also known as muscle memory, this is the memory for how to do things (ride a bike, play an instrument).

Putamen—Part of the basal ganglia, a structure in the brain involved in motor skills.

REM sleep—Stands for *rapid eye movement sleep*, a specific type of sleep where the eyes are moving under the eyelids.

Retrieval—The final stage in memory formation, where the information to be remembered is recalled.

Retroactive interference—When two new, similar skills or pieces of information are learned too close together in time, the second piece of information interferes with the ability to remember the first piece of information.

Secondary auditory areas—Areas of the brain involved in processing sound after it has been processed by the primary auditory cortex, the first stop in the brain for processing sound.

Semantic memory—Memory for information and facts.

Sensorimotor loop—A group of brain structures that work together to time and pace movements in the absence of something external (like a metronome) helping to accomplish this.

Serial practice—A practice method where the learner cycles through different skills relatively quickly in the same order each time.

Short-term memory—A type of memory for holding a small amount of information in memory for a limited time (like remembering a phone number before being able to write it down).

Sleep spindles—A type of brain activity that occurs during sleep and helps consolidate and solidify new information and skills that were learned during wakefulness.

Somatosensory cortex—Part of the brain, located in the parietal lobes, and in charge of processing incoming sensory information from the body.

Spaced practice—A practice method that incorporates frequent breaks to maximize learning.

236 GLOSSARY

Stabilometer—A seesaw-like platform to stand on and used to measure people's ability to balance.

Stage 2 sleep—A specific stage of sleep, on the lighter side but not the lightest type of sleep.

Structural cues—Information on where you are in the formal structure of a piece of music. From Roger Chaffin's list of the four types of performance cues musicians use to orient themselves while playing from memory.

Supplementary motor area (SMA)—Part of the brain, located in the frontal cortex, and involved in motor skills.

Synapse—The tiny space in between two neurons where the communication between them happens.

Transcranial magnetic stimulation (TMS)—A method of brain stimulation that delivers a magnetic pulse to the brain to manipulate brain activity in a noninvasive, safe way.

Variable practice—A practice method where the details and parameters of the skill are slightly varied each time rather than repeated exactly.

Walker, Matthew—One of the leading neuroscientists on the study of sleep.

Working memory—A type of memory similar to short-term memory, but where the information being held in memory is also being used and/or manipulated (e.g., remembering the key signature and accidentals while using that information to sight-read accurately).

Wulf, Gabriele—The research psychologist who first discovered, studied, and described external versus internal focus.

Zimmerman, Barry—The research psychologist who articulated the three-step model for effective practice: goal setting, self-monitoring, self-reflection.

Notes

Introduction

1. Ericsson, K. Anders, Ralf T. Krampe, and Clemens Tesch-Römer. "The role of deliberate practice in the acquisition of expert performance." *Psychological Review* 100, no. 3 (1993): 363–406.
2. Ericsson, K. Anders, and Kyle W. Harwell. "Deliberate practice and proposed limits on the effects of practice on the acquisition of expert performance: Why the original definition matters and recommendations for future research." *Frontiers in Psychology* 10 (2019): 2396.

Chapter 1

1. Laubach, Mark, Johan Wessberg, and Miguel A. L. Nicolelis. "Cortical ensemble activity increasingly predicts behaviour outcomes during learning of a motor task." *Nature* 405, no. 6786 (2000): 567–571.
2. Walker, Matthew. *Why we sleep: Unlocking the power of sleep and dreams*. Simon and Schuster, 2017: 121–122.
3. ul Hasnain, Musarrat, Sumera Badar Ehsan, and Ali Ishaq. "Role of overlearning in skill retention of cardiac first response course." *Annals of Punjab Medical College (APMC)* 12, no. 2 (2018): 162–167. Marcucci, Vincent, Lawrence Greenawald, Jorge L. Uribe, Faiz U. Shariff, Scott D. Lind, Patricia A. Shewokis, Sharon Griswold, and Andres E. Castellanos. "Overlearning enhances skill retention in a simulated model of laparoscopic cholecystectomy." *Journal of the American College of Surgeons* 221, no. 4 (2015): e74. Schendel, J. D., and J. D. Hagman. On sustaining procedural skills over a prolonged retention interval. *Journal of Applied Psychology* 67, no. 5 (1982): 605.
4. Fields, R. Douglas. "The brain learns in unexpected ways: Neuroscientists have discovered a set of unfamiliar cellular mechanisms for making fresh memories." *Scientific American* 322, no. 3 (2020): 74. Santos, Erin N., and R. Douglas Fields. "Regulation of myelination by microglia." *Science Advances* 7, no. 50 (2021): eabk1131.

Chapter 2

1. Duke, Robert A., Amy L. Simmons, and Carla Davis Cash. "It's not how much; it's how: Characteristics of practice behavior and retention of performance skills." *Journal of Research in Music Education* 56, no. 4 (2009): 310–321.

238 NOTES

2. Cleary, Timothy J., and Barry J. Zimmerman. "Self-regulation differences during athletic practice by experts, non-experts, and novices." *Journal of Applied Sport Psychology* 13, no. 2 (2001): 185–206.
3. Ibid., 192–193.
4. Ibid., 192–193.
5. Jonker, Laura, Marije T. Elferink-Gemser, and Chris Visscher. "Differences in self-regulatory skills among talented athletes: The significance of competitive level and type of sport." *Journal of Sports Sciences* 28, no. 8 (2010): 901–908.
6. Miksza, Peter. "Relationships among achievement goal motivation, impulsivity, and the music practice of collegiate brass and woodwind players." *Psychology of Music* 39, no. 1 (2011): 50–67. Suzuki, Akiho, and Helen F. Mitchell. "What makes practice perfect? How tertiary piano students self-regulate play and non-play strategies for performance success." *Psychology of Music* 50, no. 2 (2022): 611–630.
7. For example: Cleary and Zimmerman, "Self-regulation differences," 189.
8. Cleary, Timothy J., Barry J. Zimmerman, and Tedd Keating. "Training physical education students to self-regulate during basketball free throw practice." *Research Quarterly for Exercise and Sport* 77, no. 2 (2006): 251–262.
9. Boucher, Mathieu, Andrea Creech, and Francis Dubé. "Video feedback and the self-evaluation of college-level guitarists during individual practice." *Psychology of Music* 49, no. 2 (2021): 159–176.
10. Suzuki and Mitchell, "What makes practice perfect?"
11. Kitsantas, Anastasia, and Barry J. Zimmerman. "Comparing self-regulatory processes among novice, non-expert, and expert volleyball players: A microanalytic study." *Journal of Applied Sport Psychology* 14, no. 2 (2002): 91–105.

Chapter 3

1. Wills, Andy J., Aureliu Lavric, G. S. Croft, and Timothy L. Hodgson. "Predictive learning, prediction errors, and attention: Evidence from event-related potentials and eye tracking." *Journal of Cognitive Neuroscience* 19, no. 5 (2007): 843–854.
2. Lyndon, Harry. "I did it my way! An introduction to 'old way/new way' methodology." *Australasian Journal of Special Education* 13, no. 1 (1989): 32–37.
3. Milanese, Chiara, Stefano Corte, Luca Salvetti, Valentina Cavedon, and Tiziano Agostini. "Correction of a technical error in the golf swing: Error amplification versus direct instruction." *Journal of Motor Behavior* 48, no. 4 (2016): 365–376.
4. Milot, Marie-Hélène, Laura Marchal-Crespo, Christopher S. Green, Steven C. Cramer, and David J. Reinkensmeyer. "Comparison of error-amplification and haptic-guidance training techniques for learning of a timing-based motor task by healthy individuals." *Experimental Brain Research* 201, no. 2 (2010): 119–131.
5. Hanin, Yuri, Tapio Korjus, Petteri Jouste, and Paul Baxter. "Rapid technique correction using old way/new way: Two case studies with Olympic athletes." *Sport Psychologist* 16, no. 1 (2002): 79–99.

NOTES 239

6. Hanin, Yuri, Marko Malvela, and Muza Hanina. "Rapid correction of start technique in an Olympic-level swimmer: A case study using old way/new way." *Journal of Swimming Research* 16 (2004): 11–17.

7. Baxter, Paul, Harry Lyndon, Shelley Dole, and Diana Battistutta. "Less pain, more gain: Rapid skill development using old way new way." *Journal of Vocational Education and Training* 56, no. 1 (2004): 21–50.

8. Lameiras, João, P. Lopes de Almeida, and Alexandre Garcia Mas. "The efficacy of the old way/new way methodology on the correction of an automated technical error and its impact on the athlete's psychological skills: Case study in tennis." *Cuadernos de Psicología del Deporte* 15, no. 2 (2015): 79–86.

9. Guadagnoli, Mark A., and Robert M. Kohl. "Knowledge of results for motor learning: Relationship between error estimation and knowledge of results frequency." *Journal of Motor Behavior* 33, no. 2 (2001): 217–224.

10. Sherwood, David E., and Timothy D. Lee. "Schema theory: Critical review and implications for the role of cognition in a new theory of motor learning." *Research Quarterly for Exercise and Sport* 74, no. 4 (2003): 376–382.

Chapter 4

1. Ebbinghaus, Hermann. *Über das gedächtnis: untersuchungen zur experimentellen psychologie*. Duncker & Humblot, 1885.

2. Boettcher, Michael, Johannes Boettcher, Stefan Mietzsch, Thomas Krebs, Robert Bergholz, and Konrad Reinshagen. "The spaced learning concept significantly improves training for laparoscopic suturing: A pilot randomized controlled study." *Surgical Endoscopy* 32, no. 1 (2018): 154–159.

3. Moulton, Carol-Anne E., Adam Dubrowski, Helen MacRae, Brent Graham, Ethan Grober, and Richard Reznick. "Teaching surgical skills: What kind of practice makes perfect? A randomized, controlled trial." *Annals of Surgery* 244, no. 3 (2006): 400–409.

4. Spruit, Edward N., Guido P. H. Band, and Jaap F. Hamming. "Increasing efficiency of surgical training: Effects of spacing practice on skill acquisition and retention in laparoscopy training." *Surgical Endoscopy* 29, no. 8 (2015): 2235–2243.

5. Aziz, Wajeeha, Wen Wang, Sebnem Kesaf, Alsayed Abdelhamid Mohamed, Yugo Fukazawa, and Ryuichi Shigemoto. "Distinct kinetics of synaptic structural plasticity, memory formation, and memory decay in massed and spaced learning." *Proceedings of the National Academy of Sciences* 111, no. 1 (2014): E194–E202.

6. Buch, Ethan R., Leonardo Claudino, Romain Quentin, Marlene Bönstrup, and Leonardo G. Cohen. "Consolidation of human skill linked to waking hippocampo-neocortical replay." *Cell Reports* 35, no. 10 (2021): 109193.

7. Kramár, Enikö A., Alex H. Babayan, Cristin F. Gavin, Conor D. Cox, Matiar Jafari, Christine M. Gall, Gavin Rumbaugh, and Gary Lynch. "Synaptic evidence for the efficacy of spaced learning." *Proceedings of the National Academy of Sciences* 109, no. 13 (2012): 5121–5126.

240 NOTES

8. Willis, Ross E., Eileen Curry, and Pedro Pablo Gomez. "Practice schedules for surgical skills: The role of task characteristics and proactive interference on psychomotor skills acquisition." *Journal of Surgical Education* 70, no. 6 (2013): 789–795.

9. Shadmehr, Reza, and Henry H. Holcomb. "Neural correlates of motor memory consolidation." *Science* 277, no. 5327 (1997): 821–825.

10. Walker, Matthew P., Tiffany Brakefield, J. Allan Hobson, and Robert Stickgold. "Dissociable stages of human memory consolidation and reconsolidation." *Nature* 425, no. 6958 (2003): 616–620.

Chapter 5

1. Walker, Matthew P., Tiffany Brakefield, Alexandra Morgan, J. Allan Hobson, and Robert Stickgold. "Practice with sleep makes perfect: Sleep-dependent motor skill learning." *Neuron* 35, no. 1 (2002): 205–211.

2. Walker, Matthew P., Tiffany Brakefield, Joshua Seidman, Alexandra Morgan, J. Allan Hobson, and Robert Stickgold. "Sleep and the time course of motor skill learning." *Learning and Memory* 10, no. 4 (2003): 275–284.

3. Simmons, Amy L., and Robert A. Duke. "Effects of sleep on performance of a keyboard melody." *Journal of Research in Music Education* 54, no. 3 (2006): 257–269.

4. Genzel, Lisa, Amelie Quack, Eugen Jäger, Boris Konrad, Axel Steiger, and Martin Dresler. "Complex motor sequence skills profit from sleep." *Neuropsychobiology* 66, no. 4 (2012): 237–243.

5. Smith, Carlyle, and Christine MacNeill. "Impaired motor memory for a pursuit rotor task following stage 2 sleep loss in college students." *Journal of Sleep Research* 3, no. 4 (1994): 206–213.

6. Ibid.

7. Smith, Carlyle. "Sleep states and memory processes." *Behavioural Brain Research* 69, no. 1–2 (1995): 137–145.

8. Farhadian, Negin, Habibolah Khazaie, Mohammad Nami, and Sepideh Khazaie. "The role of daytime napping in declarative memory performance: A systematic review." *Sleep Medicine* 84 (2021): 134–141. Schmid, Daniel, Daniel Erlacher, André Klostermann, Ralf Kredel, and Ernst-Joachim Hossner. "Sleep-dependent motor memory consolidation in healthy adults: A meta-analysis." *Neuroscience and Biobehavioral Reviews* 118 (2020): 270–281.

9. Nishida, Masaki, and Matthew P. Walker. "Daytime naps, motor memory consolidation and regionally specific sleep spindles." *PLoS ONE* 2, no. 4 (2007): e341.

10. Morita, Yuko, Keiko Ogawa, and Sunao Uchida. "Napping after complex motor learning enhances juggling performance." *Sleep Science* 9, no. 2 (2016): 112–116.

11. Korman, Maria, Julien Doyon, Julia Doljansky, Julie Carrier, Yaron Dagan, and Avi Karni. "Daytime sleep condenses the time course of motor memory consolidation." *Nature Neuroscience* 10, no. 9 (2007): 1206–1213.

NOTES 241

12. Lahl, Olaf, Christiane Wispel, Bernadette Willigens, and Reinhard Pietrowsky. "An ultra-short episode of sleep is sufficient to promote declarative memory performance." *Journal of Sleep Research* 17, no. 1 (2008): 3–10.

13. Brooks, Amber, and Leon Lack. "A brief afternoon nap following nocturnal sleep restriction: Which nap duration is most recuperative?" *Sleep* 29, no. 6 (2006): 831–840.

14. Eichenlaub, Jean-Baptiste, Beata Jarosiewicz, Jad Saab, Brian Franco, Jessica Kelemen, Eric Halgren, Leigh R. Hochberg, and Sydney S. Cash. "Replay of learned neural firing sequences during rest in human motor cortex." *Cell Reports* 31, no. 5 (2020): 107581.

Chapter 6

1. Gerbier, Emilie, Thomas C. Toppino, and Olivier Koenig. "Optimising retention through multiple study opportunities over days: The benefit of an expanding schedule of repetitions." *Memory* 23, no. 6 (2015): 943–954.

2. Gallagher, Anthony G., Julie Anne Jordan-Black, and Gerald C. O'Sullivan. "Prospective, randomized assessment of the acquisition, maintenance, and loss of laparoscopic skills." *Annals of Surgery* 256, no. 2 (2012): 387–393.

Chapter 7

1. Hall, Kellie Green, Derek A. Domingues, and Richard Cavazos. "Contextual interference effects with skilled baseball players." *Perceptual and Motor Skills* 78, no. 3 (1994): 835–841.

2. Abushanab, Branden, and Anthony J. Bishara. "Memory and metacognition for piano melodies: Illusory advantages of fixed- over random-order practice." *Memory and Cognition* 41, no. 6 (2013): 928–937.

3. Carter, Christine E., and Jessica A. Grahn. "Optimizing music learning: Exploring how blocked and interleaved practice schedules affect advanced performance." *Frontiers in Psychology* 7 (2016): 1251.

4. Soderstrom, Nicholas C., and Robert A. Bjork. "Learning versus performance: An integrative review." *Perspectives on Psychological Science* 10, no. 2 (2015): 176–199.

5. Shea, John B., and Robyn L. Morgan. "Contextual interference effects on the acquisition, retention, and transfer of a motor skill." *Journal of Experimental Psychology: Human Learning and Memory* 5, no. 2 (1979): 179–187.

6. Porter, Jared M., and Esmaeel Saemi. "Moderately skilled learners benefit by practicing with systematic increases in contextual interference." *International Journal of Coaching Science* 4, no. 2 (2010): 61–71.

7. Lin, Chien-Ho Janice, Barbara J. Knowlton, Ming-Chang Chiang, Marco Iacoboni, Parima Udompholkul, and Allan D. Wu. "Brain–behavior correlates of optimizing learning through interleaved practice." *Neuroimage* 56, no. 3 (2011): 1758–1772.

242 NOTES

8. Song, Sunbin, Nikhil Sharma, Ethan R. Buch, and Leonardo G. Cohen. "White matter microstructural correlates of superior long-term skill gained implicitly under randomized practice." *Cerebral Cortex* 22, no. 7 (2012): 1671–1677.

Chapter 8

1. Kerr, Robert, and Bernard Booth. "Specific and varied practice of motor skill." *Perceptual and Motor Skills* 46, no. 2 (1978): 395–401.
2. Wulf, Gabriele. "The effect of type of practice on motor learning in children." *Applied Cognitive Psychology* 5, no. 2 (1991): 123–134.
3. Douvis, Stavros J. "Variable practice in learning the forehand drive in tennis." *Perceptual and Motor Skills* 101, no. 2 (2005): 531–545.
4. Willey, Chéla R., and Zili Liu. "Long-term motor learning: Effects of varied and specific practice." *Vision Research* 152 (2018): 10–16.
5. Landin, Dennis K., Edward P. Hebert, and Malcolm Fairweather. "The effects of variable practice on the performance of a basketball skill." *Research Quarterly for Exercise and Sport* 64, no. 2 (1993): 232–237.
6. Pigott, Robert E., and Diane C. Shapiro. "Motor schema: The structure of the variability session." *Research Quarterly for Exercise and Sport* 55, no. 1 (1984): 41–45.
7. Zipp, Genevieve Pinto, and A. M. Gentile. "Practice schedule and the learning of motor skills in children and adults: teaching implications." *Journal of College Teaching and Learning (TLC)* 7, no. 2 (2010): 35–42.
8. Wrisberg, Craig A., and Barbara J. Mead. "Developing coincident timing skill in children: A comparison of training methods." *Research Quarterly for Exercise and Sport* 54, no. 1 (1983): 67–74.
9. Sánchez, Carla Caballero, Francisco Javier Moreno, Raúl Reina Vaíllo, Alba Roldán Romero, Álvaro Coves, and David Barbado Murillo. "The role of motor variability in motor control and learning depends on the nature of the task and the individual's capabilities." *European Journal of Human Movement* 38 (2017): 12–26.
10. Guadagnoli, Mark A., and Timothy D. Lee. "Challenge point: A framework for conceptualizing the effects of various practice conditions in motor learning." *Journal of Motor Behavior* 36, no. 2 (2004): 212–224.
11. Schöllhorn, W. I. "Applications of systems dynamic principles to technique and strength training." *Acta Academiae Olympiquae Estoniae* 8 (2000): 67–85.
12. Wymbs, Nicholas F., Amy J. Bastian, and Pablo A. Celnik. "Motor skills are strengthened through reconsolidation." *Current Biology* 26, no. 3 (2016): 338–343.
13. Wu, Howard G., Yohsuke R. Miyamoto, Luis Nicolas Gonzalez Castro, Bence P. Ölveczky, and Maurice A. Smith. "Temporal structure of motor variability is dynamically regulated and predicts motor learning ability." *Nature Neuroscience* 17, no. 2 (2014): 312–321.

Chapter 9

1. Pascual-Leone, Alvaro, Dang Nguyet, Leonardo G. Cohen, Joaquim P. Brasil-Neto, Angel Cammarota, and Mark Hallett. "Modulation of muscle responses evoked by transcranial magnetic stimulation during the acquisition of new fine motor skills." *Journal of Neurophysiology* 74, no. 3 (1995): 1037–1045.
2. Elbert, Thomas, Christo Pantev, Christian Wienbruch, Brigitte Rockstroh, and Edward Taub. "Increased cortical representation of the fingers of the left hand in string players." *Science* 270, no. 5234 (1995): 305–307. Schwenkreis, Peter, Susan El Tom, Patrick Ragert, Burkhard Pleger, Martin Tegenthoff, and Hubert R. Dinse. "Assessment of sensorimotor cortical representation asymmetries and motor skills in violin players." *European Journal of Neuroscience* 26, no. 11 (2007): 3291–3302.
3. Smith, Dave, Caroline J. Wright, and Cara Cantwell. "Beating the bunker: The effect of PETTLEP imagery on golf bunker shot performance." *Research Quarterly for Exercise and Sport* 79, no. 3 (2008): 385–391.
4. Frank, Cornelia, William M. Land, Carmen Popp, and Thomas Schack. "Mental representation and mental practice: Experimental investigation on the functional links between motor memory and motor imagery." *PLoS ONE* 9, no. 4 (2014): e95175.
5. Bernardi, Nicolò Francesco, Alexander Schories, Hans-Christian Jabusch, Barbara Colombo, and Eckart Altenmüller. "Mental practice in music memorization: An ecological-empirical study." *Music Perception: An Interdisciplinary Journal* 30, no. 3 (2012): 275–290.
6. Iorio, Claudia, Elvira Brattico, Frederik Munk Larsen, Peter Vuust, and Leonardo Bonetti. "The effect of mental practice on music memorization." *Psychology of Music* 50, no. 1 (2022): 230–244.
7. Bernardi, Nicolò F., Matteo De Buglio, Pietro D. Trimarchi, Alfonso Chielli, and Emanuela Bricolo. "Mental practice promotes motor anticipation: Evidence from skilled music performance." *Frontiers in Human Neuroscience* 7 (2013): 451.
8. For example, see Olsson, C.-J., and Lars Nyberg. "Motor imagery: If you can't do it, you won't think it." *Scandinavian Journal of Medicine and Science in Sports* 20, no. 5 (2010): 711–715.
9. Skelton, Geoffrey. *Paul Hindemith: The man behind the music.* Camelot Press, 1975: 157. Zatkalik, Miloš, Melina Medić, and Denis Collins, eds. *Histories and narratives of music analysis.* Cambridge Scholars Publishing, 2013: 406.
10. Bernardi et al., "Mental practice promotes motor anticipation," 11.
11. Keller, Peter E., and Mirjam Appel. "Individual differences, auditory imagery, and the coordination of body movements and sounds in musical ensembles." *Music Perception* 28, no. 1 (2010): 27–46. Kageyama, Noa, host. "Peter Keller: On becoming more skilled ensemble musicians with insights from cognitive science." *Bulletproof Musician* podcast. June 5, 2022. Accessed June 5, 2022. https://bulletproofmusician.com/peter-keller-on-becoming-more-skilled-ensemble-musicians-with-insights-from-cognitive-science/.

244 NOTES

12. Gallese, Vittorio, Luciano Fadiga, Leonardo Fogassi, and Giacomo Rizzolatti. "Action recognition in the premotor cortex." *Brain* 119, no. 2 (1996): 593–609. Di Pellegrino, Giuseppe, Luciano Fadiga, Leonardo Fogassi, Vittorio Gallese, and Giacomo Rizzolatti. "Understanding motor events: A neurophysiological study." *Experimental Brain Research* 91, no. 1 (1992): 176–180.

13. Eaves, Daniel L., Martin Riach, Paul S. Holmes, and David J. Wright. "Motor imagery during action observation: A brief review of evidence, theory and future research opportunities." *Frontiers in Neuroscience* 10 (2016): 514. Marshall, Ben, David J. Wright, Paul S. Holmes, and Greg Wood. "Combining action observation and motor imagery improves eye–hand coordination during novel visuomotor task performance." *Journal of Motor Behavior* (2019): 333–341.

14. Romano-Smith, Stephanie, Greg Wood, D. J. Wright, and C. J. Wakefield. "Simultaneous and alternate action observation and motor imagery combinations improve aiming performance." *Psychology of Sport and Exercise* 38 (2018): 100–106.

15. Clark, Shannon E., and Diane M. Ste-Marie. "The impact of self-as-a-model interventions on children's self-regulation of learning and swimming performance." *Journal of Sports Sciences* 25, no. 5 (2007): 577–586.

Chapter 10

1. Hardwick, Robert M., Svenja Caspers, Simon B. Eickhoff, and Stephan P. Swinnen. "Neural correlates of action: Comparing meta-analyses of imagery, observation, and execution." *Neuroscience and Biobehavioral Reviews* 94 (2018): 31–44.

2. O'Shea, Helen, and Aidan Moran. "Does motor simulation theory explain the cognitive mechanisms underlying motor imagery? A critical review." *Frontiers in Human Neuroscience* 11 (2017): 72.

3. Ibid.

4. Hardwick et al., "Neural correlates of action," 31–44.

5. Lotze, Martin, Gabriela Scheler, H.-R. M. Tan, Christoph Braun, and Niels Birbaumer. "The musician's brain: Functional imaging of amateurs and professionals during performance and imagery." *Neuroimage* 20, no. 3 (2003): 1817–1829.

6. Zatorre, Robert J., and Andrea R. Halpern. "Mental concerts: Musical imagery and auditory cortex." *Neuron* 47, no. 1 (2005): 9–12.

7. Wright, David J., Sheree A. McCormick, Samantha Birks, Michela Loporto, and Paul S. Holmes. "Action observation and imagery training improve the ease with which athletes can generate imagery." *Journal of Applied Sport Psychology* 27, no. 2 (2015): 156–170.

8. Guillot, Aymeric, Christian Collet, Vo An Nguyen, Francine Malouin, Carol Richards, and Julien Doyon. "Functional neuroanatomical networks associated with expertise in motor imagery." *Neuroimage* 41, no. 4 (2008): 1471–1483.

9. Grospêtre, Sidney, Célia Ruffino, and Florent Lebon. "Motor imagery and cortico-spinal excitability: A review." *European Journal of Sport Science* 16, no. 3 (2016): 317–324.

NOTES 245

10. Williams, Jacqueline, Alan J. Pearce, Michela Loporto, Tony Morris, and Paul S. Holmes. "The relationship between corticospinal excitability during motor imagery and motor imagery ability." *Behavioural Brain Research* 226, no. 2 (2012): 369–375.

11. Lebon, Florent, Winston D. Byblow, Christian Collet, Aymeric Guillot, and Cathy M. Stinear. "The modulation of motor cortex excitability during motor imagery depends on imagery quality." *European Journal of Neuroscience* 35, no. 2 (2012): 323–331.

12. Fourkas, Alissa D., Valerio Bonavolontà, Alessio Avenanti, and Salvatore M. Aglioti. "Kinesthetic imagery and tool-specific modulation of corticospinal representations in expert tennis players." *Cerebral Cortex* 18, no. 10 (2008): 2382–2390.

13. Guillot, Aymeric, Kevin Moschberger, and Christian Collet. "Coupling movement with imagery as a new perspective for motor imagery practice." *Behavioral and Brain Functions* 9, no. 1 (2013): 1–8. Ferreira Dias Kanthack, Thiago, Aymeric Guillot, Leandro Ricardo Altimari, Susana Nunez Nagy, Christian Collet, and Franck Di Rienzo. "Selective efficacy of static and dynamic imagery in different states of physical fatigue." *PLoS ONE* 11, no. 3 (2016): e0149654.

14. Driskell, James E., Carolyn Copper, and Aidan Moran. "Does mental practice enhance performance?" *Journal of Applied Psychology* 79, no. 4 (1994): 481–492.

15. Debarnot, Ursula, Laura Maley, Danilo De Rossi, and Aymeric Guillot. "Motor interference does not impair the memory consolidation of imagined movements." *Brain and Cognition* 74, no. 1 (2010): 52–57. Debarnot, Ursula, Kouloud Abichou, Sandrine Kalenzaga, Marco Sperduti, and Pascale Piolino. "Variable motor imagery training induces sleep memory consolidation and transfer improvements." *Neurobiology of Learning and Memory* 119 (2015): 85–92. Wohldmann, Erica L., Alice F. Healy, and Lyle E. Bourne Jr. "A mental practice superiority effect: Less retroactive interference and more transfer than physical practice." *Journal of Experimental Psychology: Learning, Memory, and Cognition* 34, no. 4 (2008): 823–833.

Chapter 11

1. Wulf, Gabriele. *Attention and motor skill learning.* Human Kinetics, 2007.

2. Wulf, Gabriele, Markus Höß, and Wolfgang Prinz. "Instructions for motor learning: Differential effects of internal versus external focus of attention." *Journal of Motor Behavior* 30, no. 2 (1998): 169–179.

3. Ibid., 171.

4. Ibid.

5. Wulf, Gabriele, Nancy McNevin, and Charles H. Shea. "The automaticity of complex motor skill learning as a function of attentional focus." *Quarterly Journal of Experimental Psychology Section A* 54, no. 4 (2001): 1143–1154.

6. Zachry, Tiffany, Gabriele Wulf, John Mercer, and Neil Bezodis. "Increased movement accuracy and reduced EMG activity as the result of adopting an external focus of attention." *Brain Research Bulletin* 67, no. 4 (2005): 304–309.

7. Lohse, Keith R., David E. Sherwood, and Alice F. Healy. "How changing the focus of attention affects performance, kinematics, and electromyography in dart throwing." *Human Movement Science* 29, no. 4 (2010): 542–555.

246 NOTES

8. Wulf, Gabriele, Janet S. Dufek, Leonardo Lozano, and Christina Pettigrew. "Increased jump height and reduced EMG activity with an external focus." *Human Movement Science* 29, no. 3 (2010): 440–448.

9. Wulf, Gabriele, Barbara Lauterbach, and Tonya Toole. "The learning advantages of an external focus of attention in golf." *Research Quarterly for Exercise and Sport* 70, no. 2 (1999): 120–126.

10. Zarghami, Mehdi, Esmaeel Saemi, and Islam Fathi. "External focus of attention enhances discus throwing performance." *Kinesiology* 44, no. 1 (2012): 47–51.

11. Mornell, Adina, and Gabriele Wulf. "Adopting an external focus of attention enhances musical performance." *Journal of Research in Music Education* 66, no. 4 (2019): 375–391.

12. Ibid., 379.

13. Atkins, Rebecca L., and Robert A. Duke. "Changes in tone production as a function of focus of attention in untrained singers." *International Journal of Research in Choral Singing* 4, no. 2 (2013): 28–36. Atkins, Rebecca L. "Effects of focus of attention on tone production in trained singers." *Journal of Research in Music Education* 64, no. 4 (2017): 421–434.

14. Atkins and Duke, "Changes in tone production," 28.

15. Atkins, "Effects of focus of attention," 421.

16. Wulf, Gabriele, Nancy H. McNevin, Thomas Fuchs, Florian Ritter, and Tonya Toole. "Attentional focus in complex skill learning." *Research Quarterly for Exercise and Sport* 71, no. 3 (2000): 229–239.

17. Bell, James J., and James Hardy. "Effects of attentional focus on skilled performance in golf." *Journal of Applied Sport Psychology* 21, no. 2 (2009): 163–177.

18. Singh, Harjiv, and Gabriele Wulf. "The distance effect and level of expertise: Is the optimal external focus different for low-skilled and high-skilled performers?" *Human Movement Science* 73 (2020): 102663.

19. Schücker, Linda, Norbert Hagemann, Bernd Strauss, and Klaus Völker. "The effect of attentional focus on running economy." *Journal of Sports Sciences* 27, no. 12 (2009): 1241–1248.

20. Freudenheim, Andrea Michele, Gabriele Wulf, Fabrício Madureira, Silmara Cristina Pasetto, and Umberto César Corrêa. "An external focus of attention results in greater swimming speed." *International Journal of Sports Science and Coaching* 5, no. 4 (2010): 533–542. Stoate, Isabelle, and Gabriele Wulf. "Does the attentional focus adopted by swimmers affect their performance?" *International Journal of Sports Science and Coaching* 6, no. 1 (2011): 99–108.

21. Personal communication with Jeffrey Sykes.

22. Wulf, Gabriele, Nathan McConnel, Matthias Gärtner, and Andreas Schwarz. "Enhancing the learning of sport skills through external-focus feedback." *Journal of Motor Behavior* 34, no. 2 (2002): 171–182.

23. Ibid., 174.

24. An, Jongseong, Gabriele Wulf, and Seonjin Kim. "Increased carry distance and X-factor stretch in golf through an external focus of attention." *Journal of Motor Learning and Development* 1, no. 1 (2013): 2–11.

NOTES 247

25. Ibid., 5.
26. Ong, Nicole T., Alison Bowcock, and Nicola J. Hodges. "Manipulations to the timing and type of instructions to examine motor skill performance under pressure." *Frontiers in Psychology* 1 (2010): 196.

Chapter 12

1. Mishra, Jennifer. "Playing from memory: Development of a 19th-century performance practice." *American Music Teacher* 65, no. 6 (2016): 12–16.
2. Squire, Larry R. "The legacy of patient HM for neuroscience." *Neuron* 61, no. 1 (2009): 6–9.
3. Baird, Amee, and Séverine Samson. "Memory for music in Alzheimer's disease: Unforgettable?" *Neuropsychology Review* 19, no. 1 (2009): 85–101.
4. Craik, Fergus I. M., and Endel Tulving. "Depth of processing and the retention of words in episodic memory." *Journal of Experimental Psychology: General* 104, no. 3 (1975): 268–294.
5. Guida, Alessandro, Fernand Gobet, and Serge Nicolas. "Functional cerebral reorganization: A signature of expertise? Reexamining Guida, Gobet, Tardieu, and Nicolas' (2012) two-stage framework." *Frontiers in Human Neuroscience* 7 (2013): 590.
6. Chaffin, Roger, Tânia Lisboa, Topher Logan, and Kristen T. Begosh. "Preparing for memorized cello performance: The role of performance cues." *Psychology of Music* 38, no. 1 (2010): 3–30. Noice, Helga, John Jeffrey, Tony Noice, and Roger Chaffin. "Memorization by a jazz musician: A case study." *Psychology of Music* 36, no. 1 (2008): 63–79. Chaffin, Roger, and Gabriela Imreh. "Practicing perfection: Piano performance as expert memory." *Psychological Science* 13, no. 4 (2002): 342–349. Chaffin, Roger, and Topher Logan. "Practicing perfection: How concert soloists prepare for performance." *Advances in Cognitive Psychology* 2, no. 2 (2006): 113–130. Chaffin, Roger, and Gabriela Imreh. "'Pulling teeth and torture': Musical memory and problem solving." *Thinking and Reasoning* 3, no. 4 (1997): 315–336.
7. Thank you to Peter Slowik for this suggestion.
8. Lotze, Martin, Gabriela Scheler, H.-R. M. Tan, Christoph Braun, and Niels Birbaumer. "The musician's brain: Functional imaging of amateurs and professionals during performance and imagery." *Neuroimage* 20, no. 3 (2003): 1817–1829.
9. Haueisen, Jens, and Thomas R. Knösche. "Involuntary motor activity in pianists evoked by music perception." *Journal of Cognitive Neuroscience* 13, no. 6 (2001): 786–792.

Chapter 13

1. Allen, Sarah E. "Memory stabilization and enhancement following music practice." *Psychology of Music* 41, no. 6 (2013): 794–803.
2. Callender, Aimee A., and Mark A. McDaniel. "The limited benefits of rereading educational texts." *Contemporary Educational Psychology* 34, no. 1 (2009): 30–41. See

248 NOTES

also: Brown, Peter C., Henry L. Roediger III, and Mark A. McDaniel. *Make it stick: The science of successful learning.* Harvard University Press, 2014.

3. Ginsborg, Jane. "Classical singers learning and memorising a new song: An observational study." *Psychology of Music* 30, no. 1 (2002): 58–101.

4. Kornell, Nate, Matthew Jensen Hays, and Robert A. Bjork. "Unsuccessful retrieval attempts enhance subsequent learning." *Journal of Experimental Psychology: Learning, Memory, and Cognition* 35, no. 4 (2009): 989–998. Yan, Veronica X., Yue Yu, Michael A. Garcia, and Robert A. Bjork. "Why does guessing incorrectly enhance, rather than impair, retention?" *Memory and Cognition* 42, no. 8 (2014): 1373–1383.

5. Beilock, Sian L., and Thomas H. Carr. "On the fragility of skilled performance: What governs choking under pressure?" *Journal of Experimental Psychology: General* 130, no. 4 (2001): 701–725.

6. Ibid.

7. Ibid.

8. Englert, Christoph, and Raôul R. D. Oudejans. "Is choking under pressure a consequence of skill-focus or increased distractibility? Results from a tennis serve task." *Psychology* 5, no. 9 (2014): 1035–1043.

9. Ibid. Masters, Richard S. W. "Knowledge, knerves and know-how: The role of explicit versus implicit knowledge in the breakdown of a complex motor skill under pressure." *British Journal of Psychology* 83, no. 3 (1992): 343–358.

10. Lewis, Brian P., and Darwyn E. Linder. "Thinking about choking? Attentional processes and paradoxical performance." *Personality and Social Psychology Bulletin* 23, no. 9 (1997): 937–944.

Chapter 14

1. Rao, Stephen M., Deborah L. Harrington, Kathleen Y. Haaland, Julie A. Bobholz, Robert W. Cox, and Jeffrey R. Binder. "Distributed neural systems underlying the timing of movements." *Journal of Neuroscience* 17, no. 14 (1997): 5528–5535.

2. Phillips-Silver, Jessica, and Laurel J. Trainor. "Hearing what the body feels: Auditory encoding of rhythmic movement." *Cognition* 105, no. 3 (2007): 533–546.

3. Phillips-Silver, Jessica, and Laurel J. Trainor. "Vestibular influence on auditory metrical interpretation." *Brain and Cognition* 67, no. 1 (2008): 94–102.

4. Trainor, Laurel J., Xiaoqing Gao, Jing-jiang Lei, Karen Lehtovaara, and Laurence R. Harris. "The primal role of the vestibular system in determining musical rhythm." *Cortex* 45, no. 1 (2009): 35–43.

5. Kirschner, Sebastian, and Michael Tomasello. "Joint drumming: Social context facilitates synchronization in preschool children." *Journal of Experimental Child Psychology* 102, no. 3 (2009): 299–314.

6. Benedetto, Alessandro, and Gabriel Baud-Bovy. "Tapping force encodes metrical aspects of rhythm." *Frontiers in Human Neuroscience* 15 (2021): 633956.

Chapter 15

1. Ballard, Dennis L. *Relationships between college level wind instrumentalists' achievement in intonation perception and performance.* Doctor of Music Education diss. Indiana University, 2006.
2. Morrison, Steven, and Janina Fyk. "Intonation," in *The science and psychology of music performance: Creative strategies for teaching and learning,* ed. Richard Parncutt and Gary McPherson, (New York, NY: Oxford University Press, 2002), 183–198.
3. Micheyl, Christophe, Karine Delhommeau, Xavier Perrot, and Andrew J. Oxenham. "Influence of musical and psychoacoustical training on pitch discrimination." *Hearing Research* 219, no. 1–2 (2006): 36–47.
4. McLachlan, Neil, David Marco, Maria Light, and Sarah Wilson. "Consonance and pitch." *Journal of Experimental Psychology: General* 142, no. 4 (2013): 1142–1158.
5. Jones, Scott Allan. *The effect of vocalization on pitch discrimination among high school instrumentalists.* PhD diss. University of Minnesota, 2003. Bennett, Schultz Jackson. *Can simple vocalization help improve the intonation of wind players?* DMA diss. Arizona State University, 1994. Silvey, Brian A., Jessica Nápoles, and D. Gregory Springer. "Effects of pre-tuning vocalization behaviors on the tuning accuracy of college instrumentalists." *Journal of Research in Music Education* 66, no. 4 (2019): 392–407.
6. Lyons, Abby Bush. *An examination of middle school band students' ability to match pitch following short-term vocal technique training.* Master's thesis. Louisiana State University, 2013. Scherber, Ryan Vincent. *Pedagogical practices related to the ability to discern and correct intonation errors: An evaluation of current practices, expectations, and a model for instruction.* PhD diss. Florida State University, 2014.
7. Elliott, Charles A. "Effect of vocalization on the sense of pitch of beginning band class students." *Journal of Research in Music Education* 22, no. 2 (1974): 120–128.
8. Schlacks, William Frederick. *The effect of vocalization through an interval training program upon the pitch accuracy of high school band students.* PhD diss. University of Miami, 1981.
9. Schlegel, Amanda L., and D. Gregory Springer. "Effects of accurate and inaccurate visual feedback on the tuning accuracy of high school and college trombonists." *International Journal of Music Education* 36, no. 3 (2018): 394–406.
10. Ibid., 398.
11. Janata, Petr, and Kaivon Paroo. "Acuity of auditory images in pitch and time." *Perception and Psychophysics* 68, no. 5 (2006): 829–844.
12. Woods, David L., and Robert Elmasian. "The habituation of event-related potentials to speech sounds and tones." *Electroencephalography and Clinical Neurophysiology/ Evoked Potentials Section* 65, no. 6 (1986): 447–459.
13. Cebrian, Ana Navarro, and Petr Janata. "Electrophysiological correlates of accurate mental image formation in auditory perception and imagery tasks." *Brain Research* 1342 (2010): 39–54.

250   NOTES

14. Pfordresher, Peter Q., and Andrea R. Halpern. "Auditory imagery and the poor-pitch singer." *Psychonomic Bulletin and Review* 20, no. 4 (2013): 747–753.
15. Pruitt, Tim A., Andrea R. Halpern, and Peter Q. Pfordresher. "Covert singing in anticipatory auditory imagery." *Psychophysiology* 56, no. 3 (2019): e13297.

Conclusion

1. Alex Pang summarizes this well in his book *Rest*. Pang, Alex Soojung-Kim. *Rest: Why you get more done when you work less*. Basic Books, 2016.
2. Huberman, Andrew, host. "The ideal length of time for focused work." *Huberman Lab* podcast. September 10, 2022. Accessed September 11, 2022. https://www.yout ube.com/watch?v=5HINgMMTzPE.
3. Personal communication.
4. Milkman, Katherine L., Julia A. Minson, and Kevin G. M. Volpp. "Holding the hunger games hostage at the gym: An evaluation of temptation bundling." *Management Science* 60, no. 2 (2014): 283–299.
5. Fig, Joe. *Inside the painter's studio*. Princeton Architectural Press, 2009: 42.

Index

For the benefit of digital users, indexed terms that span two pages (e.g., 52–53) may, on occasion, appear on only one of those pages.

Figures are indicated by an italic *f* following the page number.

action observation, 118, 121, 122*f*, 123*f*, 125
action observation and motor imagery (AOMI), 118–19, 131–32
amplification of error technique, 37–38
AOMI. *See* action observation and motor imagery
at-tempo chunking, 196–97
audiation/auditory imagery, 117, 125–26, 185–88
auditory cortex, 125, 155
auditory memory, 153, 154–55
auditory-motor coactivation, 155–57

Bach, J. S., 1, 2, 10, 56*f*, 56–57, 68, 79
bad habits, 20, 36–37
    amplification of error technique for correcting, 37–38
    old way/new way technique for correcting, 38–42, 40*f*, 41*f*, 42*f*
    persistence of, 36–37
    role of feedback in correcting, 43–44
Bartók, Béla, 197, 198*f*
basic cues, 152, 153
Bjork, Robert, 83
blocked practice, interleaved practice *versus,* 79–89, 82*f*, 84*f*, 87*f*
brain. *See also* neural pathways; neurons; synapses
    activation, 86–89, 121–25, 173–75
    anterior and posterior areas of, 121–22
    auditory-motor coactivation, 155–57
    during breaks, 51–53, 54, 55–57
    cerebellum, 125
    damage, memory and, 146–47, 148, 159
    four lobes of, 121, 124*f*
    frontal lobe, 122–25

hippocampus, 147, 159
    mental practice and, 107–11, 121–28
    metronome and, 173–75
    microscopic structure of, 11–15
    parietal lobe, 121–23
    practicing and, 36, 51–53, 86–89, 87*f*, 107–11, 121–25, 122*f*
    putamen, 88–89, 125, 126
    SMA and PMC, 123–25, 124*f*
    structure of, 11–15
breaks, in practicing, 47–51, 50*f*, 52*f*, 54–55, 67
    brain during, 51–53, 54, 55–57
    microbreaks, 51, 52*f*, 70, 75–76
    practice schedules and, 71–72, 73, 76–78, 203–5
    retroactive interference and, 55–57, 68–69

Carter, Christine, 83
cerebellum, 125
Chaffin, Roger, 152–53, 155, 162
challenge point, 99–100
choking, 167–70
chord progressions, 151
chunking, 149–52, 179–80
    at-tempo, 196–97
Close, Chuck, 210
Concerto for Viola (Bartók), 197, 198*f*
consolidation, in memorization, 159–61
constrained action hypothesis, 134–35
contextual interference, 81–82
COVID-19 pandemic, 3–4, 71

Dalcroze, 177–78
DanceStage, 64
Davies, Dennis Russell, 110–11

252 INDEX

declarative memory, 147–48, 155
deep encoding, 149–50, 153, 157
deliberate practice, 2
desirable difficulties, 99–100, 192–93, 195–96
dissonant intervals, 182–83
distraction hypothesis, in choking, 168
drones, tuners *versus*, 184–85

Ebbinghaus, Hermann, 48, 72
encoding, 149–52, 157
    deep, 149–50, 153, 157
encoding strategies
    for musicians, 152–55
    performance cues, 152–53
    strengthening auditory
        memory, 154–55
    strengthening declarative memory, 155
    strengthening muscle memory, 154
episodic memory, 147
Ericsson, Anders, 2
ERPs. *See* event-related potentials
event-related potentials (ERPs), 186
explicit monitoring, 168–69
expressive cues, 152–53
external focus, 133–44
    feedback in, 140–42
    internal focus *versus*, 133–38, 135f, 136f,
        138f, 140–42, 142f, 143f, 143
    memorization and, 169
    in musicians, 137–40, 138f
    skill level and, 138–39
    teaching and, 140–44

feedback, 144, 182–83, 185
    in error correction, 43–44
    in external focus, 140–43, 143f
fMRI machine, 86, 174
focus
    internal *versus* external, 133–38, 135f,
        136f, 138f, 140–42, 142f, 143f, 143
    during practice, 205–6
forgetting curve, the, 71–73
frontal lobe, 55, 88–89, 122–25

Gingold, Joseph, 190

habit bundling, 209
Hahn, Hilary, 151–52

haptic guidance, 38
Hindemith, Paul, 110–11, 117
hippocampus, 147, 159
H.M., 147, 148, 159
homunculus, 108–9, 109f

illusion of mastery, 83–84, 86, 89, 100–1
interleaved clicking up, 193–96, 194f
interleaved practice
    blocked practice *versus*, 79–89, 82f,
        84f, 87f
    for speed, 193–96, 194f
    strategies, 89–94
internal focus, external focus *versus*, 133–38, 135f, 136f, 138f, 140–42, 142f, 143f, 143
interpretive cues, 152, 153
interval timer practice, 90–91, 166–67
intonation
    audiation and, 185–88
    mental practice and, 130–31
    overlearning and, 21
    pitch and, 181, 183
    singing to improve, 181, 183–84
    tuners *versus* drones for
        improving, 184–85
irregular groupings, 197

Kageyama, Noa, 103, 169–70
knowledge structures, 151–52

Lang, Lang, 151–52
Liszt, Franz, 146
long-term memory, 148, 149, 165–66
long-term potentiation (LTP), 18, 53–54
Lyndon, Harry, 36, 37

memorization, 73, 103, 129–30, 145–67.
        See also encoding strategies
    choking and, 167–70
    chunking in, 149–52, 179–80
    consolidation in, 159–61
    retrieval in, 161–67, 164f
    sleep in, 160f, 160–61, 161f
memory
    auditory, 153, 154–55
    brain damage and, 146–47, 148, 159
    declarative, 147–48, 155
    encoding and, 149–55

episodic, 147
long-term, 148, 149, 165–66
motor, 68*f*, 88, 148
muscle, 135, 147–48, 150–51, 154, 155
semantic, 147
short-term, 148, 149, 165–66
types of, 145–49, 146*f*
working, 148–49
mental practice, 107–11, 111*f*, 112–14, 118–19
AOMI in, 118–19
block of time devoted to, 129
for children, 131
closing *versus* opening eyes during, 129–30
of experts *versus* novices, 125–28, 127*f*
intonation improved by, 130–31
listening to recordings *versus*, 131–32
moving *versus* stillness during, 128–29
physical practice and, 114–17, 115*f*, 116*f*, 121–25, 122*f*, 165
retrieval practice and, 167
MEP. *See* motor-evoked potential
metricality, 179–80
metronome, 31, 173–75, 191–95
microbreaks, 51, 52*f*, 70, 75–76
Minuet in G (Bach), 56*f*, 56, 68
mirror neurons, 118
mistakes/errors, 23–26, 28–31, 32–33, 36
amplification of, 37–38
retrieval and, 163–64, 164*f*
role of feedback in correcting, 43–44
mock performance, 92–94
motor cortex, 108*f*, 108–10, 111*f*, 155–56
motor cortex excitability, 88
motor-evoked potential (MEP), 126–28, 127*f*
motor imagery, 118, 122*f*, 123*f*
motor memory, 68*f*, 88, 148
muscle activation, 126–27, 128, 136*f*, 136–37
muscle memory/procedural memory, 135, 147–48, 150–51, 154, 155
myelination, 18–20

naps, 67–70, 68*f*
neural pathways, 14–15
myelination and, 18–20
practice habits and, 20–22

practicing and, 15–18, 20
neuronal ensembles, 13
neurons. *See also* synapses
communication between, 11–13, 53–54
LTP and, 53–54
mirror, 118
structure of, 12*f*, 12
neurotransmitters, 11–12, 18–19
NREM sleep, 63, 64, 65–66, 67–68

old way/new way technique, 38–42, 40*f*, 41*f*, 42*f*
overlearning, 17, 52–53

parietal lobe, 121–23
performance cues, 152–53
performance psychology, 169–70
pitch
discrimination, 181–83
intonation and, 181, 183
perception, 181, 182, 187
pizza wrist, 37–38, 38*f*
PMC. *See* premotor cortex
practice habits
effective, 9–10, 26–28
habit bundling, 209
ineffective, 10–11, 28–33
neural pathways reinforcing, 20–22
practice journal, 201–3
practice mistakes, common, 28–33
metronome in, 31
mindless repetitions, 32–33
playing through best spots, 32
running through, 31
practice schedules
breaks in/spaced, 71–72, 73–78, 77*f*, 165–66, 203–5
creating, 73–78, 74*f*, 75*f*
the forgetting curve and, 71–73
for heavy day, 205
for ideal day, 204
for light day, 204–5
motivation and, 207–8
practice strategies
audiation, 130–31, 187–88
for brand new music, 92
external focus, 144
general, 28–33
interleaved, 89–92, 193–96

254 INDEX

practice strategies (*cont.*)
  interval timer practice, 90–91, 166–67
  intonation, 21, 175, 183–84,
    185, 187–88
  irregular groupings, 197
  late night/early morning mock
    performance, 92–94
  memorization, 153, 154–55, 156–
    57, 165–67
  mental practice, 113, 118–19, 130–31
  microbreaks, 52–53
  perform in random order, 91–92
  prevent choking, 169
  red-yellow-green method, 30, 209
  repetitions, 17
  retrieval and, 165–67
  serial practice, 90, 166
  for speed, 189–99
  for steady tempo, 175, 177–78, 180
  time-constrained practice, 91
  variable practice, 101–4
  Zimmerman's three-step model, 26–28
practicing. *See also* blocked practice;
    breaks, in practicing; interleaved
    practice; mental practice
  brain activation during, 52, 70, 86–89,
    87*f*, 121–25, 122*f*
  brain and, 36, 51–53, 86–89, 87*f*, 107–11
  effective practice skills,
    learning, 26–28
  focus during, 205–6
  LTP and, 54
  motivation for, 206–11
  myelination and, 19–20
  neural pathways and, 15–18, 20
  sleep and, 59–64, 61*f*, 62*f*, 66–67
  as social time, 210
  synapses during, 13
prefrontal cortex, 55, 88–89
premotor cortex (PMC), 123–25, 124*f*
proactive inhibition, 36
proactive interference, 36–37, 55–56
procedural memory. *See* muscle memory
pulse, improving sense of, 176–80
putamen, 88–89, 125, 126

Red-Yellow-Green method, 30, 209
REM sleep, 63, 65–66

repetitions, in practicing
  mindless, as common practicing
    mistake, 32–33
  neural pathways and, 16–18
  microbreaks, 52–53
  overlearning, 17–18
retrieval, in memorization, 161–67, 164*f*
retrieval, strategies for practicing
  interval timer practice, 166–67
  mental practice and, 167
  playing in random order, 166
  serial practice, 166
retroactive interference, 55–57, 68–69, 100
rhythm, 173–74, 176*f*, 176–77, 179*f*, 179–
    80, 190, 191*f*
Rodland, Carol, 110–11
running through, 28–31

Scarlatti, Domenico, 114, 115*f*
Schumann, Clara, 146
Schwanendreher, Der, 110–11
semantic memory, 147
sensorimotor loop, 174–75
serial practice, 90, 166
short-term memory, 148, 149, 165–66
sightreading, 148–49
singing, intonation and, 181, 183–84
sleep
  deprivation, 65*f*, 65–67
  in memorization, 160*f*, 160–61, 161*f*
  naps, 67–70, 68*f*
  NREM, 63, 64, 65–66, 67–68
  practicing, performing and, 59–64, 61*f*,
    62*f*, 65–67
  REM, 63, 65–66
  Stage 2, 63, 64, 67–68
sleep spindles, 64, 67–68
slurring patterns, 190, 192*f*
SMA. *See* supplementary motor area
somatosensory cortex, 108*f*, 108–10
spaced practice, 48, 50–51, 54, 71, 73–
    74, 76, 78
  interleaved practice and, 80
  schedules, 71, 76–78, 77*f*, 165–66
speed, practice methods for
  at-tempo chunking, 196–97
  interleaved clicking up, 193–96, 194*f*
  irregular groupings, 197

metronome clicking up, 191–95
rhythms, 190, 191*f*
slurring patterns, 190, 192*f*
techniques for fast tempos, 197–99,
198*f*, 199*f*
stabilometer, 134, 135–36
Stage 2 sleep, 63, 64, 67–68
structural cues, 152, 153
super chunks, 151–52
supplementary motor area (SMA), 123–
25, 124*f*
Suzuki method, 23–24, 145, 156
Sykes, Jeffrey, 103
synapses, 11–12, 12*f*, 13
LTP and, 18, 53–54

tempo, 174–75, 177–78, 179, 189, 191–
96, 197–99
at-tempo chunking, 196–97
improving sense of pulse, 175, 177–78, 180
speed techniques for fast, 197–99,
198*f*, 199*f*

time-constrained practice, 91
TimeGuru, 175
TMS. *See* transcranial magnetic
stimulation
transcranial magnetic stimulation
(TMS), 122–23
tuners, drones *versus,* 184–85

variable practice, 95–97, 97*f*, 98*f*, 99*f*
skill level in, 97–101, 101*f*
strategies, 101–4
vestibular system, 177–78
video-recording
practices, 169

Walker, Matthew, 59–64
working memory, 148–49
Wulf, Gabriele, 133–37

X-factor stretch, 141, 142*f*

Zimmerman, Barry, 26–28